SURVIVING INSIDE
CONGRESS
THIRD EDITION

A guide for prospective, new and not-so-new
Congressional staff – and a guided tour for those
who just want to learn how it all works

Mark Strand
Michael S. Johnson
and **Jerome F. Climer**

Published by
The Congressional Institute, Inc.
© 2013

Founded in 1987, the Congressional Institute, Inc. is a not-for-profit 501(c)(4) corporation dedicated to helping Congress better serve its constituents and helping their constituents better understand the operations of the national legislature. The Institute sponsors major conferences for the benefit of Members of the U.S. Congress as well as a number of smaller gatherings, all devoted to an examination of important policy issues and strategic planning. The Institute conducts important research projects consistent with its mission, develops resources such as a House Floor Procedures Manual and this book and sponsors Oxford-style bipartisan Congressional debates. The Congressional Institute sponsors the annual Congressional Art Competition.

A volunteer Board of Directors chaired by Dan Meyer governs the Institute. Mark Strand is the Institute's President. Jerry Climer is the former president. Michael S. Johnson served as Chairman from 2000-2009.

The Library of Congress has catalogued the first edition as follows:
Strand, Mark (Mark N.)
Surviving inside Congress : a guide for prospective, new and not-so-new congressional staff—and a guided tour for those who just want to learn how it all works / Mark Strand, Michael S. Johnson, and Jerome F. Climer.
Alexandria, Va. : Congressional Institute, c2008
273 p. ; 24 cm.
ISBN: 9780963305718
Introduction—In the beginning—A job or a career?—Who's who—Power stations—Genesis of a law—Formal introductions—Managing to succeed—Plotting course—Keys to communication—Strategic communication—Public opinion and public judgment—Leading major change—Playing by the rules—Working with the private sector—The big picture.
Includes glossary and index.
Subjects: United States. Congress.—Officials and employees. United States. Congress.
LC Classification: JK1083 .S87 2008
Other System Numer: (OCoLC)ocn317067573

Table of Contents

3

Table of Contents

The 21ˢᵗ century finds leaders at all levels of government challenged by increasingly complex issues. Joblessness, debt, pension security, poor healthcare, international terrorism, worldwide economic uncertainty, an aging population, education mediocrity, and the nation's crumbling infrastructure are just a few of the challenges demanding we do more with less. Ideological rigidity and tough partisan tactics have become the norm in the struggle for political domination, testing the ability of the elected to govern and to do so with civility. The media's inability or unwillingness to present complex, substantive issues to the public, focusing instead on the drama of conflict, has decreased the nation's capacity to resolve major problems. As a result, low public confidence in institutions, including government and its leaders, has made it all but impossible for the elected to communicate effectively with those who elected them.

Introduction

Unelected professional staff members, who meet the diverse, sometimes critical, needs of elected officials and their constituents, also face these challenges. Most new members of congressional staffs are ill equipped to handle such demands. There are few comprehensive training programs and no curriculum that adequately addresses the multiple roles they play and functions they perform. This is largely due to the uniqueness of their roles and the environment in which they work. As a result, the academic credentials and professional experiences they bring to Capitol Hill often have little relevance to the tasks they're about to undertake.

Many of those tasks will be defined by the elected officials they serve, and these elected officials, for the most part, have little training for the positions they hold, let alone the supervisory experience required to guide subordinates to the same level of professional efficiency and effectiveness that is demanded in the private sector.

This handbook explores what professional staff in the public arena can do to prepare themselves for the challenges facing them and those they work for. Although it focuses primarily on work within the United States Congress, what is written here may be of value to everyone interested or involved in government, whether as a student, an elected official, a member of a government agency or a constituency hoping to influence an elected official's actions.

The authors owe a debt of gratitude to a number of experienced public policy experts whose works contributed to this volume as well as the many elected officials with whom the authors once worked. The extent to which their comments and suggestions were taken to heart is reflected in the number of places where they will recognize their thoughts woven into the fabric of the text—often without attribution.

We are deeply grateful to the contributions of past and present Congressional Institute staff: Dan Risko, Amy Hinderliter and Patrick Deitz.

Tim Lang of the Congressional Institute staff deserves special praise and thanks for editing the third edition of Surviving Inside Congress as well as doing yeoman's work on the second edition two years ago—managing multiple drafts and changes made by three authors. His contribution was essential to the success of the project. Finally, the authors would like to acknowledge the research performed by interns Natalie Warrick and Robert Kelly on generational differences on congressional staffs.

The authors also acknowledge a debt of gratitude to George Pica, the editor of our first edition. It was not easy to harmonize the very different writing styles of three strong-willed individuals, but we believe his contribution formed the solid foundation upon which these subsequent editions have been built.

When British statesman and philosopher Edmund Burke observed, "Those who don't know history are destined to repeat it," he wasn't talking just about students attending summer school. Many recent political scandals, for example, could have been avoided if those who initiated them had paid closer attention to the lessons provided by the scandals of the past. But it's not just notoriety that can be avoided by familiarity with the lessons of history—bad policy and bad politics can be, too. The past is where we get the knowledge that propels us into the future—if every generation reinvented the wheel, mankind would still be dreaming of flights to the moon on gossamer wings. And if that's not reason enough to invest a few minutes exploring the heritage of the Congress, do it out of respect for the traditions that have made the institution a beacon in mankind's search for government of, by and for the people.

It began in 1789 when the 65 Members of the House of Representatives and the 26 Senators of the 1st Congress convened in the nation's capital— New York City. No personal staff members were provided in those days. House Members didn't need much help. They represented districts that included a mere 30,000 or so people, many of whom couldn't read or write, thus limiting the volume of correspondence Congressmen had to deal with.

Senators were chosen by the legislatures in the states they represented. They too operated without the benefit of personal staff.

Although 48 percent of House Members and 56 percent of Senators had college degrees, those without degrees were far more representative of the overall population at that time.

Frederick Muhlenberg of Pennsylvania was the first Speaker. His father, a German immigrant, established the Lutheran Church in the American colonies. Muhlenberg was an ordained minister who served in the Continental Congress. The second Speaker was Jonathan Trumbull, Jr. of Connecticut, the brother of the famous painter John Trumbull (yes, it must have been confusing around the family dinner table).

"There are few shining geniuses," wrote Fisher Ames of Massachusetts, who described his colleagues as sober, solid folks. "There are many who have experience, the virtues of the heart and the habits of business. It will be quite a republican assembly."

The first Speaker, Frederick Muhlenberg of Pennsylvania

Not by today's standards: All 91 Members were white, male land-owners. The average age in the House was 43, and in the Senate, 46. They were paid $6 a day for their efforts.

Like many who would follow in his footsteps, Ames discovered soon into the 2nd Congress that familiarity could breed contempt—especially in the Legislature, where he complained about the yawning listlessness of many who served there.

"Their state prejudices, their over-refining spirit in relation to trifles, their attachment to some very distressing formalities in doing business," he said in tallying the reasons for his growing disenchantment. "The objects now before us require more information, though less of the heroic qualities than those of the 1st Congress."

Whether heroism was uppermost among the goals of the Constitutional Convention of 1787 is debatable, but it was very much in evidence. Those in attendance had been tasked with rewriting the Articles of Confederation. Instead, they closed the doors and windows, and, under the cloak of secrecy, wrote a new Constitution.

One of the original Members of the House of Representatives, Fisher Ames kept an extensive diary during the first Congresses.

Today many Americans hold the Constitution to be an almost sacred document, and it should never be lost on us just how impressive the drafting of our foundational charter was. Intelligent and strong-willed men offered myriad ideas and differing opinions. Every aspect of it was forged in compromise and consensus. As historian Paul Johnson noted, "no delegate was always on the losing side, and no delegate was always on the winning side." At times they had such significant disagreements that at one point Benjamin Franklin proposed hiring a chaplain in the hope that the Almighty could help bridge the divide. Yet the delegates always respected each other, and in the end, their final product has been declared an act of genius.

The inspirations for their masterpiece were numerous. They drew upon the experiences of the Continental Congress and the Congress of the Confederation, both of which had been unicameral, each consisting of a single legislative chamber rather than two separate houses. They drew upon the political philosophers and parliaments of Britain and other European nations. They drew upon the governing documents of North Carolina, Pennsylvania, and Virginia. James Madison even drew upon the Bible, citing Isaiah 33:22 specifically, as a model for three separate branches of government.

The creativity and the genius of the Founders are worth studying. The debate at the Constitutional Convention ranged from terms of office, to which officials would be elected directly by the people (if any), to how many chambers in the legislature.

The Articles of Confederation allowed each state one vote. At the Constitutional Convention, the New Jersey Plan, supported by the smaller states, desired to continue this arrangement. The Virginia Plan, advocated by the larger states, proposed a single legislative chamber based on population. The Great Compromise of 1787, proposed by Roger Sherman of Connecticut, merged the two ideas creating a Senate with equal representation between the states and a House of Representatives based on proportional representation.

And in the process, they evolved a clear and definite role for the Congress to play: It would be the first branch of government, the one that was truly representative of the people.

"The grand depository of the democratic principles of government" is how George Mason of Virginia envisioned it. "The requisites in actual representation are that the Representatives should sympathize with their constituents, should think as they think and feel as they feel and that for these purposes should even be residents among them."

Among the most important of the 18 congressional powers enumerated in the Constitution is the power of the purse—the authority to tax and the authority to spend. The authors of the Constitution insisted that this power reside in the House of Representatives. It also gave the Congress the power to impeach and, to the Senate, the power to confirm or deny Presidential appointments, and ratify treaties.

(Sometimes, it seems, the Founders thought of everything, including term limits, which had been among the provisions of the Articles of Confederation. The Constitutional Convention considered weaving term limits into its document. Instead it limited Members of the House of Representatives to two-year terms, naively assuming that would guarantee a constant flow of new blood into the Congress.)

At the Constitutional Convention of 1787, James Madison proposed the plan to divide the central government into three branches. He discovered this model of government from "the Perfect Governor," as he read Isaiah 33:22:

"For the LORD is our judge, the LORD is our lawgiver, the LORD is our king; He will save us."

There can be no confusion as to the intent of the Founders. They established the legislative branch as the seat of the government and the font from which the nation's newly won independence would flow. Its importance is reflected in the fact that Article One of the Constitution, which creates the legislature, is twice as long as Article Two, which establishes the executive branch, and four times as long as Article Three, which defines the judiciary.

Throughout the history of what the Founders referred to as the Republic, the balance of power has shifted back and forth among the executive, legislative and judicial branches. Factors such as the leadership abilities of those in charge, the political alliances they formed, and national and world events have contributed to shifts in the power structure that defines the three branches.

A famous political scientist, Richard Neustadt said the United States did not have a separation of powers, but rather "separate institutions sharing power." Sometimes they share better than others. As one Senate staffer said, "It is more like separate institutions competing for power."

Several Presidents have exercised substantial influence over the Congress, usually in times of national emergency, but the Congress has exercised substantial influence over Chief Executives, as well. Sometimes both occur during a single administration, as was the case with President Bill Clinton, a Democrat, who at times dominated the Republican-controlled Congress, which turned the tables on him, too. More recently, President Barack Obama achieved his legislative priorities in the first two years—healthcare, economic stimulus and financial regulation—but was unable to accomplish much of anything when the public elected a Republican Congress in 2010.

The relationship between the legislative and executive branches was less tempestuous in the early days of the Republic, particularly when the Legislature was dominated by supporters of the first President. George Washington is said to have been significantly influenced in the writing of his first inaugural address by James Madison, who at that time represented Virginia in Congress. The day following Washington's address, Madison was appointed to head a committee of the House to prepare a response to the President's message he'd helped to write.

Although Madison might be better remembered as a President, he exemplified the leadership potential and influence a person can assert as a legislator. As legislator, Madison headed a panel that drafted the first rules of the House and was a driving force behind the Bill of Rights, originally introduced as 12 amendments to the Constitution. Individuals from both the Federalist and Anti-Federalist factions opposed Madison's amendments. Anti-Federalist Aedanus Burke of South Carolina captured the spirit of the debate when he called the amendments "little better than whipsyllabub, frothy and full of wind, formed only to please the palate."

But Madison prevailed and the 12 amendments were submitted to the States for ratification on the last day of the 1st Congress. Ten were ratified. One of the two that were not adopted would have prohibited Congress from giving itself a pay raise while in session, which meant a raise could not take effect until after the next election. It was resurrected in 1992, and became the 27th and most recent amendment to the Constitution. (The non-ratified amendment is discussed below.)

Without Madison's dedication, the Constitution might never have been ratified. Those demanding that a Bill of Rights be added carried enough weight to permanently table the entire document. His success cleared the way for the 1st Congress to flex its oversight muscle early, instructing the executive departments it had just created to report back to it on various matters under the President's jurisdiction. The House also appointed a committee on Ways and Means to advise it on fiscal matters but dissolved it eight weeks later in favor of relying on advice from Secretary of the Treasury Alexander Hamilton—a reflection of the still-unresolved ambiguity in the roles played by the branches of our Federal Government.

The 1st Congress apparently had more confidence in other actions it took. It created three Federal departments—Treasury, War, and Foreign Affairs. It established the nation's court system, passed laws dealing with trade, patents, crime, mail, the military and bankruptcies, admitted two additional states into the Union and deliberated over slavery and relations with the native peoples they called Indians.

The Congress also established rules governing its internal operations. The House and Senate devised ways to communicate with each other and set salaries. The House also created the first permanent committee, the Committee on Elections to judge the qualification of its elected Members.

Interesting Firsts

In 1917, Jeannette Rankin of Montana was the first woman to serve in Congress as a Member of the House of Representatives.

Octaviano Ambrosio Larrazolo of New Mexico was the first Hispanic elected to the U.S. Senate. Joseph Marion Hernández of Florida, a Whig, was the first Hispanic elected to the House.

In 1869, Joseph H. Rainey became the first African-American Member of the House. In 1966, Edward Brooke of Massachusetts became the first African-American elected to the Senate.

The first time President Washington visited the Congress, he witnessed events that made it clear once and for all that, while the legislative, executive and judicial branches of government would be equals, the legislative would be more equal than the others, just as the Founders had intended. Washington and Secretary of War Henry Knox went to Federal Hall in New York City, which at the time was the nation's capital, to seek the Senate's advice—but more importantly, its consent. At issue was creation of a commission to negotiate a treaty with the Creek Indians, who at the time laid claim to much of what eventually would become Florida, Georgia and Alabama. If Washington and Knox expected a rubber stamp, they were sadly mistaken. Several Senators indicated that they wanted to see documents related to the plan and since no such documents were available, it was agreed that the issue ought to be referred to committee. There ensued an uncomfortable period of silence and muttering, during which Senator William Maclay of Pennsylvania observed that Washington was visibly irritated. When Washington and Knox retreated from the Chamber a short time later, the President vowed never to return. But he did, two days later, when the Senate approved the commission. The incident established the independence of the Senate in regard to meeting its Constitutional responsibility to provide advice about and consent to treaties—and it also marked the last time a President has shown up in person to petition that body for such a purpose.

Despite President Washington's disappointment, harmony, civility and willingness to compromise stood as hallmarks of decision-making in the 1st Congress. It considered 168 bills, of which 108, or 64 percent, were enacted. Its accomplishments were recorded in a little more than 500 days, with almost no incidents of incivility. (In fact, there were no political parties until the 3rd Congress when candidates began identifying themselves with Alexander Hamilton and John Adams' Federalists and Thomas Jefferson and James Madison's anti-Federalists.)

"There is less party spirit, less of the acrimony of pride when disappointed of success, less personality, less intrigue, cabal, management, or cunning than I ever saw in a public assembly," wrote Fisher Ames. "There was the most punctual attendance of the Members at the hour of meeting. Three or four have had leave of absence, but every other Member actually attends daily, till the hour of adjourning."

The Upper House—Literally!

It was at Federal Hall in New York City, site of the meeting of the first Congress, that the terms Upper House and Lower House were first used in reference to the Senate and the House of Representatives. It is commonly assumed that these designations refer to the power vested in these governing bodies, but in fact, they are the result of the building's architecture. The Senate could be accommodated within the comparatively modest confines of the structure's second floor, but the House required the more spacious first floor. Thus, the Senate was referred to as the Upper House and the House of Representatives the Lower House.

IN THE BEGINNING

"Small wonder they completed so much in such a short time," historian Robert V. Rimini writes in *The House: The History of the House of Representatives,* "and all this without a staff of assistants to aid them."

They got away with it because, despite the contentiousness surrounding various issues, life was simpler then—if only because there weren't as many people, lobbyists or TV cameras looking over the shoulders of those in the Congress and making demands upon their time and energy.

The addition of staff in the intervening years reflected the nation's growing population, more populated congressional districts, larger federal government activities and the expanding demands on the time of Members.

Today, elected officials and their staffs represent most every major segment of society and U.S. geography, most every religious belief, professional pursuit, education and political persuasion. Critics point out, however, that the proportion of lawyers far exceeds the ratio of lawyers to the rest of the nation's population and that women and minority representation is nowhere near their proportion in the population as a whole. Yet, the Congress is more representative now than it ever has been.

In our nation's earliest days, this fact of life didn't represent a significant problem. In general, the Congress and the people it represented subscribed to the philosophy of political theorist John Locke, who believed government ought to have as little influence as possible on the lives of the governed.

Abraham Lincoln enunciated it thusly: "The legitimate object of government is to do for a community of people whatever they need to have done, but cannot do at all, or cannot do so well, for themselves, in their separate and individual capacities."

Finding things the community of people could not do at all or not very well, Lincoln's definition of the role of government has become one of the driving raisons d'être of the Federal Government. Its search has been very successful—perhaps too successful, in the view of many. From the Constitutional Convention to the present, two major issues defining the differences between political factions have been the role of government in the lives of individual Americans, and the role of government in the economy.

By the time the 2nd Congress convened in 1791, the legislative branch began drifting away from the Lockean model. The influence of the Federal Government has been expanding ever since. Journalist Saul Pett points out that during the Civil War the offices of all the people who worked for the Federal Government would have fit comfortably in a building the size of the modern Pentagon. But it was growing at a hectic pace even then. The cork was out of the bottle, so to speak.

Yet, it wasn't until 1884 that Senators were finally authorized to employ staff, and even then it was only for the period when the Congress was in session. The Legislative Appropriations Act of 1891 specified that Senators who were not chairmen of committees would be provided with one clerk—that's it, just one—to handle administrative duties and free up the Senator to focus on the work he was elected to perform.

In 1893, the House of Representatives followed suit, allocating funds enough to employ a clerk for each Congressman. Representatives were earning $7,500 a year by this point, and it was their clerks who were being paid just $6 a day. It is worth noting that by the time the Congress got around to providing lawmakers with clerical help, many already had support staff and paid them out of their own pockets. The decision to pay these employees with tax dollars did more than just relieve these lawmakers' financial burden. It signaled the realization that the role of government and the demands that were being placed upon it were changing.

To avoid confusion, we'll pause here to explain that even though Senators are Members of the Congress, the term Congressman is generally reserved for Members of the House, unless, of course, they're women, but at the time we're talking about there wouldn't be any Congresswomen for another 23 years. (Actually, a handful of women in the House even prefer the term Congressman.) Individual Senators, by the way, are always referred to as Senator. Congressional staff, on the other hand, refers to employees of either the House or the Senate—or both.

In 1893 the Senate extended its authorization for clerical help from the period when the Congress was in session to year-round status, and by

1910, Senators were allowed to hire an additional staff member. Four years after that, they were authorized to increase their staff size to three.

Members of the House of Representatives didn't get three staff members until 1940, but they saw that number rise to six less than a decade later.

Senate staff allotments were increased to eight in 1947. A year later, limits on how many people a Senator could employ were abandoned altogether. Since then, the Senators have been provided an allowance and it is up to them to decide how to spend it. From 1951 onwards, the size of the allowance has been determined by the population of the Senator's state.

Comparatively speaking, staff sizes exploded in the 1960s, when the number of staff in the House of Representatives reached 12 per office before increasing to 18 in 1975. Four years later, each office was allowed to hire four additional temporary, part-time, or shared employees.

Those limits stand today and result in about 8,500 House staff and 4,800 Senate staff. In the House, staff sizes for personal offices average close to 18 but fluctuate as staff move on to jobs outside of government or are transferred to committee assignments—and to committee budgets—creating temporary vacancies that last until replacements can be found. Senators generally employ approximately 40 staffers.

Although staff sizes will probably remain stable, the workload will not. By the time Senate staff allotments reached eight in 1947, the ranks of executive branch agencies were increasing at such a rapid clip that tongue-in-cheek prognosticators predicted that by the year 2025, every resident of the United States would be working for the government.

Even if that prediction is realized, it is unlikely they'll be working for the Congress. There are a number of reasons, some political and some fiscal, why Members of Congress are reluctant to increase their staff. And the institution will probably not grow. Since membership in the Senate is limited to two from each state, the size of the Senate is not going to increase without a constitutional amendment, unless new states are admitted to the Union. The size of the House of Representatives is only slightly more likely to change if legislation is enacted to provide Washington, DC, with representation in the House or the number of districts is increased.

Between 1790 and 1910, the number of Representatives grew almost every decade to reflect increases in the nation's growing population. That process came to an abrupt halt in 1913, when Congress capped House membership at 435 in an attempt to retain rural dominance over the House.

Some historians claim the Founders never intended the population of a congressional district to exceed 50,000, let alone over 700,000, which is about the size of the districts today. The one amendment proposed by Madison in the Bill of Rights that was never ratified specifically limited the size of congressional districts to 50,000. Yet, if districts were limited to only 50,000 constituents the House would now have over 6,000 Members today!

"The principle of proportionally equitable representation has been abandoned," observes Thirtythousand.org, an advocate of reducing the size of constituencies. In that organization's view it is impossible for one person to adequately represent so many people.

You don't have to explain that to the overworked congressional staff members whose job it is to accommodate the needs of the ever-increasing

Madison's Failed Amendment

One of the 12 amendments originally proposed by Madison was never ratified. It would have limited the size of congressional districts.

"After the first enumeration required by the first article of the Constitution, there shall be one Representative for every thirty thousand, until the number shall amount to one hundred, after which the proportion shall be so regulated by Congress, that there shall be not less than one hundred Representatives, nor less than one Representative for every forty thousand persons, until the number of Representatives shall amount to two hundred; after which the proportion shall be so regulated by Congress, that there shall not be less than two hundred Representatives, nor more than one Representative for every fifty thousand persons."

Eighteen Enumerated Powers of Congress

Article I, Section 8 of the U.S. Constitution specifically enumerates 18 powers of Congress:

The Congress shall have Power To lay and collect Taxes, Duties, Imposts and Excises, to pay the Debts and provide for the common Defence and general Welfare of the United States;...

To borrow Money on the credit of the United States;

To regulate Commerce with foreign Nations, and among the several States, and with the Indian Tribes;

To establish an uniform Rule of Naturalization, and uniform Laws on the subject of Bankruptcies throughout the United States;

To coin Money, regulate the Value thereof, and of foreign Coin, and fix the Standard of Weights and Measures;

To establish Post Offices and Post Roads;

To promote the Progress of Science and useful Arts, by securing for limited Times to Authors and Inventors the exclusive Right to their respective Writings and Discoveries;

To constitute Tribunals inferior to the Supreme Court;

To define and punish Piracies and Felonies committed on the high Seas, and Offences against the Law of Nations;

To declare War, grant Letters of Marque and Reprisal, and make Rules concerning Captures on Land and Water;

To raise and support Armies, but no Appropriation of Money to that Use shall be for a longer Term than two Years;

To provide and maintain a Navy;

To make Rules for the Government and Regulation of the land and naval Forces;

To provide for calling forth the Militia to execute the Laws of the Union, suppress Insurrections and repel Invasions;

To provide for organizing, arming, and disciplining, the Militia...;

To exercise exclusive Legislation in all Cases whatsoever, over such District (not exceeding ten Miles square) as may, by Cession of particular States, and the Acceptance of Congress, become the Seat of the Government of the United States,...

To make all Laws which shall be necessary and proper for carrying into Execution the foregoing Powers, and all other Powers vested by this Constitution in the Government of the United States, or in any Department or Officer thereof.

number of constituents that each Member represents. Yet the need to increase the size of legislative staffs is not predicated solely on population growth. Without adequate personnel, Members of Congress simply cannot both serve their own constituencies and maintain oversight of countless Federal bureaucracies.

Congressional aides will not run out of work overseeing the bureaucracies or serving constituents, but not everyone considers tax dollars well spent when they are used to hire staff. Even the Congress sometimes expresses doubts, as it did in 1993 when congressional staffing became the focus of a joint committee inquiry. The only significant cut in staff ever made occurred the next year after the Republican takeover when the new majority cut all committee staffs by one-third. When the Republicans retook the House in 2011, they cut the office budgets by 11 percent for the 112th Congress, though it did not specifically cut the staff allotments. Furthermore, House Members are not required to spend all the funds allotted to them, so there is pressure to return money to the Treasury. In 2011 office expenditures ranged from a low of $870,000 to a high of nearly $1.7 million, according to calculations based on numbers gleaned from the Sunlight Foundation's report on congressional expenditures. According to a January 2012 Congressional Research Service report, Senate allowances ranged from about $3 million to $4.7 million for fiscal year 2012.

Despite occasional pressure from the public, the staff who help Members of Congress serve the needs of their constituencies and help shape laws that serve the changing needs of the nation probably would argue that they're anything but bloated.

Ambitious?

Yes!

Idealistic?

Obviously!

Overworked?

Always!

But bloated?

Not likely. The salaries paid on Capitol Hill may seem exorbitant to people in Peoria but not to those trying to make ends meet in one of

---

The Articles of Confederation and the European Union

After years of war, a group of sovereign states decided to form a loose political union where issues are decided by unanimous vote. Because the sovereign states maintained their independence, each had a different tax system and many had their own currencies. While they agreed to allow the free flow of people across borders, they often conducted their own foreign and trade policies. They maintained their own militaries and coastal navies. Several of the states had severe sovereign debt problems—owing much to foreign governments—while some of the sovereign states were nearly debt-free and resentful of the financial demands of their indebted neighbors. To deal with these issues, the political union formed its own currency, but, without the backing of sovereign states and the ability to directly tax citizens, it eventually became worthless.

A description of the European Union (E.U.)? Well, no—not intentionally. This describes the first American government under the Articles of Confederation, from 1783-1789. The Americans were faced with a choice either to become closer knit by ceding more sovereignty to a central government or to go their separate ways, and likely fall back under the influence of Great Britain, which still had troops on American soil and in Quebec.

The comparison is most assuredly not an exact one. But, the European Union, facing a sovereign debt crisis, a currency crisis and an ineffective governing system, probably will need to consider the same decision the early Americans did—should they become a United States of Europe, or should they go their separate ways? This is a question that only Europeans can decide, but—thanks in part to the United States—at least they can do so without the external threat of the former Soviet Union, unlike the post-Revolutionary Americans who were looking over their shoulders at the British. Ironically perhaps, "Euroscepticism"—resistance to tighter European integration—is strongest today among the British. Just one more thing the early Americans and the E.U. have in common?

the world's most expensive cities. Following the 2010 Census, several news outlets reported that the Washington, DC, area had displaced Silicon Valley as the nation's most affluent regions. At the same time, many congressional staffers earned much less than their private-sector counterparts, according to "Keeping Congress Competent," a December 2010 study on compensation in Washington produced by the Sunlight Foundation, a watchdog group advocating greater transparency in government. For instance, a corporate executive may earn nearly $190,000 per year, while a Hill chief of staff will earn about $25,000 less than that. The second in command in a congressional office, the legislative director, could earn about $86,000, whereas a general manager in the private sector might receive $128,000 yearly.

Congress remains the branch of government that is truly representative of the people it serves, and as a result those who work on the Hill, elected or non-elected, get their share of complaints, criticisms, second-guessing, and sometimes nastiness, from the media, interest groups and their constituencies. Some organizations exist for the sole or primary purpose of criticizing Congress and they are able to raise money doing it if they are good at it.

There is even one organization that relishes in declaring to the world the salaries of each congressional employee—including college interns and receptionists. They would probably print the dating history and list of Facebook friends of every Hill employee if they thought they could get away with it.

It's easy to become defensive when you're on the receiving end of this sort of carping—but it's a fact of life that comes with the job. As Harry Truman noted, "If you can't stand the heat, get out of the kitchen."

If being misunderstood hurts your feelings, find another line of work. Those who benefit most from the experience of working for Congress are the ones who develop a thick skin, the ones who are undaunted by the slights of those at whose pleasure they serve and the ones with enough self-confidence to believe that what they're doing makes a difference. They are also the ones who provide constituents with the best service and devote more of their time to informing and educating those they serve, so that communication stays positive and the work is productive.

Chapter One Summary

- The 1st Congress convened in 1789 when the 65 Members of the House of Representatives and the 26 Senators met in the nation's capital—New York City. Neither the House nor the Senate had personal staff support. Today there are 435 Members of the House and 100 Senators.

- At the time of the nation's founding, only white, land-owning men were allowed to vote and they, for the most part, fell into just a few occupational classes: merchants, farmers and ranchers. Most were not formally educated, communications were poor and Congress received little advice or feedback from the governed. Today, the education level of the constituents almost equals that of Members, communications are instantaneous and citizens frequently know more about specific topics than the Members.

- Twelve amendments were originally proposed to the U.S. Constitution. Ten were initially ratified and are known as the Bill of Rights. Another was ratified in 1992 and specifies that when Congress votes itself a pay raise, another election cycle must occur before it takes effect. Only one of the first twelve proposed amendments has not been adopted. That amendment would have established a constitutional process for limiting the size of congressional districts that have grown from their original 30,000 citizens to over 700,000 today. That growth has significantly changed the nature of being a Member of Congress and both dictated the number and duties of congressional staff.

- Congress' oversight authority was first deployed when President Washington visited the Senate for what he assumed would be quick "advice and consent" to his proposed commission to negotiate a treaty with the Creek Indians. Washington sat in dismay as the proposal was questioned and documents were sought by an ad hoc committee to study the treaty.

- Congressional staff was unheard of in the early days of the republic. Not until 1891 did the Senate authorize the hiring of one staff member for each Senator. The House followed suit and authorized the payment of $6 per day for one staff person per Member in 1893.

- The need for oversight is one reason Senate staff allotments increased to eight in 1947. A year later, limits on how many people a Senator could employ were abandoned altogether. Since then, the Senators have been provided an allowance, to be used at their discretion. From 1951 onwards, the size of the allowance has been determined by the population of the Senator's state.

- Comparatively speaking, staff sizes exploded in the 1960s, when the number of full-time staff in the House of Representatives reached 12 per office before increasing to 18 in 1975, the current limit. Four years later, each office was allowed to hire four additional temporary, part-time or shared employees. The Senate now averages around 40 staff members per personal office.

- The only significant cut in staff ever made occurred after the Republican takeover in 1994 when the new majority cut all committee staffs by one-third.

There's no shame in using an appointment to the congressional staff as a stepping-stone. Nearly everyone who works for the Congress is a temp, most of all the elected officials who run the show but whose futures are as uncertain as the next election. If the boss is defeated, the entire staff is fired, though many stay on the Hill, working for another Member. What little job security there is usually derives from a staff member's dedication, talent and experience—not to mention the gerrymandering of congressional districts to protect Members from opposition and keep them in office.

Despite these harsh realities, congressional offices have little problem filling vacancies. They typically receive anywhere from several hundred to several thousand applications a year from people intent on serving the public by serving the institution and those elected. Although patronage no longer is the surest means to a job in government, elected officials still put a premium on ideological compatibility and familiarity within the district or state they represent—especially among those in their inner circle. Yet, education, professional skills and the ability to produce results are in greater demand than ever before, and there are many people with those skills eager to fill any slot that comes open.

People start their careers in different ways. They can start at the bottom as an intern or at the top as chief of staff. For most, however, the advice aspirants hear most often from veterans is: "Just get your foot in the door."

This is good advice. The problem with Hill jobs is that they are rarely advertised. You have to be in the right place at the right time—you drop by an office to apply the day the front desk staffer walked out, for example—or you have to work your way into the informal grapevine that spreads the word when there's a vacancy.

For individuals in college or just graduated, the best avenue is an internship or entry-level staff assistant job. Prepare a resume that lists your education and experience—include summer jobs and volunteer activities that demonstrate a willingness to work hard and make sacrifices for others. For heaven's sake, use spell-check and grammar review software—it is amazing how many people do not and wonder why they never are called.

It is essential to prepare for an interview, including research on the Member and the district. There are numerous books with biographies and information on the state or district, but the best place to start is usually the Member's own website.

Prospects should be able to explain why they would want to work for the Member they are interviewing with, what they like about the Member, and what they may have in common and what skills they bring to the office.

The person conducting the interview—most likely the legislative director or chief of staff—will not expect an encyclopedic knowledge but will be looking for certain skills. Preparation and research are two of the most important ways of communicating enthusiasm and diligence.

Your appearance and how you present yourself are important, as well. Dress in business attire—even if the House and Senate are in recess, and be on time. Don't look at your watch and turn off all of your electronic gadgets before you enter the office.

And finally, the interviewer will realize you're nervous and trying to make a good impression, so be yourself. If you are arrogant, abrasive or rude, it will be assumed that you would be a disruptive influence and not a good hire.

Hill offices are always looking for interns, especially in the non-summer months. A summer internship is a great experience—in the Senate, it even pays enough to cover your expenses in DC—but offices need interns most during the spring and fall. Most colleges have internship programs and often offer college credit for a semester in the nation's capital. Take advantage of them.

Hill veterans will quickly sort interns into three categories:

1) Offspring of a friend of the Congressman, or FOCs.

2) Nice kid, but not cut out for the Hill.

3) Potential staff material.

Every moment an intern serves in a congressional office, he or she is often auditioning for a permanent job—whether he or she understands that or not. Offices typically promote from within first.

Coming to work with a hangover one day can irreparably damage a reputation. Blowing off a request for help from a permanent staff member will also earn a permanent mark against you. Saying something offensive to a constituent that a senior staff member has to apologize for will probably get an intern sent home.

Staff, new or old, permanent or temporary, must always be on their best behavior, even after checking out for the day. Everyone, from the newest intern to the chief of staff, learns quickly that even their private actions can have consequences—if only because reporters and political opponents will exploit to the detriment of the Congressman. In 2011, a group of young staffers rented a beach house in Annapolis and trashed the place while claiming to neighbors they were on congressional business. Even though the irresponsible staffer's boss had no idea what they were up to, the Congressman suffered the consequences.

On the other hand, working hard, lending a hand wherever it's needed and taking every opportunity to learn something new will get an intern noticed. A good attitude and great manners—especially around constituents—also go far.

When an entry-level opening does occur—usually at the staff assistant or legislative correspondent level—an intern who caught the eye of superiors is often times on the short list of candidates. That's because an internship provides far better evidence of an applicant's talents and abilities than a good resume, a thirty-minute job interview and solid references.

If you can't relocate to Washington, DC, look into the possibility of interning in a district or state office. Sometimes an internship at that level can be even more advantageous than one in DC. When Members are in their home offices, their schedules may be less intense and provide opportunities to get to know the intern driving them from one town to another to meet with constituents.

Another popular method of attracting attention is to work on a campaign. Campaigns are incredibly intense but at the same time fun. The camaraderie between campaign workers is similar to the bond between soldiers. As Winston Churchill once observed with tongue firmly in cheek: "Politics is just like war, except in war you can only die once—in politics many times."

There are key differences between working on a campaign and working in a congressional office—some of which are discussed later in the book—but a smart, hard-charging staffer will usually be noticed, appreciated and rewarded.

Politics is really the last of the great meritocracies. Academic credentials are nice—but they don't mean all that much in a Hill office. It doesn't matter where you came from, what your background is, or your gender, religion or race. If you help a Member succeed, he or she is going to find a way to keep you in the political family.

People who come to Washington without a job often are unable to land one right away. Don't be discouraged. Sometimes the timing is just wrong. The next best thing is to get into the orbit that revolves around the Hill. Political party organizations, think tanks, and lobbying and consulting groups, as well as the thousands of associations and non-profit groups headquartered in Washington, are always looking for research assistants. Many of these organizations work directly with the Hill and offer the opportunity to develop contacts, friendships and networks that form the Capitol Hill job grapevine.

Some will take a more direct route to the Hill, but these are people who, for the most part, will occupy senior level positions. A campaign manager, for example, might be hired as chief of staff—but it's not as common as you might assume—or a campaign spokesman might become press secretary, which is a far more natural fit. Someone with expertise in a topic near and dear to a Member's heart might be hired into a policy position or onto a committee staff. Almost every situation is unique.

The greatest challenge facing those fortunate enough to be hired lies in fulfilling expectations. The public's demand for efficient, cost-effective government often exceeds what mere humans can produce. That's why it's a good idea to bring more than altruism to a job on the Hill.

Typically, staff members share a desire to:

- Immerse oneself in public-policy issues and the art of governing;
- Make more money;
- Follow in the footsteps of a relative or mentor;
- Acquire celebrity, fame or notoriety;
- Amass and exercise power
- Promote a partisan or philosophical agenda;
- Or simply serve the public.

Some new staff members consider themselves devotees of the art of politics: They are there to advance a party or ideology.

Others consider themselves issue specialists or policy experts and advocates: They are there to promote issue-related outcomes.

The most successful congressional staff members possess the best qualities of both—political and policy savvy and the intelligence to use it productively. Such staff members are essential to the successful operation of the Congress and make it possible for the elected to legislate.

Yet circumstances dictate that the vast majority of those working at any one time in a congressional office will take the experience and contacts they've accumulated to other jobs. They may find themselves employed in the executive branch, in academia, or the private sector.

Some staff leave public service, only to return through elective office. President Lyndon B. Johnson was a House staffer before serving in both Chambers and as President and Vice President. Vice Presidential candidate Paul Ryan began his career as an intern in the Senate and later as a legislative assistant to the late Jack Kemp, who was himself a Vice Presidential candidate. Bob Michel of Illinois, who was the House's GOP leader before his retirement, and former Senate Republican Whip Trent Lott of Mississippi began their careers on congressional staffs. Actor and former Senator Fred Thompson worked on the Hill as a junior counsel for the House Judiciary Committee. So did Democrats Tom Harkin and Hillary Clinton. All in all, according to the Congressional Research Service (CRS) 105 Members of the 112th Congress had been congressional staffers and 9 had been pages earlier in their careers.

Congressional staff anticipating they'd be there until retirement are often lured away by industry, other branches of government or the vast range of agencies that benefit from the skills and knowledge of those who've been intimately involved in the lawmaking process. Those who stay, though fewer in number than those who move on, may have arrived on Capitol Hill with plans of cutting their teeth there, then moving to the higher-paying, high-visibility jobs, but discover themselves better suited to working behind the scenes and end up remaining.

The staffers who do stay, for the most part, fit well in the unique role of congressional aide. They come to terms with the role of subordinate and the ego-bursting reality that they will seldom get credit or recognition for the ideas, concepts and innovations they bring to public policy. Their ideas see the light of day only when adopted, articulated and advanced by elected Members of the institution. They are agents of the constitutionally elected people they serve and the good staff are comfortable and effective in that role. Their job satisfaction derives from the fact that their opinions are considered and sometimes their ideas are implemented and the process is better for it.

These career professionals are the nucleus of Capitol Hill. They are the glue that holds the Congress together, the unseen, unheard, unsung heroes of the legislative branch. They know the ins and outs of the legislative process, as well as the history of almost every Federal policy, from environmental issues to tax laws.

Like all professions, theirs has distinctive cultural aspects, and archaic codes unique to the Hill. For example, among Congress' archaic codes is an antiquated system of bells, buzzers and lights that is used to summon Members of the Congress for a vote on the Chamber floor. In the old days, this was the only means to guarantee that every Member within earshot knew his or her presence was required.

Because voting is the one task a Member may not delegate, each Member must make his or her way to the floor when summoned—usually within 15 minutes. Members learn quickly how long it will take them to get to the Chamber from anywhere on the congressional campus and often cut their departure as close as humanly possible to give them time to finish whatever they were doing when summoned. There was a time when staff members were expected to be experts on the system of bells, lights and buzzers so they could remind the boss in case he or she lost track of time. Modern staffs rely on emails, portable electronic devices and closed-circuit telecasts of what's taking place on the floor and keep their bosses updated by email or text message.

The system of bells, buzzers and lights, the Mace, the bowing protocols and other pomp and circumstance surrounding the House and Senate distinguish the institution and preserve its unique and revered place in our national body politic. Some of these may seem anachronistic to the uninitiated—they definitely can prove mind numbing to master and downright disturbing when they unexpectedly shatter your concentration—but they aren't likely to be abandoned just to make life easier for newcomers. Eventually, they'll contribute to the richness of your memories, whether your stay on a congressional staff proves to be a temporary oasis or the last job you ever have.

One dying tradition that could use resuscitation is the encouragement of staff friendships across the partisan aisle. And why not? For the most part staff from both sides have a remarkable amount in common: similar education levels and majors, similar salaries and working conditions, similar social circles—it's entirely possible that they find themselves on the same soccer sideline cheering their kids on towards the goal. They happen to have differing opinions on some issues—not unlike most family gatherings at the Thanksgiving dinner table. These relationships allow cooler heads to prevail during heated debates by creating informal communication channels that allow staff to work on compromises without exposing their bosses to public attack. Today, far too few staff in the Congress have friends in the other party. This is one of the consequences of an environment that breeds partisan polarization and governmental gridlock, which will be discussed in more detail later in the book.

The good career professionals build relationships, but they also become expert mechanics in the craft of legislating. They obtain a working knowledge of parliamentary procedure and historical precedents. They develop expertise in particular areas of public policy and process making them indispensible to Members of Congress and other staff colleagues who do not have the luxury of honing the sharpness of those tools. The same holds true for communications directors and press secretaries who become important resources to the media and the public.

Whatever roles they might play in an office, star staffers should be skilled communicators able to communicate with people both inside and outside Congress. A good staffer will know how to communicate with colleagues in either Chamber, whether they serve on personal, committee, or leadership staffs, each of which has a unique character and a language all its own. The best aides also perfect communications with counterparts in other branches and other levels of government, private sector organizations that have an impact on public policy and most importantly, the private citizens whose welfare is the reason for their service.

Their knowledge and skills enable the best staff to survive the daily challenges, as well as the winds of change that blow through the nation every decade or so, or, in the case of 2006, 2008, 2010 and 2012, every two years (rarely in our history has Congressional turnover been so dramatic so often as it has the last eight years).

New Members bring with them new staffs, but invariably they rely on the veterans to help them navigate through unfamiliar rules, procedures and protocols, to say nothing of the small fiefdoms and principalities that dot the landscape, from the massive enclaves of the Library of Congress to the offices of the Clerk, the Sergeant at Arms and the through the lines at the Longworth Cafeteria. Newcomers also find a universe that bears little resemblance to their expectations. They come to the nation's capital with dreams of conquering the panoply of complex issues facing America, from globalization's cultural and economic ramifications to educational needs in a rapidly changing scientific and technological environment. They quickly learn that answering constituent mail can be their most urgent priority on any given day.

Genuine Politics

In a speech in 1993, famous dissident and later President of the Czech Republic Václav Havel said: *"Those who claim that politics is chiefly the manipulation of power and public opinion, and that morality has no place in it are wrong. Political intrigue is not really politics, and, although you can get away with superficial politics for a time, it does not bring much hope for success... Genuine politics—politics worthy of the name—is simply a matter of serving those around us: serving the community, and serving those who come after us. Its deepest roots are moral because it is a responsibility, expressed through action, to and for the whole..."*

Less daunting than coming up with solutions to the world's problems is the need to review the lessons you learned in high school civics:

- The entire House of Representatives must be elected every two years, forming a completely new Congress that must elect (or re-elect) its party leaders, adopt its own rules and appoint its officers; Members of the Senate serve six-year terms, but the terms are staggered so that approximately one-third of the Senate is elected every election cycle—making the Senate the only ongoing legislative body in the world.

- Senators represent entire states; House Members represent districts within each state—districts that are a fraction the size of the states and whose inhabitants tend to be more cohesive in their attitudes (with the obvious exception of single-Member states—Alaska, Delaware, Montana, North Dakota, Rhode Island, South Dakota, Vermont and Wyoming).

- Senators serve on more committees and have larger staffs to support their efforts; House Members typically don't even have committee specialists on their staffs until they achieve seniority—nor are they required to develop expertise in as broad a range of committee topics.

- Some believe that all House Members want to be Senators and all Senators want to be President. However, the election of 2008 was the first in nearly half a century to elect a Senator as President.

The Culture of the House and Senate

Staff will have a very steep learning curve when they first start out, but they are expected to have a cursory knowledge of institutions of government and how they work. For example, they should know the answer to some very basic questions:

Can appropriation bills be initiated in the Senate?

Does the House ratify treaties?

Do House Members vote to confirm nominees to the Federal court system?

Can a supermajority of the Senate and House amend the Constitution?

Can a simple majority vote of both houses can override a veto?

Do House members serve for four years?

Do all Senators and House Members run for office at the same time?

Was the capital of the United States always Washington, DC?

(The answer to all of these questions is no, by the way.)

Most of your peers will assume you understand such basics and will not take time to explain them. This assumption is so firmly entrenched, in fact, that it has led to conversational shorthand to describe congressional actions. Were a House colleague to say, for example, that a bill has gone to Rules, he or she would mean the legislation has been approved at the committee level and submitted to the Rules Committee where it will be scheduled for debate on the floor.

The same expression will not be heard in the Senate, which does not rely on a committee to control the flow of work on the Senate floor or determine how long debate will be. In most cases, the rules of the Senate do not vary from one bill to the next, and the Senate majority leader handles scheduling.

Keep in mind that the Constitution says that Members of Congress answer only to their constituents for their official actions, including how they vote or manage their offices, unless their Chamber sanctions them for misbehavior.

Become familiar with the culture of the legislative branch as a whole, as well as distinctions between the culture of the Senate and the culture of the House.

The House consists of 435 independent players representing all of the people in 435 congressional districts in the nation. In addition, the House has five non-voting delegates from the territories and one from the District of Columbia. It is a majoritarian institution—meaning it was deliberately designed to allow a unified majority to push its agenda through, even if it means steamrolling the minority.

The 100 U.S. Senators are equally independent. However the Senate is deliberately designed to protect the rights of the minority party, even if it occasionally frustrates the will of the majority party.

The stature of the offices these men and women hold affords them a semblance of respect among fellow citizens, their colleagues and staff. Maintaining appearances is essential and part of the culture. Congressional employees may be on a first-name basis with the boss in the office but are expected to address him or her formally in the presence of outsiders: Say "Congressman Smith" or "Congresswoman Applegate," for example, when speaking to a constituent, other Members or the media. Always address other Members formally unless invited to do otherwise—and even then, follow the same rules that apply in your relationship with your boss.

Familiarize yourself with the roles of other staff in your congressional office, as well as personnel in other offices, committees and the leadership. Employees of the legislative branch are much more interdependent than, for example, those in the Department of Agriculture, which has somewhere in the neighborhood of 100,000 employees with a range of specialties and a measure of autonomy working in offices scattered around the world. A congressional employee, on the other hand, might oversee her office's computer operations while the staffer sitting next to her might manage scheduling and another neighbor might be a central player in legislation or constituent services. Mutual respect is vital to peaceful and prosperous co-existence.

Successful staffers respect the history of the Congress. They become sensitive to its ebb and flow. They recognize it as a living part of the body politic, one with muscles and nerves that give it elasticity and ever-changing form. Successful staffers understand the goals and aspirations of the Member they serve and how those hopes affect the behavior of not only the Member but his or her staff and everyone else working on the Hill.

Learn to recognize formal and informal power structures and the relationships among the staffs of Members, between the staffs of Members and those of leadership. Leaders in both parties may do their best to persuade Members to march in lock step, for example, but they have limited leverage to do so. That is why former Senator Trent Lott titled his book on leadership *Herding Cats*.

Be aware most of all that the Congress is a well-lighted fishbowl that is monitored 24 hours a day by lobbyists, traditional media, independent bloggers, political adversaries and dozens of non-profit organizations whose existence is dependent upon their self-appointed role as over-seers of the body politic. Those in government are often painted with broad strokes and harsh tones. Sometimes it seems that as far as these watchdogs are concerned, whatever public servants are doing is never enough and usually wrong.

The Balancing Act

Members of Congress serve their constituents in many ways, but the most difficult is making tough decisions for the good of the nation. Some of the more cynical political observers, such as political scientist David Mayhew, believe that Member of Congress are solely motivated by the desire to be reelected. In reality, it is impossible to apply a common motivation to each Member of Congress.

In making decisions, legislative staff members must learn to balance political awareness, sensitivity to voter attitudes, the legislative process and constituent service.

All power is situational and temporary. Members of the House and Senate get to the Congress by a variety of routes and for a variety of reasons. The same holds true for their staff. The positions they hold are not necessarily based on skill, experience or knowledge. Their tenure is subject to the whim of the electorate or their boss. Decisions made in

---

Who are the House Buildings Named For?

Nicholas Longworth from Ohio was a prominent Republican politician active during the first few decades of the 20th century. He served as House majority leader from 1923 to 1925 and subsequently as Speaker of House from 1925 to 1931. He was married—not always happily—to Teddy Roosevelt's daughter Alice (who campaigned against him for reelection).

Republican Joseph "Uncle Joe" Cannon served as Speaker of the House from 1903 to 1911, and historians generally consider him to be the most authoritarian Speaker in United States history. At the time of Cannon's election, the Speaker of the House concurrently held the chair of the Rules Committee. He lost his power in a Republican revolt led by George Norris and Nicholas Longworth.

Sam Rayburn, also known as Mr. Democrat, was a Democrat from Texas, who served as the Speaker of the House for seventeen years, the longest tenure in U.S. history. He was a close friend and mentor of LBJ. Rayburn's career as Speaker was interrupted twice: 1947–1948 and 1953–1954, when Republicans controlled the House. During those periods he so disliked the term *Minority Leader* that he asked to be referred to as the *Democratic Leader,* a practice that continues to this day. He was known for fairness and integrity and had close friends in both parties.

the Congress are based on consensus. Because power there is transient, there are no accepted rules for how a Member should decide whether to support or oppose a measure. It should come as no surprise then that when a Member is forced to take a position, it is as much shaped by outside pressures, and the imperative to compromise as by simple logic.

Among the reasons it's hard to decide whether a Member should vote his or her conscience or his or her constituency's sentiment is the leeway provided by the Founding Fathers when they took what they considered the best qualities of a republic and best qualities of a democracy and created our democratic republic.

- A democracy is directly governed by majority rule: In our case, the ballot box is used to elect individuals and adopt or reject initiatives or referendums.

- A republic is indirectly governed: In our case, the U.S. Constitution puts the burden on those elevated to positions of authority to make decisions based on their best judgment.

In the Federalist Papers, James Madison defined a republic as a representative democracy as opposed to a direct one. Reflecting both forms is not easy, particularly when a representative knows more about an issue than the constituents. Thus, there is a never-ending tension between following the people and leading them—and conflicting obligations, as well. Members of Congress are sometimes challenged to weigh their beliefs and their knowledge against public opinion. There are circumstances in which a Member must make a choice between voting a conviction that one course of action is in the best interests of the country and his or her district or state, or voting for another course that seems to be the more popular among his or her constituents. In the former case, the Member is then obligated to return to the district or state and convince the constituency that his or her judgment should prevail over theirs. A third situation can arise where the House Member or Senator feels obligated to vote on an issue in the best interests of the country, but maybe not in the best interests of the district or state. In that case, again the Member is obligated to return home and explain his or her vote. These are the challenges that face a representative in a republic form of government. There is often no right or wrong course, only choices to be made. However, they all must bear in mind that many elected officials and their staffs have

Three Perspectives on Representation

- "A portrait is excellent in proportion to its being a good likeness—the legislature ought to be a most exact transcript of the whole society."
  —James Wilson (Signer of Declaration and Constitution and one of the original Supreme Court justices)

- "Your representative owes you, not his industry only, but his judgment; and he betrays instead of serving you if he sacrifices it to your opinion."
  —Edmund Burke, Member of Parliament

- "Members of Congress need to be at least as clear on the reasons why they would risk losing as they are on the reasons why they wanted to come here in the first place."
  —The late Representative Henry Hyde of Illinois

been doomed when a strongly held belief or principle conflicted with the equally adamantly held opinions of voters back home. Just ask the Blue Dog Democrats who lost their seats in 2010 when they voted for President Obama's health care reform bill.

Whether or not a Member is motivated solely by the desire to be reelected, or perhaps gain power within the Congress by pleasing their party's leadership, or even just try to enact good policy, political decision-making seems similar to what a business school graduate would refer to as the rational choice model of decision-making. According to this theory, a decision maker analyzes the situation, examines the possible alternatives, weighs the cost and decides on the best solution. While not exactly the same, like a businessman, the seasoned legislator does indeed use a form of a rational decision-making model where outcomes are measured in the currency of politics: votes and political support, not dollars and cents. Politicians will seek to propose the solution that maximizes political gains and minimizes political costs. (Political gains may include gaining power within the Congress or setting up a run for higher office as well as trying to get reelected).

Of course government is not a business, and cannot be run like one. But that is not the point here. While politicians have specific reasons for the positions they take that may or may not produce the typical business outcome, they are rational people making decisions that maximize political benefits. Whatever their political motivation, however, there is an expectation by the media and the public that they rationally explain their actions in terms that maximize the public benefit. Think of it as "rational justification."

The public, therefore, uses the rational choice model as the standard of accountability. The irony is that even if they arrived at their own policy preferences through non-rational or emotional means they will still want to justify their opinions in a rational way.

In short, whether or not a policy proposal actually is made consistent with the rational choice model, politicians will need to justify their actions according to it.

The health care debate in the 111th Congress is a good illustration. Let's use the example of medical liability (the authors are not commenting on the merit of the proposal, but it's a good example because it tends to divide the Congress along party lines). A purely rational decision-making process based on finding the best solution at the lowest cost might have included medical liability reform. Proponents argue that tort reform eliminates defensive medicine and needless diagnostic tests. Defenders of medical liability claim that cost savings brought about by tort reform would prevent innocent victims of medical malpractice from obtaining justice. Both sides were backed by strong political proponents. However, for the Democrats, who controlled the legislative process and drafted the bill, the political cost of including a rational economic decision opposed by one of their key coalition groups—the trial lawyers—would be too great and would split their governing coalition. Nonetheless, the policy-makers in charge would need to make an argument to the public about why it is not cost effective to include tort reform. Ultimately the public judges that explanation at the ballot box.

Just to make sure we are being fair, try to imagine the reaction to a member of the Republican Party suggesting his party support tax increases to reduce the deficit. Whether an actual economic rational choice can be made to justify it, proposing tax increases would involve political costs that most Republicans could not afford.

President Lyndon Johnson, who had also been Senate Majority Leader, experienced that conflict when as President he tried to convince his fellow Southern Democrats to support the Civil Rights Act of 1964. Despite the fact that Johnson previously had resisted such change in the Senate and despite their assurances that they would support the measure when it came to a vote, many of those Democrats voted nay. Had it not been for Johnson's long-time political adversary (but not enemy), Republican Leader Everett Dirksen of Illinois, he probably would not have been able to produce the votes he needed to win passage of the Civil Rights Act. Johnson rightly calculated that while many Southern Democrats thought the political costs too high for supporting the Voting Rights Act, the majority of Republican Senators did not, and therefore he could appeal to them to pass the landmark legislation. More recently, when President George W. Bush determined it was necessary to the survival of the world financial system to pass the Troubled Asset Relief Program (TARP) legislation he had to appeal to his political opponents in the Democratic

Party to pass the emergency legislation because the political cost of supporting what constituents perceived as a "bailout" was too great for many Republicans.

The passage of the TARP legislation was extraordinary, but often you'll find that the work can be mundane, seemingly counterproductive and sometimes counter-intuitive, with conclusions and outcomes often elusive. This sometimes produces a conflict of objectives between representing state or district interests and serving national or partisan political or policy interests. Dealing with that conflict in priorities also complicates the demands on your time. Egos, political ambitions and jealousies are magnified in this environment, usually at the expense of staff relationships and office efficiency.

And yet these quirks contribute to the human dynamic that is the U.S. Congress and make it an unparalleled gathering of Americans trying to ensure that self-government lives up to its ever expanding potential. And it is this institution of Congress that has shaped the greatest government in history for the richest country and the most blessed people.

Chapter Two Summary

- The majority of congressional staff do not remain with the Congress for a life-long career.

- Those that do remain form the nucleus of Capitol Hill. They are the glue that holds the Congress together. They know the ins and outs of the legislative process, as well as the history of almost every Federal policy, from environmental issues to tax laws. Like all professions, theirs has distinctive cultural aspects and archaic codes unique to the Hill.

- According to the CRS, 105 Members of the 112th Congress had been congressional staffers and 9 had been pages earlier in their careers.

- Job openings in the congressional world are rarely advertised; it pays to be at the right place at the right time and to know Members of the House, Senators or other staff. Internships and campaign work (voluntary or paid) are great avenues to entry.

- Politics is really one of the last great meritocracies. Academic credentials are nice, but they don't mean all that much in a Hill office.

- Staff must become familiar with the culture of the legislative branch as a whole, as well as distinctions between the culture of the Senate and the culture of the House. Successful staffers respect the history of the Congress.

- Be aware most of all that the Congress is a well-lighted fishbowl that is monitored 24 hours a day by mainstream media, independent bloggers, lobbyists, political adversaries and dozens of non-profit organizations whose livelihoods depend upon their self-appointed role as overseers of the body politic.

Every organization has a hierarchy, whether it is Microsoft or the PTA. Understanding such hierarchies can mean the difference between succeeding or merely surviving, particularly in Washington, DC.

Just as no Member of Congress owes allegiance to any other, neither is there uniformity in staff titles and their meaning or function. While each office has great autonomy, Members must respond to a maze of obligations ranging from committee assignments and party loyalties to constituent demands. Each office has its own unique hierarchy.

A Member's interests typically reflect his or her personal background and the concerns of his or her constituents. A district from Kansas or Iowa, for instance, is likely to elect a Representative interested in farm policy. Those representing western states are likely to seek appointment to the Interior or Natural Resources Committees. A lawyer or a doctor prior to election may want to serve on the Judiciary Committee or a committee involved in health issues such as Ways and Means or Energy and Commerce.

When first elected, most Members don't get their first choice and not all get a committee that addresses their home district's or state's most pressing concerns. They're more likely to be appointed to second-choice committees, where they await opportunity to move up should someone retire or be unseated. There are rare times, however, such as a change of control in the Chamber, where numerous openings are created on major committees. Many members of the large 2011 Republican freshmen class were appointed to seats on prize committees like Ways and Means, Appropriations and Energy and Commerce.

Once in Washington, a new Member looks for experienced staffers who can get the office running, handle committee chores and deal with the Federal and state agencies on behalf of constituent needs. Staff tends to reflect the Member's background, interests and state or district, but the organizational structure may typically mimic that of his or her predecessor, if they are of the same party. Obviously, the new Member brings a new direction and needs, but it's usually beneficial to look to the predecessor's staff and approach to office needs and constituent services and learn from the practices that worked and those that didn't.

Unless the new Member is replacing someone from the opposition party, it's likely some of the predecessor's staff will even be retained, in the short term at least, providing the continuity and experience that will enable the newcomer to focus on more urgent matters. At a minimum, however, the newcomer is likely to bring along a couple of trusted allies, usually people from back home and the campaign.

When the district's representation changes parties, it is not unusual to see a total turnover in staff and even a reshuffling of the location of district offices and committee preferences.

Personal Staff

Despite the fact that Senate offices typically have more than twice the staff of their counterparts in the House, the organization charts of the two Chambers are very similar.

Not surprisingly, the Member occupies the pinnacle of the power structure, but who's next in line?

In the vast majority of offices, the chief of staff is the Member's strong right-arm, the most important hiring decision the Member makes—sometimes, the only one. An effective chief influences every aspect of the Member's political and professional life.

You'll sometimes hear the position referred to as an administrative assistant. Don't be misled. In non-congressional parlance, administrative assistant may be a euphemism for executive secretary, which is an important position, but an effective chief of staff carries considerably more responsibility.

In the absence of the Member, the chief is the boss. Even in the Member's presence, the chief makes decisions affecting how things get done. On one level, the chief functions very much like a Chief Operating Officer (COO), holding everyone else within his or her domain accountable to the Member's mission and goals, supervising every aspect of the congressional office. The chief oversees the legislative and communication operations and helps coordinate relations between the Member's personal office, on the one hand, and committees and leadership, on the other. The chief also coordinates the activities of the DC office with the Member's district or state office. Sometimes the chief even coordinates interaction between the office and the Member's family.

In addition, the chief has a hand in policy initiatives and even re-election efforts. Although the chief is legally prohibited from participating in campaign activities during working hours, he or she is usually the liaison between the congressional office and the Member's campaign staff—particularly if the chief played a role in getting the Member elected in the first place.

Some chiefs are former campaign managers, but the nature of a government office and a campaign are quite different. Conventional wisdom suggests that individuals that have experience on the Hill or previously served on the Member's senior staff at another level of government may be better suited for the task. This is why there is a great deal of turnover among new chiefs of staff in the first year of a freshman legislator's term. For a campaign manager to be a successful chief of staff he or she needs to re-learn how to manage people and operate in an atmosphere that more closely resembles a small business than a political campaign.

Despite the responsibilities heaped on the chief, there are no legally mandated qualifications for the job: no experience or age requirements, no degree or certification requirement—nothing. As a result, it's not common but entirely possible for a Harvard Law School graduate to be working the phones in the front office under the supervision of a chief of staff whose academic achievements stopped at graduation from high school. Far more important than degrees are a chief's personal qualities, primarily political acumen, competence and loyalty.

Regardless of what sort of relationship exists between the Member and the chief at the time of the appointment, if they survive the first term together, they are likely to become life-long friends and confidants.

The Member will usually be less involved in the hiring of other staff, taking a collaborative role in the selection of senior positions but pretty much leaving others to the chief. The Member is likely to be involved in selecting a legislative director or communications director, for example, but far less involved, if at all, in hiring legislative correspondents, a staff assistant or receptionist.

The focus of staff members who report to the chief fall into four basic categories:

Legislative

Communication

Outreach and Constituent Service

Support and Administrative Staff

The legislative team deals with what many think of as the main job of Congress: the making and amending of laws. These staff members manage the legislative process throughout all its stages: developing policy positions, researching legislative and political options, drafting bills and amendments, and shepherding them through the legislative thicket. They review incoming constituent mail on policy issues and conduct specialized research on key measures of interest to being advanced by the Member. They meet with individuals, constituent groups and lobbyists who have an interest in issues of importance to the Member's constituents or the committees on which he or she serves.

Legislative staff must be knowledgeable in the processes and peculiarities of the Congress, its history and traditions, including myriad rules, procedures and precedents, and the jurisdiction of committees and leadership. They must possess near-encyclopedic knowledge of issues for which they are responsible and be able to respond swiftly to questions from the Member or constituents.

A "B+" may be a satisfactory grade in college, but a legislative staff member who gives the boss a memo on an issue that is only 90 percent accurate and balanced will soon feel the sting of rebuke. The legislative staff must earn and maintain a level of trust that ensures any information it provides will be accepted and acted upon.

The legislative team is usually a three-tiered hierarchy that consists of the legislative director (LD), legislative assistants (LAs) and several legislative correspondents (LCs).

The legislative director oversees the day-to-day activities of the legislative staff—four or five people in the House and more than 10 in the Senate—and is responsible for developing a strategy for pursuing the Member's legislative agenda. The LD also reviews all legislative staff work done within the office to ensure it is consistent and reflects the Member's point of view. In addition, he or she works with the Member to map out support or opposition to efforts endorsed by the leadership or the executive branch. The LD also has the task of keeping the Member abreast of key provisions in legislation being debated on the floor or under consideration within committees and subcommittees.

Although some chiefs of staff have deputies (more common in the Senate than the House), the LD is second only to the chief in most offices.

Legislative assistants commonly have several committees or topics for which they are responsible. It is their job to audit the work going on in committees and advance the Member's interest on specific legislation. In the House, they also draft answers to constituent, agency or committee inquiries associated with their areas of specialty. An LA in the Senate doesn't usually draft correspondence but works closely with staff that does.

Legislative correspondent is the entry-level position in the legislative hierarchy, but LCs are often the best-informed team members when it comes to specific bills or amendments. Their survival depends on it. They are the ones who coordinate responses to all kinds of inquiries regarding questions on which a Member has already taken a position. Such responses usually start with a pre-approved text, but the LC should conduct further research to verify that its contents are still current. That's why the LC position is considered the best place to learn about a piece of legislation and its consequences.

There are ample opportunities for LCs to learn. There are sometimes more than 10,000 pieces of legislation introduced during each Congress—and each of them is the most important measure in the world to somebody. The ability to quickly research and reduce complex issues into easy-to-understand language is among the most valuable skills in any congressional office.

The demand for such skills adds to the challenges facing the legislative director, who must teach and mentor a new LC, one fresh out of law school, perhaps, to abandon overly complex, yet accurate and precise legal writing in favor of a style that constituents find straightforward, factual and reassuring.

Constituent Mail

The biggest challenge for legislative staff is constituent mail. Every office gets lots of it. Some House offices receive up to 100,000 communications per year from their constituents. Senate offices can receive many times that. As a new legislative correspondent or legislative assistant in the House, answering constituent mail may very well take up 50 to 75 percent of your day.

Communications take many forms. There is the written letter—or what you will learn to call "snail mail." This is the traditional handwritten or typed letter from an individual constituent on an issue of great importance to him or her. It has always been as good as gold in a congressional office because someone went to a great deal of effort to exercise one of his or her prerogatives as a citizen—almost akin to a sacrament in a civil religion.

Today, the hand-written or typed letter is just as valuable, though shrinking as the main form of constituent communication. First, due to the ease with which people can communicate by email, it has supplanted the handwritten letter. Second, the September 11, 2001 attacks and the subsequent anthrax attack on Capitol Hill a month later resulted in all letters and packages being sent to an outside facility for irradiation. This terrorism protection measure has dramatically slowed the mail process on Capitol Hill since it takes 10-14 days to process mail through this facility. By the time an office receives a letter to the time it can answer and turn it around, a month has usually passed before the constituent gets a response. And that's the best-case scenario.

Finally, there are professional firms that are now counterfeiting personal letters from constituents. Jeff Birnbaum, writing in *The Washington Post,* described companies that special interest groups hire to compose letters for constituents to sign. As if to prove the market value of these letters, these operators can receive $75 to $125 for each letter they are able to convince a constituent to sign. This practice is not new, but the latest technology has taken it to a new level that will dilute the value of authentic letters since congressional offices won't know which ones are from constituents and which ones are from hired writers.

Another variation of this is the postcard campaign, where organizations generate postcards on behalf of their members. The cards are usually identical and unsigned. The silver lining is that when these postcards bombard you, an organization is essentially giving you its mailing list that can be harvested and used to communicate your own message to the constituent.

Another source of communication is constituent phone calls. Most offices will respond in writing to phone calls in the same way they respond to written correspondence. Phone calls are personal and require a constituent to take action and verbally state an opinion. A smart office will promptly write to the caller and store the name, phone, address and issue in a database.

Although "snail mail" has traditionally been constituents' favored mode of communication, the highest volume of constituent communication is now email. According to the Congressional Management Foundation, Congress received 313 million emails in 2006 and anecdotal evidence suggests that number continues to climb. Offices need to respond to emails from their district just as they would a letter.

According to a January 2010 study done by the Congressional Institute, *Helping a 221-Year-Old Institution Harness Cutting-Edge Communication Technologies: Research Findings to Enhance Congressional Contact with Constituents and the Media*, from the constituent's perspective, there's nothing really wrong with replying to an email via snail-mail. The January 2010 survey found that 73 percent of respondents told us that if they sent an email to the Member of Congress, they'd expect an email reply; however 90 percent of respondents said that if they received a written reply instead, that would be satisfactory.

However, from an efficiency and budgetary perspective, an office is better off responding to an email with an email, for a couple of reasons. First, the constituent has already shown his or her preferred means of communication. Second, sending an email instead of a letter saves much money, by avoiding the costs associated with snail mail, including paying for paper, envelopes, postage and for folding the documents.

Professional companies are generating large volumes of email on behalf of various organizations. Some companies sell web modules that allow an organization to automatically generate emails from their membership to congressional offices. While some of these efforts may be legitimate liaisons between advocates and their supporters, these emails are often generated by slick campaigns that only reveal a small portion of the information available on an issue. For instance, in 2005 a major cancer organization contracted with one of these organizations. They whipped their membership into a frenzy by telling them that Congress was trying to pass a law that would outlaw breast cancer screenings. Nothing, of course, could have been further from the truth. The underlying legislation was a small business health care bill that would have allowed any small association to form a group for health insurance purposes, and operate under the same Federal law that governed the health care plans of labor unions and large corporations. By operating under Federal law these small associations might have evaded state mandates, but all of the union and corporate plans covered under Federal law had coverage for breast cancer screenings. These email-generating campaigns are often thinly disguised fundraising efforts designed to create lots of smoke even if there is only a small fire.

That doesn't mean an office can avoid answering these emails. The more inaccurate the information the constituent receives, the more important it is to generate a response that sets the record straight. And, as with the postcard campaigns discussed earlier, an office can harvest the email addresses of constituents who've indicated they care about a certain issue.

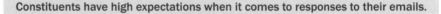

Constituents have high expectations when it comes to responses to their emails.

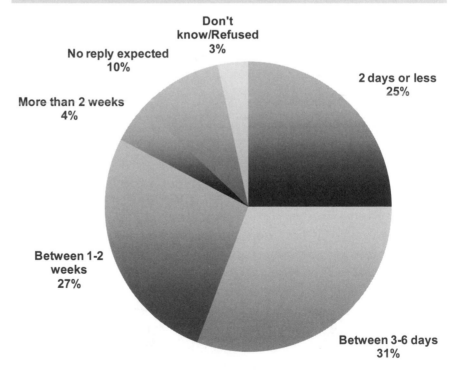

Don't know/Refused 3%

No reply expected 10%

More than 2 weeks 4%

2 days or less 25%

Between 1-2 weeks 27%

Between 3-6 days 31%

Constituents expect rapid responses to their communications. The January 2009 Congressional Institute study found that a majority (55.8 percent) expected a reply to an email query within one week. In fact, 25 percent said they expect a reply within two days—a fairly common standard for customer service departments in big corporations.

How does an office answer this massive volume of mail? It does so with enormous amounts of time, effort and technology. In the House, every legislative person writes or reviews mail. In the Senate, legislative correspondents generally draft all responses, but the more senior legislative staff will provide guidance and approval.

Generally, all messages are "logged into" a computer database. That database allows an office to identify the constituent's name and mailing and email addresses. The software also allows the user to attach an "issue code" which identifies issues that are important to a constituent. Finally, a record of previous letters and responses by that constituent is kept in the database.

The letter drafting process is different in each office, but generally speaking, offices try to answer as many letters as possible with a form response. This is an essentially identical letter written to people who have identical concerns. The Congressional Institute's 2010 study found most offices take one to two weeks to reply to a constituent query about public policy, with very specialized replies requiring up to one month. Some offices report that they can turn around 90 percent of their email in two to three days. But even at this high level of performance, some 10,000 letters—200 per week—require original text to be drafted.

The degree to which the Member directly participates in this process varies. The best offices have the Member review all major new text. For instance, a legislative assistant may notice that a lot of letters and emails are coming in regarding an upcoming tax bill. The legislative assistant will likely want to brief the Member, explain the issue and seek his or her guidance as to how to respond. The legislative assistant then drafts a response based on the Member's position. The legislative director and the chief of staff will review the letter. In most offices, the Member will make a final clearance, especially on a major issue. Once the letter is complete, it is usually mailed to letter writers and callers, and emailed to people who prefer email.

It should be noted that many Members insist on seeing and signing all correspondence. Without judging the relative merits of that noble-sounding ideal, it takes a lot of effort for these offices to keep up with constituent expectations for a response, especially when the staff is accurately reflecting the Member's views.

The process sounds redundant, and it is. That is because the written word lasts forever. A junior staffer writing an inaccurate or offensive response could cost the Member dearly. There is a guiding principle about letters and emails: Never write anything you are not prepared to defend if your worst enemy gets a hold of it, because he will.

Additionally, all of these letters make up a library of "approved text" that can be used by other staff to write portions of other individual responses.

Most importantly, once the letter has gone out, a permanent computer record is made. This can be used to generate proactive email newsletters that keep constituents informed on issues you know are important to them. How do you know what they care about? They clearly told you so themselves when they wrote their letter.

The process is cumbersome and creative staff members in congressional offices are always looking for innovative ways to reduce steps and speed up the process. Only a seriously out-of-touch Member or chief of staff would tell you their mail system could not be improved.

Communications Staff

The communications director, who's sometimes called a press secretary, handles communications of a different sort but is involved in more than just public relations. Effective communication is essential to political and legislative success, so the position has evolved into one of the most significant in any congressional office. These days, the communications director is involved in every aspect of the office. He or she has to be. No function in a congressional office can be performed well without consideration of the others.

In the information age with so many means of communicating information, an office must have a communications strategy and a comprehensive plan for accomplishing the office's goals. Without it, a communications director is likely to be found flailing about and doing little more than reacting to news made by others.

And, like Caesar's wife, it is important for the communications director to be above reproach. Members must be able to trust that they will accurately express the officials' thoughts, opinions and positions to the media. And the media must be able to trust that when a communications director speaks, it is with the Member's voice and that the information imparted is reliable. A seemingly innocuous misstep can prove fatal to a lawmaker's career. That's why most congressional offices prohibit staff other than those responsible for communications from talking to the media—even casually.

Communications directors also help manage the Members' public appearances; prepare materials for public distribution; write newspaper columns and speak on radio shows; help coordinate state or district scheduling; and sometimes act as legislative assistants, overseeing activities surrounding measures such as those involving media regulation. We write a great deal more about communication later in the book.

Outreach and Constituent Services Staff

Outreach and Constituent Services may seem to describe many of the activities that have been ascribed to members of the legislative team, but legislative activities are centered in Washington, DC, while Outreach and Constituent Services are usually executed from within the district.

Outreach is primarily a communications function directed by the district or state director and carried out by key staff members, who attend countless meetings of Rotary and other service clubs, farm groups and veterans' organizations and visit senior centers, churches and schools on behalf of the Member. They also work closely with the communications director to ensure press coverage for local events that the Member will attend. For many constituents, outreach staff is tantamount to speaking with the Member since they are immediately accessible and presumably provide a direct conduit to the Member.

Outreach staff listen to questions, concerns and needs and, when appropriate, pass them along to the constituent service staff. Constituent service has become increasingly important as government has grown in size and complexity, making it difficult for the average citizen to find his or her way through the Federal bureaucracy.

Efforts on behalf of constituents are referred to as casework. Most involve immigration law, Social Security benefits, small business issues, the military and veterans' benefits, but there are literally hundreds of situations that might lead to the Member or his staff being called upon for assistance.

Although the majority of casework is handled at the district or state level, there are congressional offices that prefer to run constituent services out of Washington, DC.

There is no right or wrong place to do it—as long as it gets results.

Obviously, staff can generate considerable good will for their boss by serving as ombudsmen for constituents in dealings with Federal agencies, but they have to know precisely how far they can go. Some of the biggest scandals in recent congressional history have resulted when Members were asked to help convince agencies to bend the rules. Past examples include ABSCAM, the Keating Five, and a more recent case where a Senator inappropriately called a U.S. Attorney to inquire about the status of a legal investigation (offices should never intervene in legal matters).

To help avoid such pitfalls, most district offices employ a director of constituent services to set parameters, but in some cases these activities are overseen by a district or state director or even the chief of staff. As a further safeguard, all employees are now required to take ethics training within a few months of joining a congressional staff.

The district director in the House and the state director in the Senate perform the role of the chief of staff at the local level. Most supervise the activities of five or so people in a congressional district and as many as 20 in a Senator's state office. It is up to the district director to track political developments at the grassroots level and to build relationships with elected officials. When a Member wants to know what constituents are thinking or how they will react to an issue, a bill or an action, it is usually the state or district director who is called. On a day-to-day basis, however, these local directors usually report to the chief of staff.

There has always been interdependence among staff at the local office as well as in DC. The Internet and other means of enhanced communications have made it possible for those who handle what are commonly referred to as the functional needs of the congressional office—the legislative and communication teams in DC and the outreach and constituent services teams at the local level—to work even more closely. Cross-functional teams have been credited with making these offices more efficient and more effective.

Websites represent one example. In most cases, these are designed by the communications director and maintained by the computer systems administrator. Legislative staff contributes by constantly updating issue and policy information and the local outreach and constituent services personnel share noteworthy activity occurring on the home front or on issues of broad concern. Legislative directors, meanwhile, have developed a close working relationship with computer systems administrators in an effort to track correspondence and response times and keep the Member informed of the volume of communication on hot issues, as well as the opinions such correspondence contains.

Support Staff

The support team facilitates the efforts of everyone else, makes it possible for other teams to do their jobs, and keeps the wheels oiled and turning. In a congressional office, the duties of support staff vary from filing to the tasks performed by the person affectionately known as the scheduler.

As with any other organization or business, each congressional office has a staff member dedicated to serving all its technological needs. Just a few short years ago, all it took to become a computer systems administrator—or IT (information technology) manager, as they're called in some offices—was to attend a class and perform data entry to support the correspondence program. This is no longer the case. Technology tools have become essential to the successful operation of every congressional office and require specialized knowledge.

Most offices have a staff member whose specialty is technological tools and is responsible for the storage and protection of confidential data requiring sophisticated backup and redundancy systems. The systems manager also must meet the challenges presented by a network that may include work stations in five or more state or district offices, used by 18 staff members in the House and an average of 40 in the Senate, not to mention a host of laptops and other high-tech devices.

Hand-held communications devices, such as the iPhone and Black-Berry, have proliferated on the Hill, eliminating hand-delivered messages and making the old bells-buzzer-lights system of communication obsolete. Hand-held electronic devices are tethers attaching Hill staff to their offices, and it is not uncommon to see them using their "Crack-Berries" at their kid's soccer games, dinners or the movies.

The scheduler, who, in some offices, is referred to as the executive assistant, is usually the gatekeeper to the Member's inner office and, not surprisingly, maintains the Member's schedule. This itinerary not only identifies where the Member is going but where he or she has been. Keeping such a schedule is not an easy task, given the fact that plans often change several times a day as unforeseen events create detours and changes of plans.

The scheduler is typically responsible for the Member's personal correspondence and phone calls, so the person who holds that position must be discreet and absolutely loyal to her boss. She usually knows more about the Member's activities than anyone except the Member and chief of staff. If the Member is thinking about a bid for higher office, chances are the scheduler knows about it. If the Member is having family problems, chances are the scheduler knows about it. If the Member is avoiding the party Whip, the scheduler definitely knows about it.

Among the challenges the scheduler faces is figuring out what events the Member can and should attend. Members receive hundreds of invitations to events in Washington, DC, and the home district or state. Almost all are worthwhile, but it's humanly impossible to be at every one. In ages past, such invitations were accepted or rejected more on the basis of expediency and personal taste than strategic planning. These days, however, activities, including sporting events, are weighed against the Member's goals—and in some instances, events are actually created to help fulfill strategic goals.

In 2003, for example, President George W. Bush signed the Medicare Prescription Drug, Improvement and Modernization Act, creating a new program to provide senior citizens aid in purchasing prescription drugs.

After this, some Members made it a priority to get to every senior center in their state or district to explain the new plan and help people with the complex enrollment process. Instead of waiting for an invitation, the staff called each senior center and asked if the Member could stop by and talk to a gathering of seniors. This sort of aggressive, well-thought-out scheduling maximizes the effectiveness of the congressional office's most precious resource, the Member's time.

It has been suggested that the scheduler's duties are so crucial to achieving a Member's strategic goals that the position should be a functional category unto itself. But in the House, at least, many of the scheduler's other duties fall into the support category and include maintaining supplies, contracting for package delivery and handling expense and payroll records. (Since 1995, Congress has been subject to most of the same labor laws as any other employer and must keep track of compensatory time, overtime, distinctions between salaried and hourly employees and mandatory leave schedules.) In the Senate, where staff sizes make support functions a full-time job, the duties handled in the House by the scheduler are usually divided between two employees.

The staff assistant is another member of the support team. It's a position most people would call a receptionist, but he or she is not a receptionist in the traditional sense. The receptionist's job in a congressional office has a lot more facets. Besides being the point person on the phones and the individual who greets guests as they enter the office, providing in the process that all-important positive first impression, the staff assistant frequently manages office interns, arranges and coordinates tours of numerous DC sites that require tickets (particularly the White House) and fields requests for flags to be flown over the Capitol.

The staff assistant position is typically entry-level, taken by people hoping to work their way into a legislative, communication or administrative position. Most are successful. That's because they're usually over-qualified for the job. Don't be surprised if you learn that the first person you meet when you walk into a congressional office holds an advanced degree from a highly rated college or university. For obvious reasons, staff assistant is a high-turnover position. Those who hold that job typically move up in a year or they move on.

Chapter Three Summary

- Each office has great autonomy and its own unique hierarchy. Staff tends to reflect the Member's background, interests and district.

- Senate offices typically have more than twice the staff of their counterparts in the House but the organization charts are very similar.

- In the vast majority of offices the chief of staff is the Member's strong right-arm and the most important hiring decision the Member makes.

- The focus of staff members who report to the chief fall into four basic categories: Legislative, Communication, Outreach and Constituent Services, Support and Administrative Staff.

- Legislative staff must be knowledgeable in the rules, procedures, processes and peculiarities of the Congress, its history and traditions. The legislative team is usually a three-tiered hierarchy that consists of the legislative director, legislative assistants and legislative correspondents.

- The biggest challenge for legislative staff is constituent mail. Congress receives nearly a million constituent communications every day. To answer this massive volume of mail requires enormous amounts of time, effort and technology.

- The communications director is involved in every aspect of the office. Effective communication is essential to political and legislative success. Without a strategy and plan, a communications director is likely to be found flailing about and doing little more than reacting to news made by others.

- Outreach is primarily a communications function carried out by key staff members who attend countless meetings on behalf of the Member.

- Constituent service has become increasingly important as government has grown in size and complexity, making it difficult for the average citizen to find their way through the Federal bureaucracy.

- The district director in the House and the state director in the Senate perform the role of the chief of staff at the local level.

- Technology tools have become essential to the successful operation of every congressional office and require specialized knowledge.

- The scheduler is usually the gatekeeper to the Member's inner office and maintains the Member's schedule.

- The staff assistant answers phones, greets guests as they enter the office and frequently manages interns, arranges tours and fields requests for flags to be flown over the Capitol.

One of the aspirations shared by many congressional staffers is to be around long enough and regarded highly enough to be named to the staff of a powerful House or Senate committee. Those who succeed are considered policy experts. They are among the best-paid congressional employees because they handle the difficult, sometimes tedious, nuts-and-bolts work of shaping legislation that moves through the Congress. If the House and Senate have bureaucracies, they most likely are composed of long-serving staff members on long-standing committees under long-serving chairmen.

There are about 1300 committee staffers in the House and 900 in the Senate. These individuals do not have civil-service-style employment protection. If they remain employed after a change in the chairmanship or party control of the committee, it reflects their professionalism and expertise.

(In order to avoid a deluge of angry emails, we'll pause here to explain congressional nomenclature. It's impossible to discuss committees without mentioning their leadership. Many observers would contend that referring to women who chair committees as *chair**men*** is politically incorrect. Yet that is precisely what the vast majority of women who lead committees prefer to be called—not *chairwoman* or *chairperson* or *chair*, but *chairman* and, on formal occasions, *Madame Chairman*. So as a concession to congressional tradition, we'll refer to those who chair as *chairmen* ... and hope for the best.)

Each committee divides staff positions based on which party is in power. In the House, the ratio in recent years has been as high as 2-to-1 in favor of the majority party. The Senate Republicans and Democrats negotiate staff ratios, so when one party has a narrow overall majority, the disparity between the number of majority and minority staff members is typically far less than it would be in the House. The minority party generally puts together a legislative staff of its own that mirrors the majority's, but typically is somewhat smaller.

Committee ratios, especially in the Senate, are often major points of contention between the parties following an election. At the beginning of a Congress, the House sets it rules, which stipulate committee sizes, ratios and jurisdiction. The Senate, on the other hand, considers itself an ongoing body whose rules, written in 1789, are perpetual and carry over from one Congress to another. As a result, new committee ratios must be established by a resolution that can be filibustered by the outgoing majority. Things got complicated in 2001, when the Senate was evenly divided between the two parties, with Republican Vice President Dick Cheney acting in the Vice President's role as President of the Senate being the tie-breaking vote. Democrat Senators did not give up their committee chairmanships for 17 days into the new session when a power-sharing agreement was finally reached.

Most committees favor the majority, but there are some notable exceptions, including the House Committee on Intelligence and the House Ethics Committee. These committees split staffs equally.

The size of the staff allotted to each committee depends on the committee's jurisdiction and clout. The House Small Business Committee, for instance, has about 30 staff members, while the Appropriations Committee, which drafts spending legislation, has around 90.

Regardless of how much clout a committee might have, the chairman holds the bulk of the power.

Since 1995, each committee chairman has been responsible for the payroll, office space and agenda. The ranking minority member has been, however, generally accorded the authority to oversee that portion of the payroll that affects his or her staff and to make personnel decisions without having to clear them with the chairman.

Committees establish their own rules at the beginning of every Congress—the majority proposes the rules and expects its Members to support them. The proposed rules are usually approved, with everyone in the majority voting yes.

Most committees have subcommittees, which in turn have their own staffs, thus increasing the size of the staff available to do the committee's work. There are about 100 subcommittees in the House and about 70 in the Senate. These numbers can change from Congress to Congress. The chairman of the full committee decides who will be hired to fill these positions but does so with varying degrees of consultation with subcommittee chairmen.

The hierarchy of committee staffs closely resembles the hierarchy of Members' personal staffs. But job titles are seldom the same. Among the exceptions are the communications director and the systems manager.

The chief of staff is typically called the staff director and usually comes to the job with a good deal of history with the chairman, familiarity with the chairman's likes and dislikes, and knowledge of his or her agenda. That's because the staff director may come from a variety of backgrounds, but he or she is first and foremost loyal to the chairman. The staff director's responsibilities (beyond making sure the chairman's agenda is carried out) include hiring and budget decisions, representing the committee at leadership meetings and coordinating the committee's activities with the chairman's personal staff. (One of the surest ways for a chairman to get into political hot water back home is to allow the committee's agenda to get out of sync with the expectations of the constituents who elected him or her.)

The chief counsel plays a role similar to the legislative director's but is more likely to be called the committee's policy director or deputy staff director. In addition to experience, the chief counsel is expected to bring to the job thorough knowledge of the rules, history and traditions of the committee; a legal background; and policy expertise in the issues under its jurisdiction. It usually is the chief counsel who assigns the committee's senior legislative staff to organize hearings, generate lists of potential witnesses, develop lines of questioning and brief their party's committee members. He or she is usually the one you see whispering in the chairman's ear in videos shot during such hearings.

It's not unusual for tension to exist between the staff director and the chief counsel. The staff director is interested in advancing the chairman's agenda, putting the chairman's mark on the committee, and making sure the political ramifications benefit the boss. Chief counsels, on the other hand, sometimes see themselves as guardians of tradition. They are the ones most likely to say, "This is the way we have always done things…"

Most committees have an abundance of legislative staff positions. Committee members rely on those who fill these positions for instant recall of minute details relating to complex policy issues and to help manage the legislative process on the floor of the House or Senate. Committee legislative staffers serve as resources for Members' personal staff as well, responding to questions concerning past and pending policies or legislation.

Providing information to non-committee members helps foster positive relations by encouraging support for legislation being drafted by the committee and more importantly, defining jurisdictional authority. A clear definition of authority over issue areas helps minimize turf wars between committees, conflicts that could otherwise become nasty, intra-party struggles requiring the leadership of the House or Senate to referee.

Some committees' legislative staffs are large enough to handle investigations. In these cases, the staff does not just rely on information provided by an agency but funds field research independent of the executive or judicial branch, into the operations of programs under its jurisdiction. Investigative staff members spend months and sometimes years overseeing Federal programs. Often recruited from the Federal agencies they'll help oversee, they are typically young lawyers with a background in legal research and accounting.

In addition, each committee hires specialists in its the area of jurisdiction. The Ways and Means Committee, which is responsible for tax legislation and bills affecting Social Security, Medicare and other entitlement programs, lists "senior economist" among its staff titles. Other committees, such as the Armed Services Committee, have just as much specialization and expertise but refer to all senior legislative staff as "professional staff members"—a practice that often confuses outsiders trying to figure out who to talk to about a specific issue before that committee.

Don't be misled by staff-title roulette or the sometimes seemingly whimsical names that are given to committee staff positions. Often, the less pretentious the title, the more power the staff person actually has. The people who fill these posts are generally knowledgeable and experienced in what they do—though figuring out who's in charge may require the help of an experienced hand.

Legislative staff that serve simultaneously on a Member's personal staff and a committee's staff are known as associate staff members. The House Budget Committee, for instance, allows each of its members to appoint one personal staff member to serve on the Committee's legislative staff, from which subcommittee staff directors typically are chosen.

The clerk of each committee is the chief archivist, the keeper of committee records and the person responsible for the logistics of committee hearings. The clerk is usually a senior employee with several years of experience and usually has an assistant if he or she is assigned to one of Congress's large standing committees. The clerk also maintains the calendar of committee activities and is responsible for everything from providing water and pencils for committee meetings to ensuring that audio and video systems are available when needed.

Recordkeeping and archiving are more critical on a standing committee than in a Member office. That's because a standing committee has a life of its own—chances are it existed before today's Members were born and will continue to operate long after they've ended their careers. The clerk maintains continuity from one generation to the next.

A committee may also have a printing clerk whose primary responsibility is the publication of committee minutes and reports. Everything that is said in committee is transcribed and forwarded to committee staff for clarification (if there's uncertainty over precisely what words were uttered) and then edited for grammar before being archived. All of this is necessary, not only because the House rules require transcripts of hearings to be published, but also because courts rely on these transcripts when considering a legal principle known as legislative intent. Committee testimony also can be used in criminal and civil court cases, including those involving perjury for lying to a committee while under oath.

Once the transcript of a committee hearing has been corrected, proofed and formally released, the committee will make it available on its website for use as a resource and reference, not only for the Congress, but also for anyone else in the world interested in the topic.

Printing tasks used to be handled by the Government Printing Office, but the era of desktop publishing has brought with it the ability to make printed and online copies available to more people more quickly and cheaply.

Finally, most committees employ an office manager who is responsible for expenses, supplies and the payroll. In addition to serving much the same needs as an office manager in a Member office, a committee's office manager must be knowledgeable in the rules governing committees.

Leadership Staff

In the House and Senate, in the minority and majority, Members are elected and appointed to leadership positions. These leaders are selected by their respective party caucuses and act as agents of their colleagues. Most of those leaders are permitted to hire additional staff, over and above staff that are allotted to them for their personal office and committees on which they serve, to assist them in meeting their additional duties as leaders.

In some cases the leadership staff allotments allow for the hiring of only one or two persons, but in the case of the top leaders, the additional appropriations for both staff and office operations are substantial.

The top leadership offices, those of the Speaker, and the majority and minority leaders in the House and Senate, perform five basic functions: (1) oversight of the management of their respective Chamber; (2) management of the House or Senate floor procedures and their respective legislative agendas; (3) media relations; (4) political operations, and (5) the development and coordination of policy positions.

Beneath the top leaders are the majority and minority Whips, who are the second ranking officers in their respective caucus or conference. The whips get their name from their counterparts in the British Parliament. The Whips help manage the scheduling and flow of legislation on the floors and are responsible for corralling the votes necessary to implement their leadership agenda. The Whips appoint a chief deputy and other deputy Whips.

Under the Whips are caucus or conference chairmen and deputy chairmen, who are primarily responsible for external communications and messaging responsibilities, as well as communications and liaison duties with their entire membership including regular meetings of the membership to discuss strategy, internal rules, the legislative agenda and other matters relevant to the entire membership.

Leadership also includes a chairman of policy responsible for the development of policy positions and research and analysis of issues coming before the legislative body.

Leadership staff, by and large, are among the most qualified and experienced staff in Congress. They provide a wide range of services to their leaders and more generally to the Members of Congress and their staffs. Leadership staff who oversee the flow of legislation on the floor, for example, can be particularly helpful to congressional staff providing legislative, communications or scheduling assistance to their Members.

Usually, the media professionals in leadership offices are the best source of information and guidance regarding national press relations, and the policy experts often times are as informed, and sometimes more informed, about where the minority or majority will be positioned on a given issue.

While it is true that most staff, in terms of their interests, expertise, disposition, ideological outlook and personalities, are a reflection of the leaders who hired them, they are more often than not inclined to be of service and helpful to congressional staff.

Leadership staff, as well, if they have an expansive view of their roles, will also be sensitive to and helpful with their leader's responsibilities to his or her constituents back home. The leader, after all, is first and foremost a representative of a constituency. Throughout history, when a Member has assumed a leadership position, it is not uncommon for him to suffer in the eyes of his constituents, so attention to their interests and needs becomes all that much more important. The most striking example is that of House Speaker Thomas Foley, who was defeated for re-election to the House in 1994, because his constituents became convinced he was paying too much attention to Washington, DC, and too little attention to the people of Spokane, Washington.

Besides Speaker, elected leadership offices in the House include:

Majority and Minority Leaders

Majority and Minority Whips

Majority and Minority Chief Deputy Whips

Chairman and Vice Chairman of the Democratic Caucus

Chairman, Vice Chairman and Secretary of the Republican Conference

Co-chairman of the House Democratic Steering and Policy Committee (the party Leader is the actual Chair)

Chairman of the House Republican Policy Committee

Chairman of the Democratic Congressional Campaign Committee (political arm)

Chairman of the National Republican Congressional Committee (political arm)

The Democrats created a new position of Assistant Leader for the 112th Congress.

During the 111th Congress, the Republicans created a new position of Republican Chairman of Leadership.

The primary elected leadership offices in the Senate are:

President of the Senate (the Vice President)

The President pro tempore

Majority and Minority Leaders

Majority and Minority Whips

Chairman, Vice Chairman and Secretary of the Democratic Caucus

Chairman, Vice Chairman and Secretary of the Republican Conference

Chairman of the of the Democratic Policy Committee

Chairman of the Republican Policy Committee

Chairman of the Democratic Senatorial Campaign Committee (political arm)

Chairman of the National Republican Senatorial Committee (political arm)

Keep in mind that when party control changes in the House—the incoming majority gains a new leadership office—the Speaker—while the outgoing majority must contract. Being in the minority means fewer leadership offices, smaller budgets and a draconian reduction in staff. Likewise, when control of a Chamber shifts from one party to another it also sets off a major round of office shuffling and furniture moving. This is because the best offices in the Capitol go to the majority party. In Congress, the spoils definitely belong to the victors.

Most of members of the leadership are provided with budgets to cover the cost of staff dedicated to their leadership responsibilities. In those

Caucus or Conference

In each Chamber, the organization for Democratic Members refers to itself as a Caucus and the organization for Republicans is called a Conference. It's a historical preference that started back in the 19th century and continues to this day.

House Leadership - 113th Congress

53rd Speaker of the House John Boehner (R-OH) born 1949, House since 1991	
Majority Leader (since 1899) Eric Cantor (R-VA) born 1963, House since 2001	Democratic Leader (Since 1899) Nancy Pelosi (D-CA) born 1940, House since 1987
Majority Whip (since 1897) Kevin McCarthy (R-CA) born 1965, House since 2007	Democratic Whip (since 1901) Steny Hoyer (D-MD) born 1939, House since 1981
Republican Conference Chairman (1863) Cathy McMorris-Rodgers (R-WA) born 1969, House since 2005	Assistant Democratic Leader James E. Clyburn (D-SC) born 1940, House since 1993
Republican Policy Committee Chairman James Lankford (R-OK) born 1968, House since 2011	Democratic Caucus Chairman (1849) Xavier Becerra (D-CA) born 1958, House since 2009
Republican Conference Vice-Chairman Lynn Jenkins (R-KS) born 1963, House since 2009	Democratic Caucus Vice Chairman Joseph Crowley (D-NY) born 1958, House since 1993
Chief Deputy Whip Peter Roskam (R-IL) born 1961, House since 2007	Chief Deputy Minority Whip Rep. John Lewis of Georgia born 1940, House since 1987
National Republican Congressional Committee (NRCC) Chairman Greg Walden (R-OR) born 1957, House since 1999	Democratic Congressional Campaign Committee (DCCC) Chairman Steven Israel born 1958, House since 2001
Conference Secretary Virginia Foxx born 1943, House since 2005	Steering and Policy Co-Chairs (the Democratic Leader is Chair) Rosa DeLauro (D-NY) Rob Andrews (D-NJ)

Senate Leadership - 113th Congress

President of the Senate Vice President Joe Biden born 1942	
President Pro Tempore of the Senate Patrick Leahy (D-VT) born 1940, Senate since 1975	
Majority Leader Harry Reid (D-NV) born 1939, Senate since 1987	Minority Leader Mitch McConnell (R-KY) born 1942, Senate since 1985
Majority Whip Dick Durbin (D-IL) born 1944, Senate since 1997	Minority Whip John Cornyn (R-TX) born 1952, Senate since 2003
Democratic Caucus Co-Chairman, Democratic Policy Committee Charles E. Schumer (D-NY) born 1950, Senate since 1999	Republican Conference Chairman John Thune (R-SD) born 1961, Senate since 2005
Co-Chairman, Democratic Policy Committee Debbie Stebenow (D-MI) born 1950, Senate since 2001	Republican Policy Committee Chairman Senator John Barrasso (R-WY) born 1952, Senate since 2007
Democratic Senatorial Campaign Committee Chairman Michael Bennet born 1964, Senate since 2009	Republican Senatorial Campaign Committee Chairman Jerry Moran (R-KS) born 1954, Senate since 2011

offices that don't have dedicated staff, the Member will usually assign an individual from his or her personal staff to help carry out leadership staff responsibilities. The political arms of the caucuses and conferences are not provided appropriated federal funds for the operation of their offices, nor are they provided staff. They are, however, considered part of the elected leadership in both the House and the Senate.

Leadership staffs must perform a delicate balancing act. Since both Chambers give leadership a great deal of power in decisions pertaining to the development and flow of legislation and policy issues, proponents and opponents of key issues, both inside and outside the Congress, want to have the ear of the leaders. And there are never enough ears to go around.

That dynamic puts increasing demands on leadership staff, many of whom are known to have the ear of the leadership and are in a prime position to influence the political and policy decision-making process. Some of the most capable senior leadership staff working for the top leaders are looked upon as non-elected members of their respective bodies. Some staff are able to keep that exalted position in the right perspective; others are not. Some are able to handle the adulation and power and keep the pomposity in check; others are not. Those who fail usually don't last long in their positions.

As will be noted throughout this book, professional staff on the Hill shoulder an extraordinary responsibility to keep what power they have in perspective; to keep their own personal opinions and political proclivities subordinate to those of their employers; and to treat their position as that of public servant, not of political powerbroker. Effective leadership staff are, indeed, servant-leaders.

Leadership staff, in the broader sense, also includes those individuals who are designated by the Constitution, statute, or the rules of the respective bodies to manage the Chambers' day-to-day activities and serve all the Members, not merely one party. Their duties vary widely, and they affect the legislative process to varying degrees.

These staffers are elected by the whole membership of each Chamber. The officers of the House, such as the Clerk, the Sergeant at Arms, the Chaplain, and the Chief Administrative Officer (CAO) are nominated by the Speaker and elected by the entire House. The Secretary of the Senate, the Sergeant at Arms, and the Chaplain are appointed by the majority leader and approved by the full Senate.

Two of the most important non-partisan officers in Congress are the Clerk of the House and the Secretary of the Senate. These offices have been in existence since the Congress first met in 1789. They provide much administrative support to the bodies they serve, particularly in maintaining records.

Like the Clerk, the Chief Administrative Officer of the House provides general support to all its Members and staff. House Speaker Newt Gingrich created the Chief Administrative Officer and his staff after the 1994 Republican takeover in an attempt to professionalize the support functions of the House and remove the politicization and potential corruption involved in the delivery of essential services.

Although not involved with the legislative process, the Sergeants at Arms of the House and Senate are vital to Congress' well being. As the names suggest, they help coordinate and oversee matters related to the security of the House and Senate and their Members in Washington and on official travel. Their original duty, now a small part of their role, was to maintain order within their respective Chambers.

In addition to these primary non-partisan officers elected by the whole body, there is a host of others who serve the Congress.

Perhaps the most important appointed officials are the Parliamentarians of the House and Senate. Rules and precedents governing debate on the floor prove to be downright vexing to learn, so the House and Senate have both hired officers, known as Parliamentarians, to master procedures and interpret and explain them to the Members. The Parliamentarians and their staffs' primary responsibility is to advise the presiding officers how to rule in debate, but they also provide counsel for Members on how they can use their body's rules to achieve their legislative goals. We will speak more about the Parliamentarians in chapter 6, which discusses the legislative process.

When Congress is in session, you can easily find the Parliamentarians on the floors of the Chambers they serve. In fact, you can find plenty of support staff near the congressional Chambers. Near the Parliamentarians are clerks and official proceedings staff who manage, monitor and record what goes on while the bodies are in session. Not far from the great halls are the Republican and Democratic cloakrooms, areas for the parties to gather before, during, and after debates and votes. Each cloakroom has a manager.

Congressional Support Agencies

There is another group of Hill employees that seldom are recognized as members of the legislative branch in part because Members have comparatively little direct control over them. These are members of the staffs of support agencies such as the General Accountability Office (GAO); the Library of Congress (LOC); Congressional Research Service (CRS); and

U.S. Capitol Police (USCP), which provides security for Members and the Capitol complex.

All told, the more than 20,000 members of the agency staffs constitute the majority of employees working for the Congress. Time was when their ranks were filled with patronage, but no more. These days they're hired and promoted on the basis of merit and answer to professional managers. Their training, performance reviews, and pay scales are administered much like any other governmental office, without regard to partisan politics.

Capitol Hill is a small city with just two employers—the House and the Senate, coexisting and cooperating to conduct the nation's business. The staff members working directly for Congress and the additional support agencies represent a cross-section of America, representing every state, every race, every religion, and every socio-economic background. They're mostly young people—ambitious, patriotic, intelligent, driven. They hold political views every bit as diverse as their bosses', but there is a common bond that generally fosters mutual respect and a kind of pride that comes with public service. Regardless of what opinion polls may say about attitudes toward Congress, you'll rarely see a Hill employee bashful about saying where he or she works.

Chapter Four Summary

- Each committee divides staff positions based on which party is in power. The size of the staff allotted to each committee depends on the committee's jurisdiction and clout.

- The hierarchy of committee staffs closely resembles the hierarchy of Members' personal staffs. But job titles are seldom the same. Among the exceptions are the communications director and the systems manager.

- The staff director's responsibilities, beyond making sure the chairman's agenda is carried out, include hiring and budget decisions, representing the committee at leadership meetings and coordinating the committee's activities with the chairman's personal staff.

- The chief counsel is expected to bring thorough knowledge of the rules, history and traditions of the committee; a legal background; and policy expertise relating to the issues before it.

- The minority party generally puts together a legislative staff of its own that mirrors the majority.

- Committee members rely on legislative staff for instant recall of minute details relating to complex policy issues and to help manage the legislative process on the floor of the House or Senate.

- Some committee legislative staffs are large enough to conduct investigations.

- Don't be misled by staff-title roulette—a practice that often confuses outsiders trying to figure out whom to talk to about a specific issue before that committee.

- The clerk of each committee is the chief archivist, the keeper of committee records and the person responsible for the logistics of committee hearings.

- A leadership staffer's primary responsibility is to ensure that leadership meets its obligations to other Members—but like committee staff, they also must be sensitive to the demands of home constituencies, particularly when those demands conflict with leadership obligations.

- Most members of the leadership are provided with budgets to cover the cost of staff dedicated to leadership responsibilities, including floor managers and other experts in House or Senate procedures, communication staff to handle the needs not only of journalists but also of congressional colleagues, and staff dedicated to the organizational responsibilities of the respective caucuses.

- Officers of the House, such as the Clerk, the Chief Administrative Officer as well as the offices of the Sergeant at Arms of the House and Senate are financed through the Legislative Branch Appropriations bill.

- House Speaker Newt Gingrich created the Chief Administrative Officer in an attempt to professionalize support functions in the House and eliminate the politicization.

- There are 20,000 nonpartisan Hill employees of the legislative branch at the General Accountability Office (GAO), the Library of Congress (LOC), Congressional Research Service (CRS) and U.S. Capitol Police (USCP).

Question: How does a bill become law?

Answer: Any way it can.

Legislation doesn't always follow the route they taught us back in high school. An idea can become law as a stand-alone bill, an amendment, an appropriations rider or any of a number of other alternatives. In fact, most legislation becomes law by being attached to one of the few so-called must-pass bills that go through the entire process required of stand-alone legislation.

What counts is getting it done.

It is impossible to provide an exhaustive explanation of the legislative process—think of this chapter as the foundation upon which you can build an understanding—an introduction, if you will—to the challenges you are likely to face and the first faltering steps you will take on your journey. Come to grips with the fact that most legislative proposals never become law. Take heart from the fact that some are approved every week that Congress is in session.

Someone has figured out the system: If you hope to become a professional legislative staffer, make sure you figure it out too—and in a hurry. As for those of you who aren't on the legislative staff and figure this chapter has nothing for you, think again. This process will affect everything you do in one way or another.

A congressional staff member must know the basics of legislating, beginning with the steps necessary to transforming an idea into a law—framing the issue, writing the language, promoting the cause, mastering the process and following the procedures. Staff must understand the role the Rules Committee plays in the House, how things get to the Senate floor ("the floor" is slang for the physical chambers in the House and Senate where debate takes place), how parliamentary procedure can be used to help a bill succeed or guarantee that it fails once it is on the floor, the importance of precedents and the ways a Member can advance an idea and even a whole agenda.

An Overview of Legislative Procedure

When the Founders were writing the Constitution, they spent little time defining how the Congress should function. They made the House of Representatives the only directly elected governing body—the President was to be chosen by the Electoral College, Senators by their state legislatures, and the Supreme Court justices nominated by the President and approved by the Senate. Fear of excessive power in the hands of the President occupied the bulk of their attention: How could they keep the balance of power from tipping in the Chief Executive's favor at the expense of the other two branches of government? They were less concerned with excesses by the legislative branch and therefore gave both Chambers discretion to establish their own rules and procedures.

As a result, the House and the Senate looked for role models and found one in the British Parliament, which greatly influenced then Vice President Thomas Jefferson in drafting his *Manual of Parliamentary Practice,* a volume that every new Member still receives. Though the *Manual* serves as a guideline for conducting business in both Chambers, its significance has been diminished in the Senate, which used it as a starting point but quickly established its own rules and customs.

Since the whole House membership is up for re-election every two years, it approves its rules at the beginning of each Congress. Minor modifications can generate significant controversy, especially if it is perceived that the majority is making changes at the expense of the minority (as is often the case). In addition to the rules of the House, each party has a set of internal rules used to determine how committee assignments are made, and who can serve as chairmen of committees and subcommittees.

While the House alters its rules every two years, the Senate is the only legislative body in the world that considers itself as constant as the seasons. Since only a third of Senate seats are up for grabs in any general election, the Chamber functions as though there is never a break in its activities. As a result, it has become traditional for rules and precedents established in one session to be perpetuated by those that follow.

Aside from discrepancies in their rule books, another dynamic drives process in each body. The two Chambers were designed to play different roles in reflecting the will of the people and safeguarding their liberties. The House is a majoritarian institution that is designed to allow a cohesive majority to pass its agenda. (Of course, a majority is not always a partisan one—it might be based on issues such as agriculture that attract support across geographic and economic lines rather than political lines.) The Senate is a body specifically designed to protect the rights of the political minority and was meant to foster consensus and cool the passions of the people that would be expressed in the popularly elected House of Representatives.

George Washington summed it up best in a conversation with Thomas Jefferson, who had been in Paris as the American ambassador during the Constitutional Convention. Washington asked Jefferson, "Why did you pour that coffee into your saucer?" "To cool it," replied Jefferson. "Even so," said Washington, "we pour legislation into the senatorial saucer to cool it."

The House

The House is a more formal body with very specific rules and procedures for conducting legislative business. A set of rules is adopted at the beginning of each Congress, and these govern the body's activity. House procedures limit debate, restrict the number of amendments that can be offered, and permit consolidation of those amendments that are accepted. Most importantly, though, they entrust significant power directly to the Speaker and the Rules Committee, which he controls. One of the most powerful legislative officers of any democratic legislative body in the world, the Speaker can dominate the body's agenda, and, when backed by a cohesive majority, almost never lose a battle on the floor. The Speaker maintains control of the House through the Rules Committee.

There are two primary means by which legislation can be considered on the floor of the House. The first is by suspending the normal rules and passing a bill. The least controversial bills are placed on what is referred to as the *Suspension Calendar*. On certain days, the Speaker (or usually his designee) will entertain motions to consider bills under suspension of the rules. Debate on these is limited to 20 minutes per side and the legislation cannot be amended. A two-thirds vote is required to suspend the rules and pass the bill. Often the House will consider multiple bills under this procedure, conduct the debates and postpone the votes on individual bills until all are completed, then vote them up or down in rapid succession. It is rare that the Speaker miscalculates and a measure on the Suspension Calendar fails to win the two-thirds vote required for approval.

Hulton Archives, Getty Images

Not your father's filibuster.

Cloture reform has dramatically changed the filibuster from the tactic used by the character played by Jimmy Stewart in Mr. Smith Goes to Washington, when he refused to surrender the floor until he collapsed.

Other measures, including most major appropriation, authorization and tax bills, are traditionally considered under regular order—that is, under the approved rules of the House adopted at the beginning of each Congress. After legislation is approved in committee, it is referred to the Rules Committee, which will adopt a *special rule* that defines how long the bill will be debated, how long Members will be allowed to speak, what amendments may be considered and how long amendments will be debated.

In addition to determining length of the debate and the amendments that can be considered, the Committee may also decide whether points of order under the rules of the House will be waived to accommodate immediate consideration. *Jefferson's Manual* has served as the foundation for House rules and activities for over well over 200 years. The Rules of the House, which are very specific and govern all floor actions, are approved by the whole membership at the beginning of each Congress. However, the modern Rules Committee is so powerful that it may effectively dispense with provisions in these foundational documents. Thus, if the Rules Committee can win a majority for a special rule, it can essentially make its own rules on an ad hoc basis.

To understand the historical development of the House of Representatives you need to understand the Rules Committee. Initially, the Committee was an ad hoc committee designed to make recommendations for changes to the Rules of the House at the beginning of each Congress. In 1880s, Speaker Thomas "Czar" Reed started using the Rules Committee to control House proceedings: "The rules of this House are not for the purpose of protecting the rights of the minority, but to promote the orderly conduct of the business of the House," he asserted. Reed did two things that modernized the House. He chaired the Rules Committee that consisted of five handpicked members. The Rules Committee would control the calendar and determine which bills would come before the entire House. Bills not approved by leadership would be placed at the end of the calendar and never voted on. He also created the Committee of the Whole House—a procedural tool that allows the House to conduct business with a quorum of only 100 members.

The House needed more structure, since, after all, the annual Federal budget had reached a whopping one billion dollars by the time Reed became Speaker. Another development would change the House: incumbency. By 1901, two-thirds of the House were returning incumbents. As a result, senior Members began demanding the right to hold membership on the most important committees - the start of the seniority system. Soon seniority became the norm by which committees were assigned. Chairmen became absolute rulers of their committees.

Reed's successor, "Uncle Joe" Cannon (for whom the oldest House office building is named) took the structure Reed created too far, and was criticized for his autocratic rule. As Speaker, Cannon was also the Chairman of the Rules Committee. The Rules Committee dictated what the House would consider, but most importantly what it would not consider. The Rules Committee even considered what amendments would be allowed on legislation—a common practice today, but a first at the time. Reed had used his power to end obstructionism so the modern House could address the increased size of the legislative workload. Cannon used the rules to prevent change and maintain the status quo in the face of an activist president, Theodore Roosevelt. In the seventh year of his speakership, as a result of the public backlash, some members of Cannon's own Republican Party led a revolt with all Democratic members that stripped him of power and changed the rules so a Speaker could no longer sit on the Rules Committee.

What ensued was a period of committee independence maintained by the seniority system. A particular problem was the Rules Committee had lost none of its power, but was no longer controlled by the Speaker. As a result, a series of senior conservative Democrats from the South, protected by the seniority system, controlled the House agenda through the 1960s. In 1961, with the help of President John F. Kennedy, Speaker Sam Rayburn finally wrestled control of the Rules Committee from the "Gatekeeper," Chairman "Judge" Howard Smith, who had made a career out of using the Rules Committee to block civil rights legislation supported by 80 percent of Republican members and 61 percent of Democratic members of the House. Though Speaker Rayburn would not live to see it, his final victory led to the long overdue passage of the Civil Rights Act and the Voting Rights Act in 1964.

By the late 1970s, Speaker Thomas "Tip" O'Neill had the House rules changed to restore the Speaker's absolute control over the Rules

Committee leading to the modern era of strong party leadership in the House of Representatives.

As a consequence of the House's reforms during the 20th century, the majority party, which dominates the Rules Committee, can refuse to forward to the floor any measure that it opposes. The ratio of majority to minority Members on the Committee is two-to-one plus one, guaranteeing control by the party in power. The Speaker handpicks every Member of the majority on the Committee, expecting, and generally receiving, absolute loyalty.

In short, the Speaker has absolute and total control of the Rules Committee and therefore most everything that happens on the House floor.

The Rules Committee may conduct a hearing on any measure that comes before it but isn't required to. If it does, the chairman and ranking member of the committee putting forth the measure will offer testimony on how it should be considered. The Rules Committee will then assign one of three possible designations:

1. An *open rule* means that all germane (relevant) amendments to the measure will be allowed but only if they are presented within an allotted period of time.

2. A *closed rule* means no amendments will be considered.

3. A *restricted* or *modified open rule* or *modified closed rule* means that amendments aimed at specified portions of the underlying bill will not be considered, but that other portions of the bill will be fair game. These are also sometimes called structured rules.

As with most activity that occurs in legislative bodies, there are varying degrees of formality to the process. The chairmen of the Rules Committee and committees putting forth legislation generally work closely since they are members of the same party. Members who want to offer amendments usually try to reach out informally to these chairmen. Whether they win their support typically depends less on the persuasiveness of the amendment's sponsors than on how controversial the amendment is and whether a deal can be struck between the Speaker and the minority leader.

Where to Learn More

You can start with the appendix in this book where you will find a Manual of Floor Procedure, published by the Congressional Institute at the beginning of every Congress. The staff of the House Rules Committee reviews it. Read it, and then keep it within reach until the next one comes out.

The classic pamphlet "How Our Laws are Made" is a more detailed version of what you probably learned in school. You can find it on the web at: http://thomas.loc.gov/home/lawsmade.toc.html

Two excellent books that provide valuable historical overviews of each Chamber are *The House* by Robert V. Remini and the first 100 pages of *Master of the Senate*, the third volume of Robert A. Caro's magisterial biography of Lyndon Johnson.

Once the Rules Committee has approved a special rule defining how long the underlying bill will be debated and other issues affecting the measure, the resolution moves, along with any proposed amendments, to the full House. There, the special rule must be adopted by a majority vote before the bill can be considered.

Since the majority party controls the Rules Committee, the special rules it produces are normally guaranteed approval when voted on in the full House. Yet, in every Congress, there typically is at least one incident in which party cohesion breaks down and a rules resolution is defeated.

Although the Rules Committee is called the House's traffic cop, in recent years it might justly be accused of police brutality. House rules, like filibusters in the Senate, have been dramatically changed by partisan polarization since the late 1970s. In 1970, only 12 percent of special rule resolutions were modified or closed. Over the last few Congresses, an average of 70 percent of special rules affecting major legislation were modified or closed. In the 111th Congress (2009-2010) there were no open rules during the entire Congress. The 112th Congress saw a return to some openness, but it remains to be seen whether this was a bounce from Congress hitting rock bottom or a trend towards more open floor debates. (For more information on the rules, partisanship and polarization, please see chapter 15.)

The Senate

The Senate, in contrast to the House, is a much more informal institution. Rather than dictating the rules of debate, the Senate Committee on Rule Administration assigns parking spaces. Legislatively, every effort is made to accommodate each individual Senator. The Rules of the Senate require that the presiding officer recognize each Senator who wishes to speak and once recognized, can hold the floor as long as he or she can stand on their own two feet. Additionally, under the rules, the Senate may not proceed to final passage of a bill until every Senator's amendments have been dealt with.

The Senate Majority Leader, a position that did not even exist until the 20th century, is perhaps the weakest leadership position in any legislative body in the world. The root of the Senate Majority Leader's power comes from the right of first recognition—the presiding officer is required to recognize him first when he wishes to speak, so he may offer legislation and amendments and make motions to achieve his party's goals. True, this prerogative makes him more influential than other Senators, but his formal powers pale in comparison with the Speaker's. Former Majority Leader Trent Lott aptly summed up the limits of the position's power by titling his memoirs *Herding Cats.*

Unanimous Consent and tradition (especially seniority) are the two most important factors in determining how the Senate operates. Unanimous consent, which is usually referred to as a "UC", is the main way the Senate does business. The name largely explains the procedure: A Senator requests that all his or her colleagues suspend the normal rules for consideration of a bill, amendment or motion. They can also override points of order against a bill. And once accepted, a UC is binding on the Senate and may only be set aside or modified by another UC. They are often used for managing Senate business in addition to legislative procedure. The Senate passes 90 percent of its procedural measures by unanimous consent.

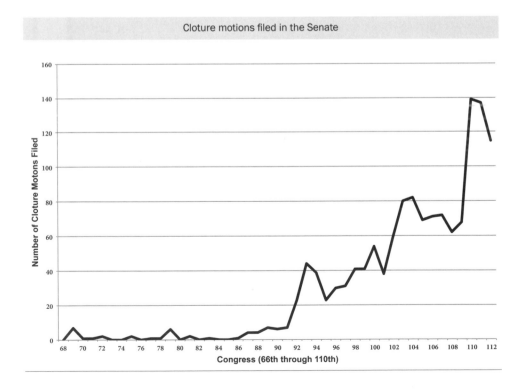

Cloture motions filed in the Senate

GENESIS OF A LAW

Unanimous consent agreements are used to create complex procedures for considering legislation, much like a special rule in the House. A UC can determine what amendments will be considered, how long debate will continue, and even the time and day a bill will be voted on. The key difference is that, unlike the House where the majority can establish procedures without the input of the minority, in the Senate both parties must unanimously agree to the terms of the debate. This offers enormous power to the Senate minority since nothing routine can be done without their consent.

The process of unanimous consent also provides another key minority right known as the hold. A hold is not an objection to a unanimous consent request, but rather a notification of intent to object should a bill be brought up without addressing the individual Senator's concerns. A hold is a prerogative of all Senators and may be placed for any reason, but there are four main reasons they are generally used.

An informational hold is one imposed by a Senator who wishes to be informed or consulted before a bill is brought up for a vote. Since every Senator has the right to try to amend any bill, a hold can be placed on a bill until the Senator has his or her amendment considered.

Other times, when a Senator wishes to negotiate, he or she will place a "Mae West" hold. "Why don't you come up and see me some time?" the Senator effectively says, imitating the famous movie star. Often times a Senator uses this hold when he or she does not want to block a bill from passing, but wants certain things clarified or wants to make sure a provision of interest is included in a bill. Committee chairs will make every effort to accommodate a Senator's concerns so that a bill can move forward to the floor.

A rotating hold is a form of filibuster where Senators take turns putting holds on bills to prevent public frustration being focused on any one individual Senator.

A retaliatory or "choke" hold is placed to kill a bill or force it to be considered in a way that subjects it to a filibuster.

Until recently holds were secret, known only to the leader of each party caucus. A "gentleman's agreement," made in January 2011, requires Senators to list their holds in the Congressional Record after 48 hours.

Senators have tried to circumvent this rule by joining together so that one places a hold and releases it before the 48 hours passes and then a colleague places another, which is then relinquished before the deadline, and so on.

The gentleman's agreement from January 2011 has tried to defang the hold, but it's still a powerful tool that allows each individual Senator to influence the course of every bill. What is the great irony of this powerful procedural tool? The concept of holds does not appear anywhere in the Rules of the Senate. It has been developed as a tradition.

Once holding Senators are satisfied, a motion to proceed to the legislation in question may be brought to the floor. At that point, the most pressing concern is for its supporters to round up 60 votes, not 51, which would be a simple majority. The famous filibuster and its antidote, cloture, are the reason for this.

To understand the daily flow of legislation in the modern Senate, it is important to understand the filibuster, what it is and what it is not.

When they hear "filibuster," many think of Jimmy Stewart in the movie *Mr. Smith Goes to Washington,* latching on to the microphone, refusing to let go, talking himself hoarse to defend himself against false charges. That is a form of the filibuster—the most dramatic, to be sure—but not the only one. Any parliamentary tactic used to slow down or stop legislation entirely is considered a filibuster. Appropriately enough, the word "filibuster" is derived from the Spanish word for "pirate", which gives you an idea of the effect the practice has on the body. (And each Congress, Senators in the majority party typically desire to treat their filibustering colleagues as harshly as real pirates.) The tradition of filibuster is so old that it's first recorded use was in the Roman Senate during the rule of Julius Caesar.

The filibuster is not found in the Standing Rules of the Senate, but is a product of tradition and the body's culture. By custom, the Senate enjoys unlimited debate. Unanimous consent agreements or statutory law can abbreviate deliberations, but, ideally, the Senate continues discussing a matter until they come to a consensus that it is time to move on. For most of the Senate's history, this practice served them well. Senators knew when to stop, because they were courteous to their colleagues—or simply because they were exhausted. Filibusters were rare and usually only a threat.

Although the filibuster was rare in the 19th century, Senators began to use the practice more frequently over the course of the 20th, a trend which prompted calls for reform at various times. Reformers scored their first victory in 1917, when Republican Senators filibustered President Woodrow Wilson's legislation to arm merchant marine ships prior to the U.S. entry into World War I. In response to an outraged public, the Senate adopted a rule allowing for a *cloture* motion, which, if successful, set a time limit on consideration of a bill or other matter. Filibustering was still permitted, and some continued to do so. Most notably, Southern Democrats filibustered civil rights legislation a half a century ago. This prompted another round of filibuster reform, allowing the Senate leadership to invoke cloture and pass long overdue civil rights bills.

Cloture, which essentially means closure, is not easy to obtain. Usually two things will be filibustered—the motion to proceed (a parliamentary means for the majority leader to call up a bill for consideration on the Senate floor) or final passage. Under Senate Rule XXII, sixteen Senators must file a cloture petition to shut off debate on the motion to proceed. After the petition "ripens," or reaches the point when a vote can be taken, three-fifths of the entire Senate (not just those present and voting) is necessary to cut off debate. Once the Senate gets 60 votes, debate continues for another 30 legislative hours (meaning the body must be in session). During those 30 hours there are some restrictions, such as a requirement that amendments be germane to the bill. Once the time expires the Senate can vote on the underlying motion. This process can take two weeks, and that can be merely on the question of whether or not to consider a bill. After that, debate and amendments can proceed before voting on final passage, which can be filibustered all over again.

At first glance, cloture seems like it should be a great blessing for the Senate majority, since they have a way to cut off debate that they had not had before. As mentioned above, it deserves at least some of the credit for the passage of the Civil Rights Act of 1964. However, it has had the unintended consequence of requiring 60 votes to cut off debate on virtually all legislation before the Senate. As a result, the various rules instituted to break filibusters have contributed to making the practice even more common.

Over the years, Senators of both parties have become more inclined to use hardball parliamentary tactics to advance their own goals and thwart their opponents'. At the same time, rule changes to make cloture easier to obtain have all but rendered the one-man filibuster, made famous by *Mr. Smith,* extinct. The onus was previously on Senators conducting filibusters to find creative ways to keep control of the floor, but the current rules have taken the work and the embarrassment out of the practice. It enables a minority party with more than 41 seats to effectively control much of the Senate agenda without being perceived by the public as obstructionist. Debate on legislation continues until the majority gets 60 votes for passage or until everyone wearies of the debate and gives up on the measure under consideration.

As a result, it is axiomatic in the Senate that the majority determines what comes to the floor and the minority determines what leaves. The 60-vote supermajority required for cloture is the main reason. It is exceedingly rare that the majority party has that many votes, and minority Senators are increasingly hesitant to cross the aisle.

The filibuster had historically forced the majority party to reach out to at least a handful of members of the minority to pass important legislation. But today, increased partisan polarization has resulted in a sharp rise in the use of the filibuster. The amount of legislation in the Senate subject to the filibuster went from 8 percent of the bills brought to the Senate floor in 1960 to an average of nearly 50 percent over the last decade.

The filibuster and cloture may be unique to the Senate, as the Rules Committee is to the House, but they illustrate why Members and staff in both Chambers need to understand the rules and how these rules can be manipulated to prevent laws and appointments from being made, for both defensive and offensive purposes.

The rules and procedures in the Senate and House are akin to the keys to your house. They aren't designed to lock you out, but that's exactly what they do if you don't take the time to learn how they operate.

Members and staff who master them know how to get measures approved and to keep measures they oppose from passing.

In the 112th Congress (2010-2012) 12,298 measures were introduced, generating 39,465 pages of *Congressional Record*. Of these 12,298 measures, 1051 were advanced to the floor of the Congress but only 238 were enacted into law—around 1.9 percent.

Don't be misled by the statistics. There were thousands of amendments attached to the 238 measures that were enacted. Very few bills of any significance make it through the House and Senate without amendments of some kind being added. The practice is so common that a revenue or tax bill is often referred to as a Christmas tree because unrelated amendments are hung on them like so many holiday decorations. As a result, it's not unusual for the volume of an omnibus appropriations bill or a revenue measure, to approach 1,000 pages.

As the numbers for the 112th Congress suggest, most legislation that is introduced does not win passage. In fact, passage isn't always the objective. There are a number of reasons to introduce legislation that is doomed from the outset. The most common are:

- To satisfy constituent interest in an issue;

- To establish a benchmark or ownership of an idea or issue in the current or a future Congress;

- To generate interest in or draw attention to an issue through its introduction and inclusion in a committee hearing;

- To establish a position that can be incorporated into legislation that is more likely to advance through the legislative process;

- To introduce an issue or an idea in an effort to attract criticism and expose its deficiencies.

Creating a Pathway to Passage

Committee chairmen have a far greater influence than other Members over whether a measure makes it into law. They control committee

Pork Barrel

There has been lots of talk about legislative earmarks or *pork barrel*. Both terms probably have their roots in agriculture. Earmarking refers to the branding of livestock to identify who owns what, as well as legislative provisions that specify projects on which appropriated funds must be spent.

Pork barrel originated in the 1800s when, before refrigeration, families stored their pork in a barrel filled with brine, and the amount of pork that was in that barrel was a sign of how well a family was doing. The term first was used on the floor of the House in 1909 when Members were accused of handing out pork to their constituents from the "Congressional Pork Barrel." From this came the phrase "bringing home the bacon."

Pork, by the way, is only used in the third person—as in "*their* pork barrel project." It is never used in the first person such as "*our* district's pork"—instead such earmarks are referred to in positive terms, such as "our district's vital road improvement."

agendas. They decide what gets voted on. More often, they decide what legislation will never see the light of day.

Every legislative measure begins life as an idea. It might be original to the Member or it might originate with a constituent. It might be the result of a planning session with staff or with other Members. It might be a response to the lead story on the 6 o'clock news. It might be an issue that has been near and dear to a Member's heart for decades. It might even be a political imperative—an initiative designed to meet a need of his or her constituency. That's sometimes called pork, but it is always important to the Member's district or state and ability to get re-elected. Whatever its derivation, success comes down to finding a way to get bills introduced and signed into law.

Coming up with a goal is the initial step in the legislative process. Only when you know where you want to go can you determine the tactics to get you there. While formulating strategy—and before drafting their proposal in legislative language—most Members test the waters by exposing the concept to various groups or individuals in their home district or state to gauge whether it will create political problems back home.

Many also try out the idea with interest groups that have a stake in what they are proposing. Such groups often have suggestions for how to increase the measure's effectiveness or suggest ways to build a coalition to support it. Interest groups with experience and expertise in the topic also can point out pitfalls and warn against approaches that will likely frustrate the Member's effort.

Members also want to touch base with colleagues in Congress who have a personal or constituent interest or serve on committees with jurisdiction over the topic. The purpose of this exercise is essentially the same as communicating with outside interest groups: to identify strong and weak points, to build support and interest in the initiative, and to determine the likelihood of success.

Generating interest and support among colleagues in Congress brings with it the bonus of potential cosponsors of a bill or, at the very least, some idea of what it will take to recruit them. Perhaps equally important is the fact that it can help identify Members of the other body who might be willing to introduce a version of the bill in their Chamber. If, for example, you are a Member of the House, you'll need someone in the Senate to introduce your measure there—and vice versa.

The odds in favor of passage increase with every cosponsor a bill attracts because every cosponsor brings along their credibility with other colleagues and constituencies. The odds increase as well by having a measure introduced simultaneously in the House and Senate and the media attention it attracts as a result.

In addition, legislative proposals should be reviewed informally with the executive branch. It is important to know at the outset whether the administration intends to provide support or opposition—how strongly and in what form—or to remain neutral on the issue.

Drafting a Legislative Vehicle

Lawyers within the Legislative Counsels' offices draft the actual text of most legislation. Both the House and the Senate have such offices. These non-partisan, non-policymaking adjuncts are for all intents and purposes legislative ghostwriters. They help couch measures in the proper legal language and will often assist congressional staff in understanding how a provision will affect laws and regulations already on the books.

Before drafting, you need to know what kind of legislative vehicle best serves your needs. Do you want your bill to be *free standing* (an entirely new concept) or *amendatory* (a modification of an existing law)?

Next, you need to decide how specific you want your legislation to be. There are three levels of specificity:

1. Hortatory or precatory language merely expresses an objective. (The Senate procedural manual refers to this as a pious hope.) For example:

   It is the sense of the Congress that the Secretary should take steps to end homelessness in inner cities.

2. *Authorizing* language empowers an individual to take action, but relies on that individual's use of discretion:

   The Secretary may take steps to end homelessness in inner cities through discretionary funding of experimental programs.

3. *Mandatory* or *obligatory* language is absolute:

    The Secretary of the Department shall take the following steps to end homelessness in inner cities and shall report to the Congress on his progress.

The Legislative Counsel's office works with Members on a confidential basis to ensure that proposed legislation conforms to Federal statutes and that the wording—and meaning—accurately reflects the intent of the sponsors. The Counsel's staff generally avoids making policy suggestions but will point out precedents and alternative means of accomplishing the stated goal.

The Legislative Counsel's staff will also help ensure that you introduce the correct kind of legislation. There are several different types: bills, joint resolutions, concurrent resolutions, and simple resolutions. Only bills and joint resolutions become law through Presidential signature or veto override, and only bills and joint resolutions can amend law. They are also the only kind of legislation that has the power to authorize or mandate actions by officials outside the legislative branch.

Concurrent resolutions—concurrent budget resolutions, for example—express the intent of both Chambers of Congress and have a binding effect only on the Congress. A simple resolution, on the other hand, is adopted by only one Chamber and therefore affects only the Chamber that adopted it.

It doesn't take long to master such distinctions, but it takes years to become proficient at drafting legislation that applies them. That is why the Legislative Counsel was created. You may, however, find yourself called upon to contribute to the process. Here are some tips that will help you avoid embarrassing yourself and your boss:

- Keep your terminology consistent. This is no time to be creative, colorful or exotic. Using different terms interchangeably will encourage judges and executive branch officials to surmise that you are making certain distinctions, and therefore interpret the law in ways you did not intend. It will be honored more in the breach than in the observance.

- If you use a technical or legalistic term, define it.

- Organize your thoughts by separating phrases and sentences based on the legal function they serve within the legislation. Designate each thought by numbers or letters so they may be easily identified.

- Avoid the use of Latinisms and legalisms. ("Whereas..." clauses are preambles, which have no meaning in law. There should be only one "Be it resolved..." clause.)

- If you want either a delayed or a retroactive effect to your legislation, you must say so. Otherwise, it will take effect upon enactment.

- If what you're proposing will require funding, your bill should authorize it.

- Be specific—avoid opportunities for interpretation wherever possible.

Following these guidelines will:

- Enable judges and lawyers to correctly interpret the meaning of the law;

- Minimize technical objections, helping to keep debate focused on policy questions and avoid unnecessary corrections that can introduce errors and ambiguity;

- Establish effective policies and avoid public embarrassment for those sponsoring the bill, enacting the law or implementing it.

Finally, when submitting material to the Legislative Counsel, the goal is not to write the legislative language but to express what it is you want to accomplish. Be brief. Make it a memo explaining the intent and options you want considered. Often, a personal meeting with the counsel assigned to the bill makes sense—especially if an idea is particularly complicated.

Chapter Five Summary

- Most legislation that is introduced never gets enacted.

- Key elements of the legislative process are framing the issue, writing the language, promoting the cause, mastering the process, and following the procedures.

- Unanimous consent and the traditions of the body govern the legislative process in the Senate.

- The filibuster now affects 50 percent of legislation going through the Senate, making cloture a key to success.

- The House Rules Committee is that Chamber's legislative traffic cop.

- Jefferson's Manual is still the Bible for procedure, especially in the House.

- Getting legislation enacted isn't the only reason for introducing a bill. Sometimes Members may wish to draw attention to an issue or establish "ownership" over a policy.

- The term pork barrel dates back to the early 1800s, when in the days before refrigeration, the amount of pork you had stored in a barrel was a sign of your prosperity. The term was used politically for the first time a hundred years later.

- Tactics for moving legislation include communicating with congressional colleagues, the executive branch and outside interest groups.

- The Legislative Counsel's Office is where legislation is drafted. They are professionals. You provide the blueprint.

At last the time has come to unveil the legislation, to tell the world what the Member is up to. The process is time-honored and almost ritualistic not so much because of tradition but because it usually works.

Introductions usually begin with a "Dear Colleague" letter, which will go to all targeted Members of Congress through the House or Senate mail system. This letter will explain the legislation, provide details and facts, and then ask Members of both parties to add their names to the list of cosponsors.

Although there's only one sponsor, a bill might have hundreds of cosponsors, adding to the bill's credibility among the leadership and committee chairs. Co-sponsorship is a form of endorsement. Theoretically, it's possible for every Member of the Congress to co-sponsor a single bill.

The sponsor's communications director, meanwhile, will earn his or her keep with a public information campaign that will target the broad range of local and national media, and he or she will invite counterparts in the offices of co-sponsors to do likewise.

Once the legislation is ready to be formally introduced, the House sponsor might seek to give a one-minute speech at the beginning of the legislative day or request time for a special order at the end of the day's business. In the Senate, a sponsor often gives a brief speech during "Morning Hour," which usually occurs before the start of legislative business.

Following this introduction process, the bill is dropped into what's known as the hopper in the House—a box on the Clerk's desk. In the Senate, it is handed to the bill clerk at the front desk of the Chamber. It is then assigned a number and referred to the appropriate committee or committees. The bill's subject matter usually determines the committee to which it will be assigned. Committee jurisdiction is defined by the rules of the House and precedent. In the House, the Speaker determines whether to refer a bill to more than one committee (although that rarely happens). In the Senate, the Parliamentarian (technically acting on behalf of the Vice President) determines committee jurisdiction. Multiple or sequential referrals require unanimous consent.

The Role of Committees

Committees are the backbone of the legislative process. They have been part of the legislative process almost from the outset. The first were ad hoc committees established by the House to address single issues that had been read or debated on the floor but needed additional study before a final decision could be reached.

It wasn't until after the turn of the 19th century that the House created standing committees to develop expertise in specific topics. The first of these was Ways and Means, followed closely by the Committee on Elections, Revised Unfinished Business, Claims, and Commerce and Manufacturing. Then came the Foreign Affairs Committee and the Post Office and Post Roads Committee.

The Senate launched its first committee in 1807 and has pretty much kept pace with the House ever since.

Over the course of their history, committees and their chairmen have assumed varying degrees of power and influence. Speakers of the House Henry Clay of Kentucky, Thomas Bracket "Czar" Reed of Maine and Joe Cannon of Illinois have been among that Chamber's most powerful leaders, exerting almost absolute control over the legislative process, the House agenda, and even the activities of committees. Since 1911, when Joe Cannon lost the reins in a bipartisan coup, however, committees more often than not dominated the agenda and the flow of legislation. In some cases, these committees frustrated the House leadership and the majority so much that committees ended up losing much of their independence to the party leadership in recent decades.

The Legislative Reorganization Act of 1946 heralded the modern committee system. This legislation consolidated the number of House committees from 48 to 19, and from 33 to 15 in the Senate. The reduction in committees increased the number and the importance of subcommittees. Power became concentrated in the hands of committee chairs and remained there until the 1970s when liberal members of the House Democratic Caucus rebelled against the power of conservative Southern Democratic committee chairs.

The reforms of the 1970s decreased the power of committee chairs and increased accountability to the party caucus. The post-Watergate

Democrat-controlled Congress removed the chairman's ability to name subcommittee chairs, replacing it with a bidding system based on seniority; set subcommittee budgets and jurisdiction independent of the committee chairman; and gave subcommittee chairman semi-autonomous authority to select their own staff and pursue their own agenda. This action was drafted in 1973 by the Hansen Committee for the Democratic Caucus and was called the "Subcommittee Bill of Rights".

These, and other changes, such as allowing the caucus to vote on chairmen, had the intended effect of reducing the power of committee chairmen and concentrating power in the hands of party leaders. However, the unintended consequence was to create jurisdictional turf battles and decentralized lawmaking. Subcommittees formed "iron triangles" where small groups of Members, unrepresentative of the Congress as a whole, would form loose alliances with outside special interest groups and the agencies they were responsible for.

When the Republicans took control after the 1994 election, a new series of reforms took place. They eliminated several committees, reduced committee staff by one-third, imposed term limits for committee and subcommittee chairs, banned proxy voting in committee (where the chairman could vote on behalf of an absent Member), opened committee hearings to the public, and required publication of recorded votes in committees. Members were limited to serving on two committees and four subcommittees (with exceptions) and jurisdictional lines were clarified.

These reforms restored some power to the committee chairs by allowing them to determine how to select subcommittee chairs and by giving them control of all committee and subcommittee staff (subject to approval of the Republican Conference and Democratic Caucus). However, term limits and requiring Conference approval of committee chairs provided a check on the independence of committee chairs.

As a result the autonomy of committees has been diminished in favor of more party loyalty and control.

Like their counterparts in the majority, ranking members—the highest-ranking minority-party Member on each committee—have seen their power ebb and flow depending upon the strength and weaknesses of their party's leadership and the chairmen's willingness to accommodate them. In some committees—especially those that serve specific constituencies like small business and veterans—relations between the two parties are generally good. In committees that deal with major policy issues, such as Education and the Workforce or Energy and Commerce, relations between the two parties can often be downright hostile.

There are three kinds of committees:

Standing committees are permanent with specific legislative jurisdiction.

Special (or select) committees are, in theory, temporary or ad hoc panels that are given broad oversight and investigative authority over a particular problem—such as aging issues or narcotics.

Joint committees consist of Members from both Chambers and have very specific oversight responsibility but negligible legislative authority to create new laws. (In 2011, pursuant to the Budget Control Act, Congress formed a joint committee with legislative authority, the Joint Select Committee on Deficit Reduction, also known as the Supercommittee. This unique creation was given original legislative jurisdiction to reduce the deficit by no less than $1.2 trillion, but it failed miserably, setting a poor precedent for joint committees with legislative authority.)

There are currently 16 standing committees in the Senate and three select (sometimes called special) committees. In the House, there are 20 standing committees and two select committees. There are four House-Senate joint committees.

There typically are 17 or 18 Members per committee in the Senate and anywhere from 13 to 56 in the House, with an average of 10 Members per subcommittee in each.

Unless a committee chairman decides the full committee should act on a measure immediately, it usually will be referred to a subcommittee for study. As a result, subcommittees bear the lion's share of the workload. It is generally at the subcommittee level that research is conducted into the measure's various components, where hearings are held to obtain expert testimony for or against it, and where fine-tuning occurs. If a majority of the subcommittee approves the measure, it is sent to the full committee for consideration.

Committee Hearings

The Congress is, by nature, reactive rather than proactive. It reacts to public pressure, to the media, to interest groups, to national emergencies, even to business left unfinished by the previous Congress. And, of course, to administration requests—as the saying goes, "The President proposes and the Congress disposes."

And what is true of the Congress is true as well of its committees.

In addition to their role in producing legislation, the primary function of committees is oversight of Federal programs. They authorize and re-authorize programs. Committees bankroll them and craft policies that regulate them. They also investigate programs, and out of all their activities, committee investigations usually generate the most controversy. In the House of Representatives alone, there are about 3,000 subcommittee and committee hearings each year, mostly in the early months of March and April and mostly in non-election years. Such hearings are generally either fact-finding exercises or policy-reviews and fall into two categories:

- Field hearings highlight a specific issue in a region where it has the greatest relevance or highlight a committee member's work in a state or district where the Member is best known. Field hearings tend to be of little real consequence in and of themselves, but when properly applied may be one of the most valuable resources for developing the case for legislative action. They are effective tools for bringing public attention to an issue.

- Washington hearings are conducted in the nation's capital either because an issue is of national importance or is such a nuisance that a hearing is the only way to make it go away.

The purpose of hearings is to accumulate facts, information and opinions, while at the same time exposing issues or policy to congressional or public scrutiny.

The most important individual at any hearing is the chairman, who determines when it will be and how long it will last, as well as who will testify and for how long. In addition, the chairman holds the gavel and controls most of the staff.

The Mark-Up

Following hearings that lead a subcommittee or committee to conclude that legislation is needed, the respective chairman creates a mark, or draft bill. Committee members then proceed to the mark-up (editing) phase, during which they offer amendments they believe will improve the bill.

A similar mark-up precedes any action on legislation proposed by a Member of the committee, a bill introduced by a Member not on the committee, a composite bill drafted by the committee staff and brought to the table as the chairman's bill (mark) or any other measure that comes before the committee.

The Committee Report

Regardless of whether a measure originates in committee or elsewhere, it cannot be submitted for consideration by the House or the Senate as a whole without an official summary called a committee report that tells other Members of the House or the Senate what the committee did and why. Such a report contains:

- A description of the legislation and why it is needed, as well as the reasoning behind the committee's conclusion;

- Background on the issue the measure addresses;

- The administration's position on the measure;

- Pertinent information that is required by the Rules Committee or otherwise deemed significant, such as cost estimates, recorded votes, economic impact, oversight findings, recommendations and how the measure will change existing law;

- Language of conciliation to opposing sides or language clarifying conditions that may be subject to litigation (since litigants look to reports and floor debate to determine congressional intent);

- Additional views—a Member may concur with the committee's action but not the reasoning behind it and choose to attach a local slant or provide further illumination of a particular viewpoint;

- Dissenting views—a Member who opposes the measure may opt to fully air his or her reasons for the benefit of future debate and deliberation;

- Minority views—statements by those who may have lost the debate in committee but hope to sway opinion when the full Chamber acts on the measure. These will provide proponents with a picture of why opponents are against the measure and will help opponents expressing their dissent through the media.

Legislative staff will find the committee report one of the most valuable resources there is for the analysis of legislation. Member views typically provide a quick means of identifying points of contention. There, explanations are usually expressed in persuasive rather than legislative language, making committee's intent accessible and easy to understand.

Navigating the Committee Process

The majority of legislation initiated by Members is quietly euthanized through the committee process. Once a bill is referred to committee, it will die there unless the chairman gives the green light for consideration. The bill also has a chance of survival if it has support from:

- A Member of the committee who has a close personal and professional relationship with the chairman– or something of value to offer, such as support for one of the chairperson's endangered initiatives;

- A Member who has the support of the majority leadership, which applies pressure on the chairman to advance the legislation;

- Or important interest groups or the media.

Non-controversial legislation such as a bill commemorating a historical event or renaming a post office often—but not always—has a good chance of survival and may even be expedited through committee.

But getting a bill through committee doesn't guarantee the individual who originated it will get any credit. In most cases, the chairman is identified as the sponsor of anything significant that comes out of the committee. Members can, however, help shape the chairman's bill.

It is possible to offer an amendment that might have originated as a separate bill but has been buried in the legislative graveyard. The caveat is that, in the House, such an amendment must be germane to the bill that's carrying it. That means that, in the judgment of the Parliamentarian, it must be directly related to the underlying bill.

Senate rules are far more lenient. There, even an amendment that's only tangentially related can often be added in committee. In 2006, for example, a Senate bill to regulate over-the-counter medical products used to make methamphetamines in home labs was attached to the Patriot Act, a measure that dealt with terrorism and intelligence services. The only thing the two had in common was that both had been referred to the Judiciary Committee and were under the jurisdiction of the Department of Justice.

An unspoken quid pro quo comes with actions of this sort. The chairman who allows such a pairing can expect the Member who originated the rider (amendment) to support and even campaign in favor of the bill that's carrying it.

House committees are considered more powerful than Senate committees for this reason. In the House, it is crucial to win the chairman's support, since it is very difficult to get a provision added to a bill once it gets to the floor, because the Rules Committee restricts the number and type of amendments that can be offered. In the Senate, if a committee refuses to act, the Senator may go to the floor where amendments, germane or otherwise, can only be limited by unanimous consent and time agreements. Thus, a Senate committee chairman does not have the same clout of a House committee chair.

These non-germane amendments added in the Senate often receive the House's stamp of approval when the House acts favorably on a conference report or by taking up a Senate bill rather than initiating legislation of its own.

Offering Amendments

If a Member has failed to get a legislative measure included on the committee agenda, he or she may still have an opportunity to get it considered on the floor. In the House, several things must happen. First, the underlying legislation to which the Member is attempting to attach his or her measure must allow for amendments. Even if it does and the amendment is accepted, restrictions can be placed on its consideration. It must also be deemed germane by the House Parliamentarian, which means it must be consistent with the rules and precedents of the House. And if it gets past the House Parliamentarian, opponents can still challenge it, in which case the Speaker will have to resolve the conflict. All this assumes the Rules Committee has not passed a special rule excluding the amendment from consideration.

An essential House publication, *Deschler's Precedents*, is often called upon to settle challenges to amendments. This volume is named for the former House Parliamentarian Lewis Deschler, who served for 50 years after being appointed by Speaker Nicholas Longworth in 1925. His book contains rulings by the Chairmen of the Committee of the Whole and the Speakers who predated him and represent standards for congressional activity much as court decisions serve as legal precedents. *Deschler's Precedents* is updated each time a new precedent is established or an old precedent modified or overturned. All precedent-setting action from the latest session of Congress is published in a new edition at the beginning of the next Congress.

It was once easier to amend legislation on the House floor. In fact, the Congressional Research Service used to train new legislative staff in the amendment process, drawing elaborate amendment tree diagrams of second-degree amendments, modified by substitute amendments and so on. Under the increasing party polarization of House floor procedures, such training is no longer necessary, as the Rules Committee dictates exactly what amendments will be allowed and which will be prohibited.

If the Speaker rules that an amendment is out of order, there's at least one other option: Working with the minority leader and ranking member of the committee, it might be possible for the advocate of the amendment to shape what is known as a motion to recommit, which would refer the bill back to committee with instructions to include the amendment attached. In reality, this motion to recommit process is a formality if the motion is adopted—the committee does not actually meet to consider the bill—instead it is deemed to have reported the bill with the amendment included in the motion to recommit. Thus, if the motion passes, the amendment is included in the bill. Such a motion is entertained after completion of all other action involving the measure on whose coattails the amendment hopes to ride. The motion must be germane and the minority can only offer one motion to recommit on any bill.

Germaneness

Germaneness is among the House's most significant legislative principles. First adopted by the House of Representatives in 1789, the Rule of Germaneness limits considerations to one item at a time. Say, for example, a bill dealing with transportation safety is being considered and an amendment is proposed that, among other things, would require states to inspect and repair bridges on a regular basis. So far, so good.

Even if the amendment contains other provisions that have nothing to do with highway safety, the amendment can be considered. But, if a Member challenges any part of the amendment, the entire measure is jeopardized. Should even part of the amendment be ruled out of order, the entire amendment is disqualified.

An amendment can be challenged for any number of reasons. If it attempts to make a temporary measure permanent, for example, it could be ruled out of order. The Parliamentarian rules on issues of germaneness. Because the burden of proof rests with the amendments' proponents, they typically consult the Parliamentarian in advance for an opinion on whether an amendment is likely to be considered germane.

The Senate does not have a Rule of Germaneness as such. Senators may add unrelated riders to any legislation except appropriation bills and any measure for which cloture has been invoked—amendments to these exceptions must be demonstrably germane.

The motion to recommit has its modern origins in 1909 when Speaker Joe Cannon, in an attempt to stave off a revolt against his speakership, offered a rules package that reserved to the opponents of a bill the final opportunity to amend the bill through a motion to recommit. A 1932 ruling by Speaker John Nance Garner specifically reserved for the minority the right to make the motion to recommit. Democratic majorities during the late 1970s through the early 1990s began restricting this traditional right by passing special rules that denied motions to recommit with instructions. This essentially reduced the motion to recommit to a redundant inverse of the vote on final passage. Donald Wolfensberger, the Director of the Congress Project at the Woodrow Wilson International Center for Scholars, detailed 83 special rules between 1977 and 1995 where the Democratic majority denied or limited the minority's ability to offer a motion to recommit with instructions. Republicans vigorously protested, and when they became the majority in 2005, affirmed the minority's right to offer a motion to recommit with instructions in the House rules, thus fully restoring this traditional right of the minority.

The Republican minority in the 110th Congress passed 24 motions to recommit—a historical number. When the Democratic majority grew to a 40-vote margin in the 111th Congress, however, it became more difficult for the Republicans to successfully use this tactic.

It is a powerful right. Its importance is magnified by the increasingly restrictive nature of special rules under which most legislation is considered, since the motion to recommit with instructions may be the only amendment opponents of a bill have the opportunity to offer. Majorities have only themselves to blame because their restrictive nature has forced the minority's frequent use of the motion to recommit.

If the motion to recommit with instructions fail and the measure under consideration is an appropriations bill, Members have at least one more arrow in the quiver. Although the rules prevent substantive amendments on such bills, a Member can strike or delete funding for a specific line item. One of the most famous examples is the Hyde Amendment that originated in the House and restricts Federal funding of abortion. Because it was an amendment to a Labor/HHS (the Department of Labor and the Department of Health and Human Services) Appropriations bill, opponents of the amendment could not add conditions or caveats. They were, however, able to temper the amendment when the Appropriations bill reached the Senate, where an exception was added to cover cases in which the life of the mother was threatened.

It has even become more difficult to influence legislation with line-item amendments to appropriation bills. During the 111th Congress, the majority took the unprecedented step of bringing appropriations bills to the floor under a closed rule. This had never happened in the 224-year history of the House of Representatives and was, fortunately, discontinued in the 112th Congress.

Parliamentary tactics that silence the minority create a vicious cycle of polarization. If Members of Congress, elected to represent hundreds of thousands of people, are denied any ability to influence the legislative process, the only option they have to make their voices heard is legislative obstruction. Then the majority, in retaliation, further restricts the minority's voice, inviting more creative means of obstruction. This results in dysfunction, and Congress does not pass important legislation. For example, during the 111th Congress, the House of Representatives failed to pass a budget resolution or a single regular appropriations bill for the first time since the Budget Act of 1974 went into effect.

While the House passed budget resolutions in the 112th Congress, they were used as an opportunity to stake a position, and were never likely to receive serious consideration in the Senate. The Senate majority arbitrarily decided the Budget Control Act of 2011 was essentially a budget, and failed to meet its statutory obligation to adopt one. In fact, the Senate has not even passed a budget resolution required by law since 2009.

As with most other procedures, bringing an amendment to the floor in the Senate is usually less tedious and less painful. The fact that a Senator must receive unanimous consent to offer an amendment doesn't mean all of his colleagues must support the amendment. It simply means all Senators agree to hear the measure.

The majority often is persuaded to give unanimous consent to a minority Member's amendment in exchange for unanimous consent for a majority Member's amendment, or for a pledge not to filibuster the bill at which the amendment is aimed.

The floor managers who shepherd the bill through to passage and who are usually the chairman and ranking member of the reporting committee typically make the decision as to whether to consider an amendment pursuant to a unanimous consent request. If they find the proposed amendment so odious that they refuse to accommodate it, there are legislative tricks they can pursue to block it. One tactic is known as filling the amendment tree. The amendment tree is a metaphor for the chart that shows the Senate procedure for what amendments may be offered to a bill and in what order they will be considered. In recent times, the Senate majority leader, who has the right to be recognized first at the start of a debate, has increasingly filled the tree with extraneous or meaningless amendments to block the consideration of a legitimate amendment he opposes.

The Role of Leadership

A Member seeking to get a bill passed should bring it to the attention of the party leadership. In the House, leadership involvement in the committee process has grown since 1994 when Newt Gingrich became Speaker. A simple reform eliminating seniority as the determining factor in who becomes committee chairman made chairmen accountable to their party in general and the Speaker in particular. If a chairman did not do what the Speaker or the party wanted, he or she could be replaced in the next Congress.

The Speaker of the House, on one hand, and the minority leader, on the other, as well as the Senate majority and minority leaders, look for opportunities to help their party's Members succeed. So do party Whips in both Chambers of Congress. Keep in mind that the assistance they provide isn't entirely altruistic.

A minority leader becomes a majority leader only if his colleagues succeed to the point that more Members of their party get elected. To retain that position, the majority leader must help other party Members succeed.

Everyone in a leadership position has skilled staff that works closely with Members and their staffs to win passage for their initiatives. When push comes to shove, they'll apply various forms of persuasion—some more pleasant than others—to get an amendment attached to a bill that has prospects of passage. In the Senate, Whips of both parties will work with floor managers of bills to get riders added.

Not only do these efforts help consolidate leadership positions, but they earn the gratitude of the Members who benefit from them—gratitude that will pay dividends in the long run.

Floor Procedure

The reason most Members seek election to the House and Senate is that they hope to shape legislation in Congress. In order to achieve this goal, they and their staffs must know what they're doing or know whom to ask for help.

An inexperienced Member, supported by an ill-prepared staff that has not worked closely with experts provided by the leadership, are likely to find themselves humbled before their colleagues and a nationwide audience watching on C-Span when they go head-to-head with someone who knows the rules and procedures better they do.

No one expects you to know everything. They do expect you to recognize your limitations, work closely with allies who know where the landmines are and learn from them as the process unfolds.

When legislation is being considered on the floor, every nuanced step has a purpose. The precedents and rules of the respective Chambers choreograph every gesture. Occasionally, there are surprises that disrupt the proceedings, but these are rare and almost always the result of someone whose actions are inconsistent with the traditions of the body—such as when a Member's words are stricken following a verbal assault on another Member or the President.

Be conversant with the rules, regulations and precedents before going into the arena.

The Role of the Administration

The role the President, the Office of Management and Budget (OMB) and the cabinet play in the legislative process isn't always obvious to outsiders, but it can be pivotal. They're interested because the executive branch will be responsible for implementing any new laws that are enacted.

The President is represented on Capitol Hill by the White House Office of Legislative Affairs (OLA), which was first established during the Eisenhower Administration. The presence of the President's people on the Hill provides two-way communication. It allows the White House to build relationships, develop intelligence and selectively use positive and negative incentives—the granting and withholding of favors, for instance—to influence legislative outcomes. At the same time, it provides Congress with a means to communicate informally with the administration to modify policy positions or avoid political traps.

Every congressional office has someone from the OLA assigned as a liaison by the White House. Legislative staff should make a point of knowing that person. Every administration sets their office up differently than its predecessor—some with better results than others.

The President has significant direct influence on the legislative process, including the legal responsibility to send a proposed budget to Congress every year. But perhaps the most effective form of leverage a President has over Congress is his veto power, which is the constitutional authority to prevent a law from going into effect by withholding his consent.

A committee chairman will usually exhaust every other available means before risking a veto of one of his or her priorities. They are even less willing to spend their hard-earned political capital on someone else's initiative by calling the President's bluff. There are times, however, when Congress or the President or both go out of their way to force the use of the veto pen to make a point.

President Clinton twice vetoed welfare reform even though as a former governor he recognized how badly it was needed. He sent the measure back to the Congress twice, to buy time and face-saving concessions sufficient to coax and coerce the left wing of his own party into accepting the reform. The third time the bill came to his desk—with a few minor tweaks, but in substantially the same form as the measures Clinton had vetoed twice in succession—it had the endorsement of a good many Democrats, and he signed it into law.

The Democratic Congress turned the tables on Clinton's successor. At the time, a united Democratic minority, along with a significant number of Republicans, sent President George W. Bush a bill that would have allowed Federal funding of embryonic stem cell research knowing full well the President wouldn't sign it. The objective was to put the issue squarely in front of voters in districts and states that favored such research in hopes of persuading them to vote for Democrats in the next election.

Of course, Congress can override a veto if two-thirds of each Chamber vote to do so. But that is a tall order. For instance, Congress's override of President Bush's 2007 veto of a $23 billion water resources bill was the first time Congress was able to muster an override in more than a decade. In fact, in U.S. history over 2500 bills have been vetoed with only 110 of those vetoes being overridden. That's just four percent.

The difficulty of securing enough votes to override a veto inspires fear in the hearts of chairmen across Capitol Hill. So, the mere threat of a Presidential veto can, and often does, change the course of legislation, particularly if the congressional majority and the President are of the same party. All a Cabinet Secretary or a White House legislative staffer has to do is whisper in a committee chairman's ear that the President will veto a bill if it includes a particular amendment the administration can't live with. If the congressional majority is made up of Members of the same party as the President, the odds are that the amendment will never make it out of committee. In such a situation, they're likely to find an opportunity for compromise on a measure that has broad support beyond the Beltway, particularly if there is plenty of glory to go around. Besides, family fights are not good politics, so compromise instead of confrontation will likely result. President Bush only vetoed one bill during his six years of unified party rule (where one party controls both chambers of Congress and the White House). President Obama did not veto any legislation during his only two years of unified government.

Even a Member of the opposing party can benefit from a compromise with the President, though they are not likely to be directly involved in negotiations; that task will likely fall to the leadership and a committee chairman. The negotiations have a greater chance of success if the administration fears being embarrassed in a public battle over the issue.

Even though the President has the power of the veto, his real influence in the legislative process tends to be the informal but substantial leverage he is able to exert. Presidential influence (or lack thereof) takes many more subtle forms as well.

Influence can take the form of popular support following a Presidential election where Members of Congress must consider the popularity of the President in their own districts. Members may not support the President's agenda, but if he outpolled them in their own districts, they may be convinced their constituents do, making opposition politically perilous. This was one of the keys to Reagan's influence in 1981-1982 when he passed his economic program of reduced tax rates, spending cuts and increased defense spending despite a divided government. Another good example is the explosion of legislation—including Medicare and the Voting Rights Act—which were initiated by President Lyndon Johnson following his landslide victory over Senator Barry Goldwater. When the President is popular his leadership enables him to influence Congress, but by the same token, high public disapproval ratings will undermine him. There was little political risk in opposing the unpopular George W. Bush in 2008 or Barack Obama in 2010.

In addition, the President can influence the legislative process by threatening to go around the Congress. The Presidency has developed pseudo-legislative powers that allow a President to bypass Congress when it is in his perceived interest. This can also include times when Congress doesn't want to take politically difficult actions—such as President Obama's 2009 Executive order permitting the use of taxpayer dollars to pay for birth control and abortion advocacy programs in foreign countries. These pseudo-legislative powers include war powers and other foreign affairs powers, but also the use of cabinets and agencies to implement and interpret the actions of Congress through the regulatory and administrative process. More direct prerogative powers include Presidential proclamations, Executive orders, signing statements, and national security directives—some of which, like signing statements, are controversial. While Congress and the Courts have the ability to overturn or countermand many of the prerogative powers, they have rarely done so. Ever since the beginning of the modern Presidency, the pseudo-legislative tools assumed under the principle of Presidential prerogative continue to evolve and expand—often at the expense of congressional power.

Resolving Differences Between the House and Senate

For a bill to be sent to the President for his signature, the House and Senate must pass the exact same bill, right down to the punctuation marks. Any differences between versions passed by each chamber must be resolved.

This can happen in one of three ways:

The easiest way is for one Chamber simply to take up and approve the bill as passed by the other Chamber. In such cases, it is usually a relatively non-controversial measure or a simple extension of current law. Of course, that is not always the case, as when the House passed the Senate's version of the controversial healthcare reform legislation in 2010. Adopting controversial legislation in such a manner is historically rare, however.

The second method is informally called congressional ping-pong. There are many instances where both Chambers have passed separate measures and then taken up the bill passed by the other, attached their language as an amendment, and sent the bill to the other chamber with the hope that the amendment will be accepted. In this case, Members hope that the disagreements between the two Chambers can be worked out through amendments that are called messages between the Chambers. If this messaging continues back and forth, it is sometimes characterized as the legislation being "ping-ponged" between the House and Senate.

If the House gets an amendment from the Senate (or vice-versa), the measure is taken up, and if they agree, the bill goes to the President.

If the House disagrees, they will send the bill back to the Senate with amendments of their own. The game of "ping-pong" can continue endlessly with no resolution and the measure would die at the end of the Congress. There is no limit to how many times a bill can be swatted across the Capitol dome until all the differences are resolved.

Scope

A point of order may be made against any conference report on the grounds that the conference agreement violates the scope of the conference—in other words, the conferees have agreed to something that is beyond the limit of their authority. "Scope" is often a contentious aspect of a conference report. In theory, the conference committee is supposed to consider a compromise between the high and lows of each bill. For example, if the House version of a bill contained $100 million for a program and the Senate version contained $300 million for the same program, the scope of the conference is between $100 and $300 million. The conferees are not supposed to approve less or more. That doesn't mean they don't and if no one objects, they can get away with it. Once debate has begun on a conference report a point of order is no longer allowed.

If an important measure bounces back and forth and cannot be reconciled, however, then a conference committee will be convened to resolve the differences

Conference Committees

One of the hallmarks of Congress is the conference committee, a temporary committee created to resolve differences between the House and Senate. But the traditional conference committee has also fallen victim to the increasing polarization. Leadership in both Chambers have increasingly sought to circumvent conference committees as a way to strengthen the hand of the Speaker in the House and the majority leader in the Senate at the expense of the committee chairs who typically run conference committees.

In 2010, for instance, the House and Senate only voted on two conference reports the entire year, compared to 22 in the House and 19 in the Senate only ten years earlier.

In theory, this is how conference committees work. When the discrepancies between the House and Senate cannot be reconciled, each Chamber appoints "managers" or "conferees" to sit on a conference committee. The House Speaker and the Senate majority leader in consultation with the minority leaders in their Chamber name the conferees. These two leaders determine how many Members will serve on the conference committee.

The rules and procedures for conference committees are choreographed as tightly as a ballet. It might seem excessively complicated, but since the most important legislation before the Congress must typically be resolved this way, the steps of this ballet must be learned.

The Chamber literally in possession of the papers - the physical bill and the amendments passed by the other body - makes the request for a conference. This is usually done by unanimous consent in the Senate, or by adoption of a rule reported from the Rules Committee in the House. The Chamber receiving the request may agree to the conference or disregard the request.

MPTV.net

A conference committee can be the closest thing you'll find to the knife fight in the motion picture *Butch Cassidy and the Sundance Kid*.

When a bill is sent to conference, the conferees are limited in the issues they may address - typically only those matters that are in disagreement between the House and the Senate.

The minority in House has the right to offer a motion to instruct conferees. However, any instructions the House issues are only advisory, not binding, and are directed only to their own conferees.

In contrast to the procedural ballet, the actual meeting of a conference committee can be the closest thing you'll find to the knife fight in the motion picture *Butch Cassidy and the Sundance Kid*—you know the scene, the one where Butch is facing off against a giant of a man and calls time out while they discuss the rules.

"Rules?" the giant demands and looks around at the ring of spectators for confirmation. "There are no rules in a knife fight."

"All right," Butch replies and kicks the giant squarely beneath his belt buckle.

While conference committees are often marked by some of Washington's best "horse trading," deliberations sometimes disintegrate into a clash of egos between Senate and House chairmen. This is particularly true when different parties have control of the House and Senate. For the sake of decorum, all this takes place behind closed doors, and in some cases no one on the outside has any idea what the measure under consideration will look like until it is sent to the floors of the two Chambers for a vote.

It is essential that a Member interested in seeing a specific provision in the conference report find an advocate on the inside of the conference committee as quickly as possible. Otherwise, the Member is likely to find all the hard work that went into introducing the legislation, getting it included as an amendment, seeing it passed and sent to a conference committee is all for naught. Why? Because those involved in the negotiations used it as cannon fodder, swapped it into oblivion, made it a hostage of the debate, and then gave it away as a concession to the other side.

It is prudent for a Member with an amendment in the bill to meet with the committee staff director or general counsel. A meeting between a Member and the chairman of the conference committee might even be arranged to finalize the deal. At the very least, the Member is expected to commit his or her support for the final conference report if it contains the Member's provision.

Conference Reports and Final Passage

Once an agreement has been hammered out, the conference report needs to be agreed to and signed by a majority of the managers of both the House and Senate. The conferees prepare a joint explanatory statement outlining the agreements, and a majority of managers from each Chamber sign it.

The Chamber that was invited to the conference calls up a conference report for a vote first. If it is agreed to, it is sent to the other Chamber for approval. If either Chamber rejects the conference report, the differences may be resolved by one Chamber agreeing to an amendment by the other, or by requesting a further conference. Once both Chambers agree the measure is enrolled and goes to the President for signature. (A little trivia: By law, the enrolled bill must be printed on parchment paper before being presented to the President.)

Follow-up and Oversight

The fat lady does not sing just because a measure is enacted into law, especially if it requires creation or changes in regulations. If the bureaucracy is not supportive, and often times even if it is, it can take months, perhaps even years, to get the necessary regulations issued or refined.

The sponsor of any change in administrative rules must stay on top of the agency responsible for implementing them. Members do that by follow-up letters, demands that bureaucrats come in for face-to-face meetings to explain themselves, and through the oversight powers of his or her committee. That way, they make sure the executive branch carries out the will of the Congress.

The Congress must jealously guard its prerogatives. Enforcement by the executive branch of laws passed by the Congress goes to the heart of the Constitution's delegation of authority. After all, the Constitution says the President's job is to "faithfully execute" the laws passed by Congress. Efforts to stall or obstruct—or outright refusal to enforce—those laws go to the heart of the Constitution as well, but bring with them dangerous consequences for the balance of power between the two branches.

Chapter Six Summary

- Members introduce a bill by dropping it in the hopper. The hopper actually exists in the House.

- When you introduce a bill, it is good to introduce it publicly with a speech on the floor of the House or Senate.

- Bills are referred to committees. On rare occasions, House or Senate leadership brings legislation directly to the floor of their Chamber.

- Committees are the backbone of the legislative process. Along with drafting legislation, the primary function of the committee is congressional oversight of Federal programs.

- Three important processes take place in committee: the hearing, the mark-up, and the preparation of a committee report.

- Germaneness—the requirement that amendments be related to the bill they target—is among the House's most significant legislative principles. It dates back to the 1st Congress and governs the ebb and flow of amendments.

- When a bill reaches the floor of the House or Senate, the procedures established by each body govern the process.

- The House rules are more restrictive than those of the Senate.

- The leadership plays a critical role in the fate of legislation in both bodies.

- The administration also shapes legislation by using or threatening a veto and by a host of other formal and informal powers. It also determines how laws will be implemented.

- The last, and often more secretive, deliberations on legislation occur in the conference committee. However, the desire of party leaders to control legislative outcomes at the expense of committee chairman are making conference committees ever more rare.

Management is discussed in great detail in hundreds of books on the subject and in MBA courses the world over. None of them prepare a person for the job of running a congressional office. Chances are you'll never aspire to such a position, but some of the insights provided here will help you work more effectively. They may even convince you to seek the job of leading a congressional office some day.

An MBA degree is not a prerequisite. In fact, there are few MBAs on Capitol Hill—at least few serving as chiefs of staff. Most chiefs of staff have backgrounds in law, political science, history or communications. What they have in common is that very little of what they learned in the classroom or in previous jobs prepared them for the role they now play.

They learn by doing—and the good ones never stop learning.

At first glance, the challenges they face are similar to those confronted by anyone who manages a creative, highly skilled, overworked, and underpaid staff toiling in offices whose amenities compare unfavorably with the mailrooms of most major corporations. But the chief of staff faces many challenges that are unique to the position. Among the greatest of these are the coordination of activities at satellites scattered across a state or district where staffs are performing a range of different functions and the need to apply management principles within a uniquely political atmosphere. Responsibilities under the chief of staff's jurisdiction might include overseeing legislative initiatives, communicating effectively with friend and foe alike, solving problems with worldwide implications, and bartering support for another Member's effort to have May designated "National Harmonica Month" in exchange for endorsement of a bill your boss is sponsoring that would have a profound impact on child safety.

And security—let's not forget security. The chief is responsible for ensuring that the workplace is safe and that there is a plan to help visitors in the event of an attack or other form of disaster, that all mail is screened, that restrictions on access to buildings and garages are maintained, and that emergency preparedness plans are updated and employees made aware of them.

All this within the confines of a comparatively miniscule operating budget, around a shrinking $1.5 million a year for the typical House office—the House has voted to cut their own budgets by 11 percent during 2011-2012—and about $4 million for each Senator's office.

Perhaps most important of all, the effective chief of staff is a facilitator, clearing obstacles from the paths of the Member and the staff alike. The chief helps them remain focused on the tasks before them and keeps them apprised of changes in strategy and circumstance. The chief makes them aware of any shifts before rumors have a chance to distort reality, undermine confidence and distract from the shared mission.

Pitfalls to Avoid

Ineffective chiefs of staff operate on the theory that knowledge is power and do everything possible to conceal information from those who work with them, a strategy that is counterproductive, at best. In an age when knowledge flows like water around obstacles, it is impossible to keep essential information secret. Secrecy only creates distrust.

This sort of misguided approach to management is not unique to the chiefs of staff who employ it. It usually is a reflection of the temperament of the Members under whom they serve. These Members want their offices to be as disciplined as the political campaigns that brought them to DC.

Political campaigns often require authoritarian management because they are structured on a military model: They have a defined objective, a single opponent, finite resources, limited time and usually are conducted in the face of enemy fire. When allowed to gain a foothold in a congressional office, such a system generally limits access to the Member by funneling everything up through the top of the pyramid, the chief of staff, who exercises complete control over the flow of information.

The Member is isolated, often by preference.

Staff has little decision-making authority and therefore little practical responsibility—unless something goes wrong. Authoritarian managers assume that no matter what the task, their subordinates aren't up to it. They assume staff will not take initiative unless pushed, that they will not recognize priorities unless they are spelled out for them, and that they will put self-interest ahead of the organization's well being.

Authoritarianism bottlenecks decisions and limits the options and perspectives available to the Member. It discourages initiative by staff and makes them less loyal to a boss with whom they have no interaction. That, in turn, undermines motivation and initiative. Staff develops slowly, if at all. As a result, decisions affecting who gets hired have little significance. Staff is expendable and easily cast off. Most don't wait for the axe to fall before beginning to look for opportunities elsewhere.

And such chiefs are often "yellers." Maybe a college football coach can yell at his players, but a manager in the modern workplace, whether it is in Congress or any other organization, should not be screaming at employees. It is the ultimate demonstration of insecurity, and no employee should have to put up with it (at least not until they find another job). If the chief is a "yeller" then he or she should stop, resolve never to yell at a colleague again, and apologize for past abuses. If they are unable to stop, they should seek counseling. Seriously.

There have been some comedic movies and television shows about bad bosses, but as the noted Harvard Business School Professor, Rosabeth Moss Kanter wrote in the *Harvard Business Review*:

> In real life, horrible bosses are the stuff of tragedy, not comedy. Workplace discontent is no joke. Some surveys show that as many as half of American workers feel low levels of work engagement, stemming in part from poor management. It's not the insults that cause the greatest harm, but rather the callousness about people's time. Horrible bosses want control. They expect subordinates to be on call 24/7 and to hit unrealistic deadlines with limited resources. When the work product is delivered, horrible bosses may ignore it for long intervals, making it clear that the deadline was artificial and the stress unnecessary.

Some micromanaging Members actually aggravate the situation by acting as their own chief regardless of who holds the title on paper. It's not unlike Benjamin Franklin's admonition: "A man who acts as his own attorney has a fool for a client."

Members should lead—chiefs should manage. These are two very different but equally important functions. There are certain things that only Members can do and they should focus primarily on those tasks.

Only the Member can participate in floor and committee proceedings.

Only a Member can appear at a press conference or do proactive interviews on television, radio, or for print and Internet.

Only a Member can meet with party and committee leaders to help pave the way for a legislative idea.

And only a Member can speak to organizations and coalitions to gather support and help build momentum for his or her ideas.

The Member should schedule his or her time doing those things that only a Member can do.

The Servant-Leader

At the opposite end of the management spectrum is what is known as the open system, which encourages professional behavior on the part of staff and increases the likelihood they will achieve desired goals. Under this system, the chief serves as a conduit rather than a faucet. He or she encourages communication and decision-making that involves the Member and those affected by decisions he or she makes. The chief's role is to equip and enable staff to perform tasks for which they are suited.

There are 541 individual offices in the House and Senate. Most are run by very capable chiefs who recognize the synergistic aspects of what their staffs do. In politics, as in most other endeavors, the whole is greater than the sum of the parts—that is, a team performs better than the best efforts of individuals operating on their own. Constituent-service personnel, for example, help provide direction for the legislative staff and the communications staffs, while legislative aides affect communicators, and communicators affect legislators.

Synergistic offices constantly seek ways to enable staff to interact with one another, for specialists in one aspect of the operation to contribute to the success of another. Interdependence built upon a common mission encourages an office-wide culture to which new staff finds it easy to adapt. When everyone, from the receptionist at a district or state office to the chief of staff, feels he or she is contributing to fulfillment of a vision and that information flows freely between the Member and subordinates, negative influences such as office politics lose credibility and their sting.

Synergistic offices are not "soft" offices—in fact the demands on staff can be greater since they have specific responsibilities that they are accountable for. An important goal for any manager, in the words of the classic 1974 Harvard Business Review article, is to *Get the Monkey Off Your Back.* Kevin Blanchard, author of The *One Minute Manager Meets the Monkey,* put it like this:

> So you're heading down the hall when one of your subordinates stops you and says, "We've got a problem." You quickly realize it's a little bigger than you can handle on the spot, so you say, "Let me think about it and I'll get back to you." Now you have the monkey (the next step) on your back and your subordinate occasionally stops to check on how you are doing with it. You accepted the responsibility and promised a progress report. Now you've become the worker and he's become the supervisor!

A good chief of staff learns to delegate to and trust the people they hire. They also learn that there are some things so important that they should not be delegated. Experience and knowledge teaches the difference. But if a chief is finding more items falling in the latter category they need to start giving the monkey back.

The decision to encourage synergy must be deliberate.

And the Member and top staff must make it.

The open management system—which often is referred to as a *flat organization*—encourages staff to make decisions and take initiative. It results in greater productivity by spreading important, high-level tasks among more people. It provides the Member with a range of perspectives on important issues.

This system also has weaknesses. People lose focus and miss deadlines if they are not held accountable for them. Staff members burn out if they take on more responsibility than they can handle. Decision-making can become unclear with more people involved and often makes employees uncomfortable if they are the kind of person who needs structure or dislikes decision-making.

Most offices fall somewhere between a pure authoritarian approach and an absolutely flat or open system. Different personalities, circumstances and electoral security influence how an office will be managed. The more open an office tends to be, the more successful and innovative it is.

Marcus Buckingham, who has written several books on management, points out that effective management is essential to what he describes as a high-trust organization. In *First, Break All the Rules,* he observes:

> Great managers need to be recognized for what they do best: reaching inside a worker and encouraging exceptional performance. That is not the same as being a great leader.... Great managers look inward, inside the company, into the individual, into the differences in style, goals, needs and motivations of each person. Then they find the right way to release each person's unique talents into great performance.

This places a premium on chiefs developing their own management and motivational skills and on hiring people they can trust.

When considering whom to hire, there are two essential components of trust: integrity and competence. Integrity is inherent. Competence, on the other hand, can be taught.

At a time when unethical behavior by a few Members of the Congress has damaged the reputations of all Members, the need for integrity is as urgent as ever in the history of this nation. Acting with integrity means acting in a consistent and ethical manner—what you do must be consistent with what you say. Integrity matters in big things but also in seemingly little things. If, for example, a Member tells the staff that correspondence must be answered within two weeks, but then takes a month to return drafts of letters, the staff quickly concludes that the Member's words and actions don't mesh.

Competence is equally essential. People trust those who accomplish what they say they will accomplish. Everyone, from the Member to the newest staff assistant, can learn to be better at what he or she does. One of the chief's jobs is to make sure staff has access to resources that will help them to learn and grow. It is even more important to keep in mind that the shortest route to results is to establish clear goals and a compensation package that rewards performance.

Next, the staff person being hired must be ideologically compatible with the Member's political philosophy and they must be personally compatible with the office culture. The smartest, most trustworthy person in the world could apply for a staff position, but if his ideology is incompatible with the boss' mission statement, then he is not going to succeed in his job. If a person is ideologically compatible, but their personality doesn't fit the office culture, it risks straining office cohesion. (We will discuss more on mission statements and office culture in the next chapter.).

There are many good management books on hiring and managing. Read some of them. The best hires occur when a person is brought in who shares the office's mission, fits the office culture, demonstrates integrity and has the potential to provide a skill the office doesn't have. The worst hires occur when insecure chiefs try to hire people whom they believe will not threaten them.

The role of the chief of staff is to help everyone else succeed. The chief of staff's job is to accomplish the office's strategic goals by managing personnel and allocating finite resources such as time and money while fostering accountability. An effective chief of staff measures personal success by the success of those around him or her.

This chief of staff is the ultimate servant-leader.

Managing Between Generations

There are lots of factors that go into management on the Hill—geographic, academic, racial, and gender to name a few. One most dynamic demographic characteristics unique to the Hill is managing between generations.

A high percentage of those working in the legislators' offices are under the age of 30—members of the generation known as Millennials. Generation Xers and the Baby Boomers complement them. There are even a scattering of people serving in Congress and on staffs who were born between the beginning of the Great Depression and the end of World War II, a generation known as Veterans, Traditionalists and Silents.

Tom Brokaw has declared the Veterans/Traditionalists "The Greatest Generation" because they not only survived the Depression but at least one of the two World Wars. That makes the *Veterans* reference obvious. They're called Traditionalists because they have a reputation for protecting traditional values such as civic pride, loyalty, respect for authority, a strong work ethic, and living within one's means. Some researchers on the subject include a generation called Silents that falls between the

Generation	Born
Veterans/Traditionalists	Early 20th Century to Mid-1920s
Silents	Mid-1920s to mid-1940s
Baby Boomers	Mid-1940s to mid-1960s
Generation X/Xers	Mid-1960s to about 1980
Millennials	About 1980 to 2000

Cuspers are people who have qualities of two generations, usually born near the beginning or end of a generation's range.

Veterans/Traditionalist and the Baby Boomers. We won't spend too much time here because there are very few, if any, staffers left on the Hill from generations born earlier than Baby Boomers.

On the Hill, it is the Baby Boomers who have been credited with inventing the 60-hour workweek.

"They have an almost Pavlovian tendency toward being driven," according to *Generations at Work* by Ron Zemke, Claire Raines and Bob Filipczak, whose conclusions are representative of the flurry of excellent books and articles that have been published in recent years on the need for managers to take into account differences between generations.

Boomers live to work.

Their sense of self is firmly connected to their job and strong attitudes about the rightness of their policy beliefs, which may help explain why they were so instrumental in winning many of the workplace rights and opportunities that are taken for granted today, particularly those affecting women. Theirs is a generation that has proven itself adept at navigating the political minefields that exist in most offices and are not bashful about voicing concerns when they feel an injustice has been done or they have not been treated fairly.

Many Members now serving in the House and Senate are Boomers. So are some committee and personal office senior staffers, who began arriving after Members were allowed to hire more employees in 1966. Boomers set the standard on the Capitol Hill with 12-hour days and frequent weekends at the office.

Generation X or Xers are the children of workaholic Boomers and perhaps the most over-analyzed and hyper-criticized sliver of society in history—and it is their parents who have criticized them the most. Xers are the first generation of America's children who arrived home after school to an empty house. Both parents were active members of the workforce and can't understand why their children aren't as dedicated to their jobs as they were—nor can they understand any of their children's other attitudes, for the matter. As a result, Xers have been called lazy, self-focused and materialistic.

Xers contend that none of these harsh labels is fair, that they're simply more independent than their Boomer parents and even their Millennial offspring. They are intelligent but cynical and despise micromanagement. Evidence suggests that they actually are as hardworking as the generation that preceded theirs and have perpetuated the 60-hour-plus workweek pioneered by the Boomers on the Hill. They simply prefer not to stay in the office unless there's something important to do.

Xers work to live.

Millennials, the most recent additions to the Capitol Hill workforce, are the most technologically savvy generation ever. They have grown up with computers and cell phones and know how to use the technology that's available to them more effectively than previous generations. It is their lifeline of sorts: They are inextricably connected to peers and family through technology.

Unlike Xers, who spent a great amount of time without parental supervision, Millennials have what they refer to as their helicopter parents, who have been almost too involved in their lives, having regulated everything from outdoor activities to dining choices. Millennials grew up on fields and in arenas where the sports they played were highly organized with matching uniforms and paid coaches. As a result, they have no idea about a spontaneous game like stickball, but they are enthusiastic collaborators and willing teammates.

They played well together, now they work well together.

Millenials dislike rigid job descriptions, are achievement oriented, and tend to be very confident in their ability to reach the goals that are set for them. Unlike the Boomers, they don't see the need to pay dues and demand to be judged on the basis of merit, not seniority. Millennials may clash with Boomers on attitudes toward the workplace and scoff at Xers' emphasis on individualism, but they have almost reverential respect for Veterans/Traditionalists/Silents.

Though each generation has its own way of looking at the world and its own way of doing things, when allowed and encouraged to work together in an open system, they do so effectively. It's not unusual, for instance, to find a Millennial in a legislative director's or a communications director's slot, a level of responsibility that's generally unheard of in the private sector, unless your father owns the business. Soon it will not be unusual for Boomers and Xers to find themselves subordinate to Millennials.

Being aware of generational differences is essential to building effective organizations, especially in an environment where staff members are likely to move into positions of authority at much earlier ages and find themselves managing the activities of men and women who are older than they are. All managers must learn to be sensitive to the distinctions, appreciate the strengths of individuals, neutralize the weaknesses of each generation, and mold those who work for them into an effective team.

When Xers and Millennials interact with Boomers, for instance, they would be wise to demonstrate respect; conduct face-to-face conversations rather than emailed exchanges and give such conversations their full attention since Boomers are uncomfortable with multi-tasking; understand that Boomers see the workplace in terms of office politics and maneuvering; and be conversant with the history of the Congress and the individual organization. The tendency of Millennials to ignore the past and focus almost exclusively on the present creates suspicion and even resentment among Boomers who contributed to that past and respect the lessons it has taught.

When dealing with Xers, other staff should say what's on their minds because Xers have a low tolerance for buzzwords and clichés. Realize as well that Xers function best when truly empowered. Give them the objective, offer support and let them determine the best way to get things done.

Most of all, make work fun.

Millennials, meanwhile, need to be challenged. They enjoy working with others as long as they are treated as an equal, a collaborator—often before their elders feels they have paid their dues. They want to be asked their opinions. Because Millennials benefit from mentoring, as opposed to instruction, managers need to take into account the fact that working with them is much more like a personal relationship than a transactional one.

Millennials need feedback. They are used to instantaneous responses from parents, teachers and the Internet. In many cases, these responses have always been excessively positive and sometimes unwarranted—like the 12-inch trophy they received for finishing 8th place in the soccer league—but there is nothing the manager can do to change their expectations. Therefore, managers should channel those expectations with constructive criticism that is couched in positive terms.

One Senate chief of staff accomplished the seemingly impossible task of behavior modification among Millennials through no-fault problem solving sessions during regular staff meetings. A situation that a Millennial—or any other staff member, for that matter—may not have handled successfully in the past or one that must be confronted in the near future was described in general terms. Staff members then took turns suggesting approaches they believed would have worked. Then the chief endorsed those that were likely to provide the greatest return on investment.

Knowledge Management

Another concern affecting the future of congressional offices involves knowledge management—the way organizations generate, communicate and use their intellectual assets. A congressional office is what the late Peter Drucker, a pioneer in management studies and author of numerous books including *Managing in the Next Society*, called an information-based organization.

In ages past, a Member and a few aides controlled most information and hired other people to support and carry out strategies based on that information. Today, a congressional office is a collection of specialists who have knowledge that Members need but can't access on their own. For example, a typical Senate office will have a military expert with top-secret security clearance and detailed knowledge of highly technical projects; an agriculture expert who knows the ins and outs of every support and loan subsidy program available for every size farm and crop; and an aide who knows transportation spending and has spent time talking with constituents, engineers, city managers and mayors, chambers of commerce and local citizen groups and businesses about specific road, rail, air, boat and bus needs.

All of this is highly specialized information that no one person can possibly acquire, let alone retain.

By default, every congressional office is, or should be, what is referred to as a "cross-functional team." Generating a news release, for example, involves a team that typically consists of the Member, the communications and legislative staffs, the scheduler and the IT manager. It only makes sense then to develop information systems that allow for easy collaboration and knowledge sharing.

Thus, the most significant intellectual asset of any congressional office is its people, but few congressional offices take full advantage of them. Here's how forward-thinking managers on the Hill perceive the situation:

- As a result of turnover, the research and development efforts of legislative staff often go away when a staff member departs. A knowledge management system can capture and distribute information pertinent to legislation, scheduling, press, administration, IT operations training, and other learning and educational resources.

- Collaboration involves working across function (information technology, working with legislative staff, working with communications, for example), as well as across space (integration of efforts by staff at the DC office and those in the home state). All staff members need access to information and the ability to compile and otherwise make use of it.

- Staff development demands access to learning, knowledge and experience. This comes from new employee orientation, office manuals, ethics training and memos, financial and personnel reports, all of which are important in preserving continuity and office culture.

- Maintaining a history of the Member's congressional career requires that critical knowledge and actions (voting record) be captured

124

through carefully kept records and the ability to correlate the information they contain.

- An *electronic organization* enables continuity of operations in the event of a terrorist attack or other incident that forces staff out of their offices.

Too often, knowledge management systems in most congressional offices consist of an inbox in the Outlook email program, an inbox whose contents disappear forever when the address of a departing staff member is eliminated. The technology needed to enable effective knowledge management programs is readily available off the shelf, including corporate mainstays such as SharePoint by Microsoft, which has been customized to serve the needs of congressional offices.

If your office doesn't have the resources it needs to take advantage of what you and everyone else that works there knows long after you've moved on, you might want to suggest to your boss that such a system would be invaluable.

COOP planning

The 800-pound gorilla in every congressional office is the ever-present threat of terrorist attack. Chiefs are responsible for the safety and security of staff. They are also responsible for cooperating with efforts aimed at making sure enemies are not able to shut down the legislative branch of government, even in the wake of the most devastating attacks.

The most important thing a chief of staff can do is be prepared. There are sources on the Hill to help offices design and implement a multi-faceted strategy called a COOP (Continuity of Operations Plan), but given security sensitivities, the less that is written about these strategies here, the better.

What you'll find readily apparent is that terrorism threats have already changed the way Members and constituents communicate with each other. Paper mail, for instance, goes through a screening process that delays delivery for up to two weeks.

Other considerations range from knowing what to do in response to various types of threats to understanding the resources available and how they should be used, from designing an evacuation plan to making sure the Member, visiting constituents and the entire staff, including interns, are secure and accounted for.

Plans need to include how the office will operate if forced out of its physical domain, particularly including phone and email communication and establishing redundant information systems and remote backups. A temporary base of operations should be identified, as well as an order or battle plan for bringing staff back to work. In addition, it should include an alternate means of communicating and coordinating with the district or state office staff.

Chapter Seven Summary

- Very little of what chiefs of staff learned in the classroom or in previous jobs prepared them for the role they play.

- A chief of staff must coordinate activities at satellite offices spread across a congressional district or state. A chief oversees legislative initiatives and external and internal communication. In general, he or she is the "chief problem solver."

- Ineffective chiefs of staff operate on the theory that knowledge is power and do everything possible to conceal information from those who work under them.

- Members should lead, but chiefs of staff should manage. These are two very different, but equally important, functions. There are certain things that only Members can do, and they should focus on those tasks.

- Under an open or flat management system, the chief serves as a conduit rather than a faucet. The chief's role is to equip and enable staff to perform tasks for which they are suited.

- Most offices fall somewhere between a pure authoritarian approach and an absolutely flat or open system.

- There are two essential components of trust: integrity and competence. Integrity means acting in a consistent and ethical manner—what you do must be consistent with what you say. Competence is equally essential. People trust those who accomplish what they say they will accomplish.

- The role of the chief of staff is to help everyone else succeed. The chief of staff's job is to accomplish the office's strategic goals by managing personnel and allocating finite resources such as time and money while fostering accountability.

- One the most dynamic demographic characteristics unique to the Hill is managing between generations.

- The majority of those working in the legislative branch are members of a generation known as Millennials. Staff representing Generation X and the Baby Boom complement them.

- Another concern affecting the future of congressional offices involves knowledge management—the way organizations generate, communicate, use, preserve their intellectual assets.

- The 800-pound gorilla in every congressional office is the ever-present threat of terrorist attack.

Chapter 8
Plotting Course

You're talking on the phone trying to unsnag paperwork for computer equipment your office has needed for the past three months when the staff assistant interrupts to say there's an emergency call from your district director. You lean forward in your seat anxiously waiting for the person at House Administration to finish his long-winded explanation for why you won't be getting any satisfaction soon and your elbow strikes one of several stacks of mail that have been accumulating on your desk. It scatters across the draft of a bill that would add five new depreciation schedules to the Internal Revenue Code, which your newest legislative assistant just presented to you. You glance at your wristwatch and realize you're missing a meeting on how to streamline your office's mail operations, which is probably just as well since your mail management software is down anyway. It's at this point that your boss walks in, orders you to drop everything and run down a rumor that money for a badly needed highway project in your district was left out of an appropriation bill before the Senate.

"This," you reason, "is why the chief of staff gets paid the big bucks."

You're not alone. Everyone in a management position on the Hill is heir to this sort of pandemonium—sometimes once a week, sometimes once a day, sometimes all day long. There are a seemingly infinite number of challenges vying for your attention. The greatest constraint is the limited amount of time available to address them.

Adrenaline may enable you to put out fire after fire, but inevitably there's a price to be paid—constituents don't get their mail answered, the advice that's given to the Member by your staff leads to a blunder on the floor of the House or Senate, schedules become confused and staff begins to send out resumes. Serving in Congress might easily become impossible were it not for strategic planning.

The key is to know where you're going and how you intend to get there. You must know, for example, what the Member's priorities are and build the entire operation around goals based on those priorities, as well as around commonly held values and issues that are important to the constituents you serve.

In short, you need a strategic vision.

If you're new to the staff of an incumbent, chances are one already exists.

Find it.

Read it.

Live it.

If you're on the staff of a newly elected Member, whether you're the chief or an entry-level staff assistant, chances are you'll have an opportunity to contribute to the development of the office strategy.

If your office (be it new or with 15 years experience) doesn't have one, doesn't have plans to come up with one, or hasn't even given a thought to one, encourage your colleagues to create one. Without a strategic vision, a set of goals based on that vision, and a plan for meeting the goals, the odds are against success.

How is it possible to make important decisions—any decisions at all, for that matter—without a common understanding of what you and other members of your staff are trying to accomplish?

How do you know what your website should contain?

What are your legislative priorities?

How do you know how much money you must budget?

The term *strategic planning* has become ingrained in the business lexicon. It often means different things to different people, however. Don't overcomplicate it. Simply put, strategic planning means determining the direction you want to go, creating goals to get you there, and then allocating the resources necessary to accomplish those goals.

The Planning Process

If you are in a position of authority and you expect everyone to work toward strategic goals, you must invite everyone whose job they will affect to have a hand in their development at an office-wide strategic planning meeting. Only by involving the entire staff can you generate the sense of ownership necessary to produce a unified force, one whose activities reflect and benefit the office's strategic goals.

For Members or chiefs, once you decide to hold a strategic planning retreat, your first step should be to invite a facilitator to lead the discussions. It may seem incongruous to suggest that the most effective way to create this unified force is to involve an outsider. But a dispassionate facilitator is essential—especially the first time you undertake an office-wide planning process. There are several reasons:

- An outside facilitator can be expected to bring to the task the skills necessary to engage everyone. It is almost impossible for a chief of staff or the Member to participate as an equal among equals and serve as moderator and overseer simultaneously. An independent moderator brings no history, no personal agenda or other baggage to the process.

- A skillful facilitator can avoid a 2-day free-for-all by applying order, logic and experience to the process.

- An experienced facilitator will be more successful than an insider at fleshing out areas of disagreement that must be resolved if the long-range plan is to succeed. Even experienced staff have issues, some of which they may not even be aware of, that can have a negative impact somewhere down the road.

- A skillful facilitator can get staff to ask questions of themselves that they would not otherwise know to ask.

Choose a facilitator wisely. The characteristics that distinguish Congress from a business will have a significant impact on the planning process and its outcome. In business, the bottom line is measured by profits and stock prices. In the political world it is measured by job approval ratings and votes. A legislator uses much different criteria in deciding how to respond to public needs and demand. Choose a facilitator who is familiar with the qualities that make Congress unique.

Logistics

Under existing congressional rules, the House and Senate do allow Members to conduct planning sessions, but there are many considerations that can affect the sort of event we're discussing here. Confer with your Chamber's ethics committee and the Federal Election Commission (FEC) to confirm that the session will not violate any codes or campaign

Keep it Simple

Strategic planning is a huge field in business and organizational management, and has been written about by hundreds of authors and experts. The strategic plan for a large corporation can amount to a book-sized document (not that bigger is necessarily better). As a result, there are multiple terms that often have overlapping meanings. There are visions, values, goals, strategies, tactics, etc. For our purposes, however, we're trying to keep things simple. There are three main focuses: the direction a Member wants to go (defined in the mission statement), the goals that embody the mission statement, and an action plan to accomplish those goals. Some offices may want to get deeper into the planning process and that is something to be encouraged. But for those offices just getting started in the planning process, we suggest working on the basics first.

laws. These rule-making bodies have constantly changing standards, so don't assume that what worked for a neighboring office or for your own office last year will work this time around.

Among the questions you'll want answered are:

- What options are available for covering costs associated with a planning session—can campaign funds or tax dollars be used?

- Is it possible for staff to attend such a session on the clock?

- Are expenses incurred by staff—transportation and meals, for example—reimbursable?

- Can related events such as a breakfast or a dinner be paid for by an outside source or the Member's campaign committee?

- Can non-governmental space or other accommodations be donated?

Once you have resolved any ethics questions, schedule the meeting in a location other than either the DC or the district office. A retreat-type setting works best, one that is a substantial distance from office phones and routine work. Sessions typically are scheduled during a workweek or weekend with little pressing business. Staff the office with a skeleton crew of interns or borrow staff from another office in exchange for covering their office when they conduct their meetings.

The DC and district staffs should participate in a single event. If that is impossible, a session for DC staff and another for district staff should be scheduled—but they will not be as productive as one for everyone.

It is important that everyone have an opportunity to contribute—and that the Member and chief be present when they do.

The Member needs to understand going in that he or she will not be making a mere guest appearance but must be a full participant in the planning session and be there from beginning to end. Failure to make and live up to that commitment will be disruptive and downright counterproductive—if the Member doesn't take the process seriously, why should anyone else? The Member must also guard against dominating the ideas shared in the sessions.

Preparations

Selecting a location and ensuring that all the relevant team members can attend might be the easiest part of preparing for the retreat. An office can't identify any goals without an accurate understanding of its constituency, so the facilitator and staff should gather information beforehand. The facilitator can be expected to require several weeks of phone conversations, face-to-face meetings and other fact-finding efforts in advance of the retreat.

With the help of appropriate office staff, the facilitator will gather information on office systems; the most recent polling data; and statistical and demographic information on the home district or state, including major employers, Federal installations and sensitive environmental sites. This information should be organized and presented to all personnel prior to the planning session. Among the topics that might be addressed are:

- What population shifts have occurred since the last election, census, or redistricting?

- Is there an influx or outflow of specific ethnic groups?

- What are the basic demographic ratios—male/female; black/Hispanic/white; under 18/18-45/45-65/over 65; etc.—and how are they changing?

- What is the unemployment rate and how has it shifted over time?

- Who are the biggest employers?

- What is the per capita income and is it rising or falling?

- How is the population broken down in terms of educational attainment?

- How are the ways constituents receive their political news changing?

- Which labor, agricultural or business groups are growing or shrinking in stature?

The Mission Statement

One of the first things a facilitator will ask for is your mission statement. If the office doesn't have one, the facilitator will likely make its creation a priority. The Member, not the facilitator or chief, should create the mission statement– after all he or she is the person whom the voters elected to represent them. It should be prepared beforehand and presented near the beginning of the retreat.

A mission statement allows an organization to articulate its core values so that it can translate them into tangible actions.

It represents what the office is all about. What is the reason the Member is in Congress? It is the foundation of the planning process and the standard against which all goals will be measured.

The mission statement is the North Star or a compass. It is a statement of principles that gives strategic focus. When an organization is guided by principles instead of personalities each person becomes more important. That is because everyone understands what the organization is about, what its priorities are, and what it stands for.

It is very liberating. It means the organization learns from its mistakes and can get back on track. If someone is taking a path and gets lost, they pull out their compass and figure out what the right direction is. The team realigns itself with its core principles and heads once again in the right direction.

In *The 7 Habits of Highly Effective People,* motivational author Stephen Covey describes an exercise that can kick start the process: *Imagine yourself a witness at your own funeral. Three people are going to speak— one from your family, one from your profession and one from your community. What do you want them to remember about you?*

Obviously, Covey is encouraging us to begin at the end by deciding what we want people to remember us for, then doing our best to ensure it's what they do remember. Recognizing the desired result enables us to focus on figuring out how to get there.

It's important to know how long a mission statement needs to be. Most experts agree, the shorter, the better. Consider one prepared by a House Member in 2012:

Our mission is to create exceptional constitutional value for the citizens of [our] Congressional District through responsive constituent services, common sense legislation, prudent fiscal stewardship, and clear communication that informs and educates.

Here's how another congressional office defined its mission:

To advocate on behalf of our constituents with integrity, professionalism and accountability while promoting policies that safeguard their basic rights to life, liberty, and the pursuit of happiness.

A mission statement should articulate principles: not specific legislation, but rather what the legislation will accomplish; not specific constituent service outreach initiatives, but what that service means and should result in; not specific committee actions, but what the world will see the office stood for. It should establish firm ethical boundaries and demands the highest moral standards and level of performance.

A mission statement sets the standard by which an office will prioritize its time and resources. It is the office's *raison d'être.*

The Session Itself

At a strategic planning retreat, an office can begin to turn the Member's mission statement into reality. Though secondary in importance to the mission statement, goal planning provides the road map to the mission's fulfillment. The mission statement tells the world where the office's compass is pointing. The planning session determines the best way to get everyone moving in that direction by developing a series of strategic goals.

There are various ways to conduct strategic planning sessions. A good facilitator will lead subtly without seeming to impose his or her will. This will discourage staff from parroting what they think the facilitator wants to hear or become suspicious of the process.

Most planning efforts begin with some kind of exercise. One favorite has participants introducing themselves, telling what they do and describing the accomplishment of the past year that they're most proud of. Participants also might be asked to share an amusing, office-related anecdote.

This gives everyone, particularly those from the DC and home offices who might not have much interaction, a chance to get to know each another. It also gets everyone talking and encourages him or her to be involved throughout the rest of the session.

If this is not the office's first planning session, the opening exercise can lay the groundwork with an assessment of past goals. This provides an element of accountability and emphasizes that the goals that come out of the current session will receive more than just lip service.

The Lay of the Land

As urgent as the need to know where you're going is the need to know precisely where you are now. In order to find out, you'll need to conduct what is known as a landscape analysis. It is important that the current operations and environment be carefully, fully and candidly scrutinized and discussed. Take inventory by assessing strengths, weaknesses, opportunities, and threats (SWOT):

- **Strengths:** What are your strengths as an organization, politically, in the district or state and within the Congress?

- **Weaknesses:** What are your weaknesses as an organization?

- **Opportunities:** What unique opportunities exist?

- **Threats:** What threats exist both from without and within?

An office creates goals by synthesizing the strengths, weaknesses, opportunities and threats that can be identified by those who work there. It does so by determining which strengths and opportunities coincide, producing what can be characterized as offensive goals, and which weaknesses and threats coincide to produce defensive goals. Offensive goals capitalize on internal strengths and external opportunities, and should be aggressively pursued. Defensive goals attempt to correct internal weaknesses and mitigate outside threats.

Identifying Destinations

Once you have a list of goals—and you will likely have 20 or more—you will filter out the unrealistic and the impractical. For instance, a goal of lowering the price of oil might be laudable, but it is not within an individual Member's capacity to attain. Introducing a bill to make it easier for local returning veterans to get enrolled in the local Veterans Affairs (VA) hospital might be a feasible goal.

Filtering the goals by means of Four Quadrants contained in the accompanying box (Fig. 8.1) is one way to accomplish this. Once you've gone through this process, you should have a pretty good idea where to focus your energies.

Figure 8.1 Filtering Goals

List factors that affect your office in the appropriate boxes of a chart patterned on the one below:

	Urgent	Not Urgent
Able to Affect	I	II
Less Able to Affect	III	IV

Quadrant I represents goals the office must achieve—these are both urgent and attainable.

Quadrant II is for goals that probably can't be fulfilled due to current limitations in time, budget or staff but that you'll work toward if you have anything left after items in Quadrant I are achieved. (These are the stuff of legacies, the accomplishments that can produce a meaningful and lasting impact, such as solving energy shortfalls or developing a plan for Social Security reform.)

Quadrant III includes issues that affect you, your office, its constituents and perhaps even the entire nation but over which you have very limited control—yet goals in this category are more urgent than those in Quadrant II.

Quadrant IV consists of goals that are worth dreaming about but have almost no chance of ever coming true—don't waste your effort.

The next stage in narrowing the list of goals is referred to as a *SMART analysis*—another acronym. It judges each goal on the basis of the following criteria:

Is it Specific? No open-ended objectives, along the lines of "Improve communication between Washington and the district." Goals must include both an objective and a strategy: "Improve communication between Washington and the district office *by setting up regular conference calls and establishing an email system for disseminating important information such as votes, floor speeches and press releases to all staff.*"

Is it Measurable? It must be possible to gauge the success of goals—your action plan should actually create accountability: "Conference calls between the DC and district offices will be made once a week. The effectiveness of these calls will be measured by a quarterly survey conducted by the communications staff, who will encourage candor by guaranteeing the anonymity of participants."

Is it Appropriate? Goals must be consistent with the mission statement and the Member's vision—no goal will succeed if the Member isn't interested.

Is it Realistic? Goals that are not attainable waste time and resources. It might not be realistic to have all mail answered in 14 days, for instance, but it might be realistic to have 85 percent of it answered in that time-frame.

Is it Time limited? A House of Representatives term only lasts two years and a Senate term only six, so goals must have a specified duration or a target date. Otherwise, it's unattainable, unrealistic, and immeasurable. "The goal of answering 85 percent of mail in 14 days will be accomplished and sustainable within 90 days," is something an office can work to complete. Without a deadline for a self-imposed goal such as that, completing the objective might be continually deferred, ultimately undermining the goal.

Goals that are SMART are more likely to be accomplished. Those that aren't undermine the process. Worse yet, goals that aren't attainable undermine the credibility of future goal-planning efforts.

Only half a dozen or so goals are likely to make it through the filter, but that is more than enough to provide your office with direction to keep it busy as long as everyone on the staff is able to feel or see the results. In future years an office may develop additional goals dealing with multiple internal and external issues—but no matter how many goals, the key is always to be SMART.

Turning Goals Into Action

Without an action plan, goal planning is little more than an academic exercise. The action plan is the strategy for accomplishing the goals: the tactics that will be used and the methods to ensure accountability.

Each goal must have a project team and each team must have a project leader.

The success of the plan's implementation depends on commitment from the top down and accountability from the bottom up. Each team needs support, resources, decision-making authority, and the opportunity

---

Why Goals Fail

The organization does not believe in the outcome—participants do not believe that once the goal is reached it will be of any value or they don't think the risk of failing to reach the goal is a serious threat or problem.

They don't believe the outcome is attainable—they think it is pie in the sky, either because the premise is flawed or it puts too much strain on resources.

They can't figure out what outcome the boss really wants.

The Member is either not on board or does not signal to all that he or she is committed to the goal.

to succeed or fail. The chief of staff's main job is to provide the tools and demand accountability.

The teams' work begins at the end—a clear picture of what it hopes to achieve and what must happen to achieve it. Then, each project is divided into stages with benchmarks and timetables for completion. These action plans should be detailed and in writing. (Some people use sophisticated software to generate PERT or Gantt charts, but this is overkill.) The likelihood of achieving a goal is directly proportional to the amount of time and thought invested in developing an action plan. As a result, there's little likelihood an action plan will be finalized at the retreat.

Although mission statements should never be compromised, goals may be, and probably will be, updated according to changing circumstances. Action plans should be flexible enough to accommodate new developments, and the chief and project team should review them regularly to gauge the success of their tactics and consider alternatives when appropriate.

Both responsibility and initiative should be recognized and rewarded. Incentives, recognition and encouragement reinforce unity throughout the ranks and show the importance of the planning process. The goals set during the planning process also create measurable standards for promotions, pay raises, and bonuses. Staff salaries are published quarterly in the House and biannually in the Senate, so there are no secrets when it comes to compensation on Capitol Hill. Be assured that staff members are always looking to see if the top management's words match their deeds. In general, if they are convinced the office is serious about its strategic plan they will enthusiastically embrace it.

The Member's involvement is critical, and so is determining precisely how involved he or she will be in their execution. On Capitol Hill at least, a successful action plan will be 90 percent the result of staff activity guided by the Member's intent and commitment to seeing it carried out successfully.

Action planning is a proven means of identifying and implementing goals, which are, in turn, the practical expression of a Member's mission statement. In an environment of constant interruptions and non-stop demands, prioritizing goals and dedicating the resources of the office to carrying them out is the only way to make a positive difference, one that gives meaning to the trust placed in Members by their constituents.

Find out what your office's goals are, what action plans are in the works, and where you fit in the process. If your office has none of the above, demonstrate your competence in your position, and then begin quietly lobbying for a session where long-range planning can occur.

If you are in a position where you must lobby for a long-term planning session, do not be especially surprised. Many offices fail to plan, which is something of a mystery. After all, planning is not anything new in business or in politics. Given the huge budgets and complexity of today's political campaigns, a smart candidate will insist on a campaign plan that accounts for media, advertising, fundraising, and expenses. Despite the fact that most Members get to Congress by having and executing a good plan, some simply do not carry over that discipline, resulting in divided and arguing staffs; an inability to be proactive instead of reactive; and, often times, a return ticket home from the constituents in the next election.

On the other hand, Members that plan effectively can gain power and prestige, perhaps becoming true national leaders as a result. One of the best examples is the Speaker of the House John Boehner. Since his early days in Congress, Boehner has been a planner—and he has always involved every single member of his staff. As he moved up the ranks, he included committee staff and leadership staff in his planning process. "Boehner-land," as his aides affectionately calls his domain, has been built on mutual respect for each person on his staff, a commitment to core principles, and the creation of plans to carry out specific goals, all of which has turned the Speaker into a successful legislator and leader and has created an entire network of people who remain loyal and supportive even when they move on to other offices. Not only has he built a staff that Members on both sides of the aisle admire for their professionalism and loyalty, they have propelled him to the highest position in Congress—not a bad example to learn from.

Chapter Eight Summary

- Everyone in a management position on the Hill is heir to pandemonium—sometimes once a week, sometimes once a day, sometimes all day long. The situation might easily become impossible were it not for strategic planning.

- If you are in a position of authority and you expect everyone to work toward strategic goals, you must invite everyone to have a hand in their development at an office-wide strategic planning meeting.

- Using an outside facilitator is essential for an office's planning session.

- A mission statement is the foundation of the strategic plan. It provides staff with a sense of what their priorities should be and how they should focus their energies. A mission statement should articulate core values that are to be translated into tangible results.

- The Member needs to be a full participant in the planning session and be there from beginning to end but not dominate.

- Goal planning provides the road map to the mission's fulfillment. The mission statement tells the staff where the office's compass is pointing. The planning session determines the best way to get everyone moving in that direction.

- An office creates goals by synthesizing the strengths, weaknesses, opportunities and threats (SWOT) that can be identified by those who work there. Offensive goals capitalize on internal strengths and external opportunities. Defensive goals attempt to correct internal weaknesses and mitigate outside threats.

- Goals that are specific, measurable, appropriate, realistic and time-limited—or SMART, for short—are more likely to be accomplished. Goal that aren't attainable undermine the credibility of future goal-planning efforts.

- An action plan, when executed, accomplishes its goals by various accountable and measurable tactics.

- Although mission statements should never be compromised, goals may be updated according to changing circumstances. Action plans should be flexible.

- Goals create measurable standards for promotion, pay raises and bonuses, and rewards, recognition and encouragement should reinforce the importance of the planning process.

Your title or job description may not contain the word communicate but it's what you do for a living. What you say and how you say it helps determine you and your employer's success or failure in the political fishbowl.

Webster's defines *communication* as: *interchange of thoughts, opinions or information by speech, writing, etc.; information, thought or feeling that is satisfactorily received or understood; the act of imparting, participating; opening into each other; connecting; personal rapport.*

In other words, communication is more than mere information. It is more than just disseminating information. It demands that information be shared in such a way that it is understood, in a way that turns information into usable knowledge. It also demands a rapport with those with whom you are communicating. The fundamentals of communication are critical to relationships in any circumstance, but particularly when you are communicating with the news media. Successful interaction with the press demands the kind of trust and comfort level that makes the recipient realize the information is credible, trustworthy and reliable. Perhaps most importantly, it demands a link that runs in two directions— he who shares knowledge gains it in return.

Listening is perhaps the least appreciated and most overlooked aspect of the communication process. "No man ever listened himself out of a job," said the famously quiet Calvin Coolidge.

If you are not on the communications team, a discussion of how those responsible for speaking to the media on behalf of your Member's office and how they can do their job effectively may not seem pertinent to the role you play, but it is.

A fundamental rule of congressional communication is this: Be circumspect. It's all right to go on and on about where you took the kids over the weekend if you're having a casual conversation with a co-worker. But if the topic is work-related and the audience is potentially larger, be brief and to the point. Avoid thinking out loud. Remember, knowledge is power—and anything that can be held against you can be used to enslave you.

We aren't trying to make you paranoid; we are just emphasizing that even paranoid people have enemies.

Not everyone you encounter is your enemy, of course. Most aren't. But by the same token, not everyone is your friend. Discretion isn't just the better part of valor; it's also the key to job security when friends and enemies alike hang on every word that is attributed to your boss and his staff.

Communication is a broad subject area. How you communicate inside an office may be more important than how you communicate outside. How you communicate with other offices and other staff members is critical to success. But for now we are going to concentrate on how you communicate with the outside world through the media. And the media is a pretty broad subject as well, stretching from news to entertainment and a morass of combinations thereof, all of which influence political thinking, political action and public-policy decisions to a greater degree than ever before.

Let's focus on a broad definition of news media, or what used to be called the press, and those who dealt with them—press secretaries (also called press assistants), or chiefs of staff who served part time as the press connection.

Four decades ago, when Members of Congress were just beginning to treat media relations as a separate professional office function, media relations were simpler if only because there were fewer media outlets. The communication staff dealt with newspapers, radio and television stations in the Member's home district or state and with wire services. They were on a first-name basis with most of the journalists they encountered.

Unless a Member was part of the leadership, exposure to national media was usually restricted to instances where he or she was in trouble or was expert in a hot issue or from an area of the country that had been ravaged by disaster. Communication staffs produced press releases, and if the media considered those press releases newsworthy—or if the media were simply desperate for something to fill a few inches of space or a few moments of airtime—they passed the information on to the public.

Even deadlines were simpler: Prime television news was mostly broadcast at noon, 6 and 10 p.m.; morning newspapers went to press at midnight, and afternoon papers went to press at noon.

Times, technology, and the volume of media have changed dramatically since then.

Traditional outlets, such as major dailies and network news no longer hold the sway over the public they once did. At his peak, Walter Cronkite was considered "the most trusted man in America," and had a 50 percent rating at an 85 percent market share! According to the Pew Research Center's State of the Media 2012 report, in 2011, his successor Katie Couric, who anchored the CBS Evening News from 2006 to 2011, had a 4.3 percent rating and an 8.0 percent market share. In fact all network news combined has a 15.8 percent rating.

Cable television has replaced network news as the top source of political news. Beginning with CNN's coverage of the first Gulf War in 1991, people discovered they could get their news when they wanted it, not when network executives scheduled it. Today Fox News has become the number one source of political news in the United States.

Newspapers, too, have shrunk in influence and many are struggling to survive financially. According to the Pew Research Center, newspaper readership is increasingly limited to older Americans, and newspapers are rarely used as a source of political news by anyone under 50.

Researchers for the Pew Project for Excellence in Journalism estimate that daily newspaper circulation declined 4.0 percent in 2011 and advertising revenue declined 9.2 percent, according to the Newspaper Association of America. Only the *Wall Street Journal* experienced a circulation increase.

New dynamics include a variety of Internet and wireless communication services and products that shape the opinions of many segments of society. In fact, a majority of all adults under the age of 50 have gone online for political news. And, their numbers grow every day. There are interactive websites and blogs. There are web pages addressing every imaginable topic. There are electronic magazines, newsletters and web commentaries. There are cyberspace gossip columns. And they are all even more unbridled than the mainstream media.

Facebook is a phenomenon—though not yet a primary source of political news. But when you consider that as of 2012 every congressional district has, on average, more than 380,000 Facebook users, it's likely only a matter of time before it becomes one. Although Twitter has nowhere

Rating Points and Market Share

A single rating point represents one percent of the total number of households with televisions. Share represents the percentage of people who were watching television in a given time slot who were tuned in for a particular program. If a program had a 10/30 rating of the approximately 115 million television households, they would have 11.5 million viewers (10 percent of the total). Of those people watching television, 30 percent were watching this show. The competitors' shows in the same time slot would have been seen by 27 million viewers. 76.5 million were not watching television at all.

near the penetration of Facebook, it has become a tool widely used by grassroots organizations, such as the Tea Party movement.

Old and new, these media are all interconnected. News in the gossip and celebrity pages becomes news in the government and politics pages. And this has contributed to the resurrection of advocacy journalism, adversarial journalism and other forms of opinionated reporting that existed during the early days of the Republic, but have been more commonly associated in recent years with the British tabloids than with American media.

Most modern day journalists will tell you that the news media serves at least three basic functions in American politics.

First, it serves as a chronicler of history in the making. Much of what we know of the political history of our country, for instance, comes from the pages of newspapers. In more recent times, the footage of broadcast media has contributed to the historical record. The news media serve the nation by recording its history. It is not the only witness to history, but it is certainly one of the primary sources on which the nation depends.

That role has brought with it an incredibly important responsibility, one that has been diminished greatly by newer forms of information dissemination via the Internet. We live in an era when raw material can be thrust into the public dialogue irrespective of its legitimacy or accuracy. A good example is is Wikipedia, a modern-day source of information to which anyone can contribute anything. While what is contained there is often used as a legitimate resource for facts and information, the information on Wikipedia is not fact-checked to the extent it should be so it is not only an unreliable source of factual information, it can also be manipulated by those with an agenda. It says something about how are society gets its news and information that Wikipedia is considered an encyclopedia and *The Daily Show* is considered a legitimate source of news.

It is incumbent on congressional staff to always be mindful of how history is recorded because they are contributing to it.

Second, news media provide oversight. They consider themselves watchdogs. They are a check and balance outside the Constitution's governmental boundaries. How many times have you heard expressions such as, "Will it play in Peoria?" patented by Richard Nixon, or "Will it pass the smell test?" or "Can you say it with a straight face?" or "Is it credible?" or "Can we say that publicly?" The media question what you say, how you say it, and, more importantly, what you do and how you do it.

In reporting on governmental activities, the media can play an important role in directing and policing the behavior of public officials. Media constantly define and redefine the term *appearance of impropriety,* and often set a standard for ethical behavior that far exceeds legal or regulatory restrictions. Right or wrong, the media can, for example, facilitate the conversion of a time-honored procedure such as earmarks into a political liability, by giving a loud voice and great credibility to those who condemn the process and little access to those who support it. The media challenge behavior, question the application of laws and regulations, and heighten the awareness of otherwise unseen and unheard of issues that have the potential for significant impact on the way we govern and the way we live. They challenge statistics, question the interpretation of facts and second-guess conclusions (granted, much of what the media do in the way of oversight originates from leads they get from advocacy groups, lobbyists, government agencies and congressional committees). At their best, the media are the ombudsmen for the people who pay your salary. At their worst, they are agents of confusion, misinformation and obstruction. Yet no other mechanism in our system is so capable of putting issues and behavior under the white heat of public scrutiny.

Third, the media disseminate information with speed and efficiency. Some turn information into junk. Others translate it into the vernacular so that readers, viewers and listeners can understand how politics and the government affect their lives. Some media use information to titillate, entertain, or incite riots (at least in Europe) and others use it to educate. But news media transmit information, lots of it, more of it than any other source available to you or your constituents.

A Short History of the U.S. Media

It is impossible to deal effectively with the media without a basic understanding of their past and what motivates them in the 21st century— and to a lesser degree, how the fundamental freedoms enshrined in the First Amendment are applied in this new era. Some of our Republic's first newspapers, and many since, were intensely partisan and ideological.

147

They were advocates rather than impartial observers. Thomas Jefferson and Alexander Hamilton launched their own dueling publications, a characterization that may be of questionable taste, given Hamilton's fate at the hand of Aaron Burr. These publications became the instruments rather than the chroniclers of the budding new political parties in America. They advanced causes that their patrons supported, smeared their adversaries and otherwise fought for the hearts and minds of early Americans. Well into the 20th century, newspapers were known for their loyalty to one party or ideology over another—some still are.

Time has tempered some of the media's politically parochial instincts, but the history of journalism in the United States is anything but a study in truth, justice and the American way. It is a study in conflicting commercial, professional, political and ideological interests brought together to advance the agendas—some noble, some not—of owners, editors and writers.

The news media have always vacillated between subjectivity and what passes for objectivity, from news to entertainment, from highly partisan allegiances to non-alignment, from independence to conglomerate ownership and from cutthroat competition to absolute monopolies. These varied interests continue to drive journalism today, sometimes along conflicting lines.

Speed Skills

There are differences not just in the roles the media play or the interests that propel them, but also in the pace at which stories develop, the questions of accountability raised by the speed with which information is transmitted, and the ferocious competition for dominance as a source of information. Clark Kent-style journalism doesn't exist anymore, if it ever did.

Today the media may exercise enormous power but when all is said and done, they are businesses, scrambling for as big a share of the market as they can get, just like any other commercial enterprise. They experience struggles between executive suites and the production line, similar to those in any other business.

Today, in order to attract audience share, they have blurred the line between news and entertainment – spawning what has been called infotainment, an entirely new way of looking at the world, including political life.

Important information isn't always interesting or easy to understand. It takes knowledge, understanding, and time to explain a comprehensive health care plan, for instance. Most journalists don't have the talent to make the complexities of a topic understandable. Even if they could, most audiences don't have the patience to absorb all the details and or appreciate the full impact of an issue on their daily lives. Our fast-paced society wants data in small, easy-to-digest doses that tickle us, that stimulate emotions and make us angry more than encourage thought and reflection. The most effective communication staffers are able to reduce legislation and policy to clear, concise and appealing messages, while at the same time preserving the integrity of the issue and relaying enough information for their audiences to draw from it intelligent conclusions and insights. While professional marketers will advise you the best messages are very few, very simple and repeated until you are sick of them, that formula doesn't always serve the media or your constituents well. Judgments must be made about the kind of communications that do more than titillate your audience, but also educate.

Audiences tune in where they can find easy answers, sarcasm or satire. Pioneering news entertainers such as Bill Maher, Don Imus, Stephen Colbert, Rush Limbaugh, Bill O'Reilly, Sean Hannity, Glenn Beck and Jack Cafferty exploit politics for fun and profit, creating ratings and a base of followers to keep them in fine clothes. But what they don't do is contribute to the kind of information dissemination that makes the public better able to self-govern, so how the infotainment world is used as a transmission vehicle for political information and insight must be done with circumspection.

The Other Revolving Door

Lobbying is no longer the only high-visibility second career available to Washington's out-of-work politicians and political operatives. The late Tim Russert was a chief of staff to Senator Daniel Patrick Moynihan and counsel to New York Governor Mario Cuomo before hosting NBC's *Meet the Press.* Chris Matthews was a one-time aide to President Jimmy Carter and House Speaker Tip O'Neill before hosting MSNBC's *Hardball.*

George Stephanopoulos was an aide to House Speaker Tom Foley and later President Bill Clinton's communication director before hosting ABC's *This Week*. Former Congressmen Joe Scarborough now hosts MSNBC's *Morning Joe*. The list keeps growing.

Newspapers used to label opinion as editorials or commentary—terms that have been used by television and radio as well—and the opinions were almost always confined to specific pages. None bother much anymore. What used to be known as objective journalism has all but become a thing of the past. The manner in which journalists, producers and editors handle information that finds its way into print or onto the airwaves is shaped by a myriad of subjective factors such as personal prejudice, gender, age, religion or lack of it, politics, ideology and experience, career enhancement, peer pressure, ratings and a host of other factors.

Nonetheless, there are a good many journalists who strive for high journalistic standards and want to serve as unbiased observers of current events. Those of you who deal directly with the media will get to know them and appreciate the role they play. Those of you who don't will benefit from the efforts of those who do. But keep in mind that dealing with them takes serious study, professional finesse, sound judgment and a lot of caution.

The World of Blogs

Blogs—which is a contracted form of the phrase *web logs*—have become a primary source of news for many Americans and a source of leads for most media. A blog is a kind of website where the author covers a particular topic, like politics or sports or cooking, by writing a series of individual articles (posts) on a periodic basis. The posts are usually short (much shorter than a magazine article), generally informal, and often take a news article or video clip as a starting point for commentary. They are a radical break from the traditional media and have sparked a revolution inside the political world.

Websites such as *The Drudge Report* and *The Huffington Post* have exposed fault lines in the news operations of traditional media, revealing errors and in some cases calling into question the credibility of such luminaries as former CBS anchor Dan Rather, whose career was destroyed when he was forced to apologize for unsubstantiated allegations involving President George W. Bush's military career.

Political blogs run the gamut from neoconservative to ultraliberal with output that ranges from urban myths to actual investigative reporting. Blogs have a strong appeal to partisans. They tend to attract audiences and commentary that share their point of view and are more forgiving of factual error than ideological apostasy. They represent an opportunity for far more personal interaction than the mainstream media, providing interactive forums where readers can comment, share opinions, ridicule political opponents, rally the troops and provide policy and other information aimed at specific political niches—all for a fraction of the cost of mainstream media productions.

While many blogs have become legitimate voices of political movements and parties, there are numerous sites that spew garbage—from vile white supremacist sites advocating hatred to ultra left sites that taunt and wish suffering on dying political opponents.

According to the Pew Internet and American Life Project, nearly 54 percent of American adults used the Internet to get news about the 2010 midterm elections. In fact, more people under the age of 36 get their news from the Internet than from newspapers. And the Internet continues to change politics—more than 39 percent of Americans have used a social networking site for political activity. During the 2012 Presidential election, 13 percent of Americans donated online or by email, and 10 percent by text or cell phone app. Since the election of Bill Clinton in 1992, the role of network television, magazines and newspapers as primary sources of political news has declined, while the role of cable television, radio and the Internet has dramatically increased.

Although the Internet has transformed the way society interacts, that doesn't mean a Member's communication director can ignore traditional media. It simply increases the range of opportunities—and challenges. So does a range of insider media that serves those working on the Hill but are accessed as well by other media, lobbyists and the executive branch. These include newspapers such as *Roll Call, The Hill* and *Politico*; online newsletters published by *Congressional Quarterly* and the *National Journal,* including *Hotline* and *Congress Daily*; and a host of other Hill-oriented outlets.

Demands of the Job

Today's communication staffs must possess the same media skills as their predecessors—creativity, salesmanship and the ability to render complex ideas in easy-to-understand prose. But they also must possess a range of high-tech skills such as the ability to quickly update Facebook pages, Twitter feeds and websites, record podcasts, make video of the boss's floor speech available, post a blog entry in a less formal and more conversational style than traditional press releases, arrange videoconferences and tele-town halls that make it possible to reach remote audiences, and produce e-newsletters. They must do all this while continuing to build productive relationships with reporters; writing columns, op-eds and traditional press releases, arranging interviews; drafting background papers, recording radio actualities (high-quality messages sent out as a podcast or over the phone) and educating staff on when and how to deal with the media.

The ever-more abundant means of communicating complicate the process of delivering messages in a timely manner. Speed is of the essence. Failure to get a Member's opinion on an important issue into the news quickly may mean missing the chance to have a voice in the debate. Worse yet, false information, if left unchallenged long enough, eventually becomes fact in the minds of many—just ask Mitt Romney, whose Presidential campaign failed to adequately respond to $100 million worth of advertising, countless hours of media reports, barrels of ink, and terabytes of bandwidth of personal attacks.

In addition to speed, accuracy is critical. In the good old days, there was time to call a reporter and clarify a comment. Even if it already had been published or broadcast, it could be corrected or rephrased or clarified. The same is not true of most websites. Once a story is published, no matter how rife with inaccuracies, it lives forever. An innocent mistake can be magnified or distorted beyond recognition and disseminated around the world in less time than it takes to say, "Congressman, we have a problem."

News has become a 24/7 process that doesn't take weekends off. Cable, then the Internet, forever changed the way Americans get information. Fox, CNN and MSNBC operate around-the-clock news operations. Newspapers must continually post new stories on their websites just to stay relevant. The Associated Press posts what used to be called bulletins, and then adds to them as information becomes available until the final report may be 10 times its original length. The millions of blogs have made potential reporters and commentators out of anyone with an Internet connection and a story to tell or an opinion to share. Television has followed suit by urging audiences to use the digital cameras in their cell phones to film news they come upon and share it with news staffs at affiliates or even the network. Even if a media outlet doesn't specifically solicit such videos, they will find them once a recording like that hits YouTube. For instance, when two Members of Congress from California got into a heated exchange in 2012, the iPhone video of the incident went viral around the world. This phenomenon should set off alarm bells to any politician or political aide. The world is indeed a fishbowl in which privacy is nonexistent.

One way to protect your Member from unfavorable media portrayals is to build working, professional relationships with reporters. Professional journalists are not likely, regardless of their personal ideology, to burn valuable relationships with a primary news source for "gotcha" politics. And if they are, they are not professional, and you shouldn't bother establishing or maintaining a relationship with them. Learn from experience—yours as well as the experience of others.

Professional journalists face intense challenges. The pressure to scoop the competition creates the temptation to run with half the facts, abuse the anonymous source, and generalize to the point of misinterpretation. The symbiotic relationship that exists between a successful congressional communication staff and these journalists demands an understanding of the influences that govern the journalists' activities, from deadlines to editors or producers to the demographics of the audiences they serve to the standards and values that guide them as a group and as individuals. In essence, it is understanding what defines news to each one of them— and understanding that what is news to one isn't necessarily news to another.

A procedural dynamic that's driving a vote on an energy bill may be of interest to a writer for *National Journal,* for example, but not to a correspondent for *NBC News.* An NBC correspondent, on the other hand, may be interested in the impact of welfare reform on a family in Iowa, while the *Journal* writer will not.

The fact that not every media outlet is interested in every story is complicated by the fact that all of them are interested in others—particularly the ones that involve controversy—and these tend to eat up space that, from your point of view, might be better devoted to the stories you'd like to tell. It's the way the world is. Don't waste time or energy being frustrated over it. Focus instead on absolutes that will benefit you in every situation:

Trust. The most important commodity a communication staff has is its credibility. Do not undermine it. Reporters must expect each member of the team to be a dependable source of information. Don't let someone else provide a reporter information that calls into question a position or a point of view you are putting forth—raise the question yourself and address it head on. Don't leave out facts, narrowly interpret them, or stretch them beyond credulity. Don't say more than you need to say, and make sure the facts and circumstances are absolutely clear in your mind before trying to impart them to someone else. Most importantly, never lie to a reporter.

Realize that trust is more than simply providing reliable information, explanations and observations. It manifests itself in returning calls, following up and providing good guidance. It manifests itself in candor and honesty as well. If you don't know the answer to a question, say so. If you know where the answer can be had, say that. And if you know the answer but can't reveal it, explain your situation.

Trust, obviously, is a two-way street. Reporters need to earn yours as urgently as you need to earn theirs. If you have even a hint of concern, probe deep enough to be sure.

Relevance. Communication staff must ensure that information provided is of value; that it is balanced, addressing both sides of an issue; and that it is of interest and importance to more than just the boss. You know what's important in your universe; know what's important in the reporter's.

Story Appeal. Not all, or even most, press relations involves responding to news or reacting to events. Communications staff must devote time and talent to pitching story ideas, selling the relevance of information that, by its very nature, might not be particularly interesting. A story idea has to have appeal. It has to be compelling to a skeptical audience. This requires easy-to-understand background information. It requires humanizing the issues. You do that by bringing information and statistics to life, giving them a human face and form that dramatizes how the issue impacts the lives of the people for whom the journalist is writing or reporting.

For instance, the concept of welfare-to-work is drab until you infuse it with life by telling the story of a formerly unemployed mother in Des Moines who is now working at a retail store, selling children's clothes. But it requires more than just an individual giving life to an issue of this sort. It also requires testimony from experts and analysts who can correlate that one success in Des Moines with thousands, perhaps millions, of others nationwide.

The challenge is to overcome the urge to proselytize, to preach, and to pack the story with partisanship. Keep personal opinions to a minimum and avoid criticism unless it's constructive and expressed in a positive way.

Judgment. Communications staff must exercise heavy doses of both political judgment and news judgment. How often have you seen or listened to a prominent politician on a news talk show getting his head handed back to him on a platter of abuse, derision, or cheap jokes? You wonder, "What on earth made that politician decide to appear on that show or be interviewed by that infotaining huckster?" Those situations do make sense if the interviewee's only objective is higher name recognition or notoriety. But more often than not, the politician and the politician's staff have made an error in judgment about the intent of the interviewer or the ability of the politician to go toe-to-toe with the interviewer. A combination of news judgment (what the media want from you) and political judgment (what you want from the media) has to be weighed very carefully before you agree to or end up trapped in a situation of public exposure from which there is no immediate avenue of escape. Public exposure is a net loser if, in your compulsion to deliver a message, you damage your brand—the reputation of the Member as a serious legislator.

Identifying worthless or harmful media opportunities might actually be the easy half of exhibiting good judgment. The ability to pitch an enticing story is probably harder. Like everyone else in Washington, journalists are crunched for time and must adapt to changing circumstances. They need to churn out a high-quality product as quickly as possible, with the utmost accuracy, for inclusion in a limited space.

In other words, each journalist loves a story that writes itself. Don't be afraid to help by providing interesting material, relevant facts and in a concise package.

Unfortunately, it's sometimes hard to come up with a story or with the time to develop it. Due to time constraints produced by day-to-day pressures and the demands of unexpected crises, coupled with the range of media to which responses must be addressed, finding a real-life story is one of the least honored absolutes in communication. You can help by identifying opportunities and passing them along to the communication staff.

A congressional district, and surely an entire state, can produce hundreds, if not thousands, of good human-interest stories, whether it involves someone helped by government, someone hurt by it, a business thriving because of it or a business impaled by it. If there is a compelling human element or a lesson that can be learned by others, or just something of drama or humor or sadness, there may well be media interest. It doesn't have to involve government, but it is government that ties the Congressman or the Senator to the story, and, obviously, that is important. The halo effect of human-interest stories is immeasurable, whether they appear in a hometown newspaper, on network news or someplace in between. Just remember that when dealing with constituent interests and needs, you and the Congressman have a clear and critical legal and moral responsibility to protect the privacy of any constituent. Don't pursue a story idea without permission and don't apply pressure to get it.

There are distinctions between a story that is primarily local and one that has national potential. Local audiences are sensitive to social, geographic, cultural and commercial concerns—parochial peculiarities and idiosyncrasies are important, right down to word pronunciation and dialects. National audiences are less concerned, however, about the correct pronunciation of "Bexar County" but share with local audiences a passion for stories that touch them on a personal level, that contain sympathetic characters grappling with challenges the audience is just as likely to face.

Human-interest stories are now evolving as the news industry shifts from papers to more modern media. In addition to the points made above about the value of "the story" one other aspect is an outgrowth of the move toward modern media versus old newsprint. Printed stories must be read, deciphered, understood, and analyzed. On the other hand, much of the new media is visceral or emotive. The old adage, "A picture is worth a thousand words," kicks in because a picture of a hungry child or a homeless family does not need a lot of words to define. There is no need to define the statistical basis for the story; it is self-evident.

For communication staff this presents a major challenge when discussing complex macroeconomic statistics versus the micro-impact of a personal story about the loss of benefits if a program is cut. Competent staff finds ways to translate that macro-economic story into a personal story with feelings suitable for exposure in newsprint or on YouTube. Otherwise, they tell a story that sounds and looks cold-hearted or only gets reported in poorly read newspapers.

Chapter Nine Summary

- Communication is much more than the transfer of information.

- A fundamental principle of communication is to be circumspect.

- Relations with media have changed dramatically with the advent of new technology. New media have blurred the lines between news and entertainment and information and opinion.

- News media provide three basic functions in the political process: chronicler, overseer, and disseminator.

- The history of news media in America puts a lot of modern-day journalism in perspective.

- Blogs have changed the world of information gathering, verification and dissemination.

- Media relations demand many skills and work, all based on trust.

- The ability to turn a complex matter into a compelling "story" can be the difference between success and failure in the policy world.

Any hope that the communication staff will have the time and resources to carry out even a fraction of their diverse mission requires that the communications director be intimately involved in strategic planning. By working backward from the goals identified in the planning phase, the communications director can identify where resources will be needed and come up with a game plan that will serve these needs. A strategic communication plan should address some or all of the following:

- The Member's priorities.

- National media relations.

- Regional/local media relations.

- Image and name recognition.

- Informing the constituency.

- Crisis communications strategy.

- Message management.

The communication component of the overall strategic plan must reflect the fact that everyone in the Member's office has a stake in successful communication and each must understand and fulfill his or her role in order for it to work. This is particularly true of the legislative staff. Communication personnel and those responsible for the office's legislative agenda must work in tandem if either hopes to be successful. You can't legislate without communication and you can't communicate without something to say. The vast majority of what is communicated is about legislation.

Elemental to the strategy is whether communication is done timidly, safely or aggressively, or somewhere in between. Are you:

- Avoiding pitfalls, playing it safe, being mundane, avoiding attention, reactive instead of proactive?

- Or are you seizing issues, establishing a brand, being proactive and engaging controversy?

The timid approach is the least popular among most communications professionals. Today's political environment simply doesn't permit a politician to be a wallflower, nor does it enhance the fortunes of a press secretary to be one either. What matters, however, is the approach or style with which the Member is most comfortable.

The Member must be comfortable with the strategy and his or her role in carrying it out. A timid or studious politician cannot carry off an aggressive media strategy, and no good communications professional would expect otherwise. But even more introverted Members need a media strategy—it will probably be more focused on written communication and new media.

Another important criteria in building a strategy is gauging what kind of Member he or she wants to be. Is he or she primarily suited to fulfilling constituent needs with little interest in national issues or political agendas? Is the Member particularly dedicated to specific issues, such as trade or health care, rather than a generalist with broader interests? Is he or she a consensus builder or primarily a communicator, a messenger, one who defines issues rather than resolves them? There are shades of gray in all of these distinctions, but regardless of where a Member falls on this scale, it is important to tailor communications to the personality, character and proclivities of the boss.

It is equally important to assess resources and points of leverage that can be applied to the benefit of the Member: for example, committee assignments, relationships with leadership and the administration in power, staff, media accessibility, existing name recognition and branding, past exposure to media and communications, attitude, and demands on time and energy.

A key element of strategy development is rooted in your ability to create an image, an identity, a brand that distinguishes your Member from others and establishes him or her as a participant in the political process and not just an observer.

Branding and name recognition can be built on the back of a legislative initiative if the Member is willing and able to devote the time and attention to it. The Member must champion an issue, develop a reputation

Do Members Have a "Brand?"

Members, Political Parties and even the Congress itself have a brand identity—whether it's intentional or not.

Keep in mind that a brand is not a marketing or campaign slogan (though a slogan that highlights a brand might be adopted). For an elected official, the brand "essence" is who he or she really is. A Member, or a political party, will often have a hard time changing public perceptions when their perceived brand (or brand essence) is different than their desired brand. A brand should conjure up certain characteristics such as attributes (committee important to this district, hard working, consistent voting record, political strength), benefits to the voter (lower taxes, better healthcare, working for their interests), values (frugal, innovative, compassionate), culture (religiosity, patriotic, appealing to images different Americans have of their country), personality (optimistic, back slapping and cigar smoking), and what kind of voter (the customer, in the business world) is likely to be attracted to that brand. The success of that brand is determined by whether people believe the elected official is what his or her brand claims he or she is, and whether they like what they believe the brand to be.

for expertise in its various permutations and be engaged in the strategy and tactics necessary to move it forward. It requires building relationships with allies, including other Members of Congress; executive branch advocates or experts; and outside organizations such as trade associations, trade media and other interests that are considered leaders in the issue area. If, for example, the initiative involves cancer research, a Member and his or her staff should build solid relationships with the American Cancer Society, American Lung Association and others who are involved in cancer research, both in Washington, DC, and at home. Many news outlets, think tanks and issue organizations have a cadre of professionals who specialize in various subjects. For instance, major news organizations have bylined healthcare reporters.

A legislative initiative has many moving parts, usually including a bill that serves as the primary mechanism for defining the issues and the ultimate goal.

The introduction of a bill can be the catalyst for press releases, interviews, blogging, tele-town halls and other forms of communication that address the problem and the need for the Member's solution. Similar proactive initiatives can be performed at each stage of the process: committee hearings, committee votes, incorporation into other legislation, floor action, action in the other Chamber, conferencing, and ultimately signing into law by the President. There are many and varying opportunities through the process to engage in tactics that help brand the Member, giving him or her a positive identity.

Other activities and events, aside from legislative vehicles, are marketable as well and can serve as useful tools in shaping images and brand. This might include walking in a local cancer fundraising walkathon or highlighting an individual's plight with a speech for the *Congressional Record,* which is distributed to the people who are interested in the issue.

Speaking at an annual Chamber of Commerce dinner, attending Boy or Girl Scout events, meeting with farmers, teaching history or government classes at high schools, town hall meetings or e-mailing information to constituents with specific topical interests are among the ways a Member builds a brand.

The best approaches to media are direct ones: a solid pitch made with an enticing story line, interesting and concise background information, a current event or occurrence that can serve as a backdrop for a story, and when possible, an element of exclusivity for that outlet. A reporter who knows he or she will be getting the story before a competitor will be more attracted to your pitch. It should go without saying, however, that exclusivity, partial or whole, should not be promised if it cannot be delivered. The enticement of exclusivity puts the reporter's credibility on the line with his or her own editors and producers.

By the way, don't be afraid to "cold call" a reporter you have never met. Calling people they don't know is something most reporters do for a living, so they are not likely to be put out if you have an interesting pitch to make.

Staff also must recognize that what works on television may not work for newspapers, magazines and the Internet. A good tool for electronic media, for example, are radio actualities—audio press releases that typically include a high-quality recording of a statement by the Member—distributed over the Internet to stations that may not have the budget for a news staff. A press conference may be a convenient way for Members of Congress to tell the media what they want them to know but scheduling one doesn't guarantee the media will attend—far from it. Press conferences should be employed sparingly and timed to accommodate deadlines and other news events. More often than not, media turnout will be disappointing. Props should be used to attract attention and clarify the message—charts, graphs, celebrities and other high-visibility supporters can distinguish what the Member has to say from what thousands of others have already said. It's called putting a face on the story.

Press events don't take place just in DC—if constituents back home don't know what the Member is doing, they're likely to perceive him or her as out of touch. Activities must be coordinated and synchronized with state and district constituencies and media.

If everything the boss does or thinks or says is presented the same way every time, the communication staff undermines its own ability to communicate. There's a time to shout and a time to whisper. There's a time for comment and a time for quiet. There's a time for emotion and a time for reason. There's a time for principle and a time for pragmatism.

No Member can afford to be the lightning rod for every issue that comes up in the Congress. In order to be effective, each Member must pick and choose which causes he'll make his own, which he'll support sub rosa and which he'll be willing to compromise on. Each Member also must decide how widely these choices should be publicized.

Calculating Risks

Communication strategy requires calculation, not only as it relates to getting the word out, but also protecting sensitive information within. Everyone, regardless of whether they're part of the communication staff, should remember:

- Never put anything in writing you don't want to appear on the front page of the *New York Times* or more importantly, your hometown's newspaper.

- Everything that is said or done should be the product of planning and should be said or done with a purpose or outcome in mind.

- Planning must take into consideration what vehicle or vehicles will be used to deliver the message: a webcast, for example, or a press release, or participation in a network roundtable, or an appearance on a late-night talk show, or a combination of the many avenues that are available. Not all avenues will be available at any given time, so alternative routes must be added to the list in descending order, thus enabling the greatest concentration of effort on the most advantageous, with the option of moving to the next tier if the top picks fall through or take less time than anticipated to attain.

- Planning also identifies who is authorized to speak publicly and under what circumstances—on the record, off the record, not for attribution, on background.

Those authorized to speak on the issue must be perpetually cautioned and eventually trained not to rush to the microphone with their mouths outrunning their brains; not to react in anger unless there's purpose behind the outburst; never to react instinctively; and to be prepared for any question, even if it must be answered with "I don't know."

Admitting ignorance is preferable to demonstrating stupidity.

You Didn't Get This From Me, But...

Prior to speaking with the media, always clarify the ground rules for the exchange. Here are the most common:

Off the Record: Nothing I say can be quoted or attributed to me or my office in any way.

Deep Background: Nothing I say can be attributed to me or my office or in any way that would lead to me.

Background: Nothing I say can be attributed to me by name, but can be sourced in a more general way.

On the record: Anything I say can be quoted and attributed to me by name and title.

Lastly, when in doubt about the ground rules, operate as if you are "on the record."

The integrity and credibility of the Member, of his or her office and communication staff depend on acquiring the facts and a willingness to share them, all of them. Provide your target audience with all sides of every issue. Put all the facts on the table and present them and interpret them in such a way that your audience can't help but reach the same conclusion you have. Some call that spin. There's nothing wrong with spin if it is practicing the art of persuasion and not perpetrating a fraud.

The effectiveness of what is said on behalf of the Member depends on the audience's ability to identify with the messenger and by extension, the message. It is not an ability the audience brings to the discussion. It is one that is produced by the medium and the message. If you are the messenger, you must be believable and able to make what you say important, interesting and persuasive. This maxim applies to news stories, feature stories, debates and any of the multitude of other communication vehicles used to ensure a message reaches its target audience in as many different ways as possible.

Basic Rules for Talking to the Press

Here are some more basic rules that will serve you well in almost every situation:

- Don't say more than you have to say to make your point. Someone once said that the First Amendment gives every American the right to make a damn fool of himself—but you don't have to exercise it. It has also been said that there is nothing wrong with having nothing to say—unless you say it.

- Stay on message. Don't be diverted. Don't digress.

- Limit the number of points you make.

- Reinforce what you say with well-selected research, expert testimony, background data, anecdotes, charts, graphs and other evidentiary material—but don't overdo it. Humanize everything you can so the story tells itself when possible.

- Be serious, but not stuffy; employ humor when possible, particularly the self-deprecating kind.

- Conclude whatever you say or do with a call to action, whether the desired action is careful consideration or actual steps—inform, educate, stimulate, and ignite passions.

- Avoid clichés. They are called clichés because they are overused and are usually hackneyed expressions whose meaning is so broad as to be meaningless. The exception is when you can give a cliché a humorous twist, as Ronald Reagan did when he freshened up the time-honored canard that suggests prostitution is the world's oldest profession: "Politics is supposed to be the second oldest profession. I have come to realize that it bears a close resemblance to the first."

- Avoid acronyms and other communication shortcuts—they often divert your audience from what you have to say to the way you're saying it. Acronyms are lazy, presumptuous, often confusing and rude interruptions to the flow. This is particularly true of those that have been made up to brand a subject, project, initiative or a piece of legislation: *Help Employ Active Retirees Time (HEART) Act.*

  Someone once said the most creative acronyms usually describe the worst programs—but they are effective in branding legislation. If you have to use acronyms, use them properly—no matter how universally understood you believe it to be, spell it out on first reference: *North Atlantic Treaty Organization (NATO).*

- Whether writing or speaking, keep it simple. Use simple sentences. Use small words. Avoid adjectives, big words and cumbersome phrases.

- Understand and appreciate your audience. Who are you trying to communicate with? Speak to them in language with which they are familiar. If you are going to use your audience as a vehicle to communicate with another audience, give the intermediary the same respect you'd give to the one you're really aiming at.

- Understand and appreciate the Member of Congress for whom you are writing. Each has his or her idiosyncrasies, styles, cadences and other peculiarities that give communications its personality and character.

- Be consistent. Get a stylebook—AP or *New York Times*—even if you're not on the communication staff. Master it. Then follow it whether speaking or writing on behalf of your boss. Be one person to all audiences.

- Be careful not to overplay your hand. You can beat an issue into irrelevance by giving it too much attention, exaggerating its implications, setting the rhetoric aflame or being overly righteous in your indignation. Keep it real.

- Always keep in mind that listening is among the most important aspects of communication. Listen carefully when asked questions. You will pick up clues about attitude, how interested the reporter is, and whether you are getting through.

- Read the book *On Writing Well* by William K. Zinsser.

Finally, if you are on the communications team, don't forget to communicate with your own office. It might sound obvious, but many a staff assistant has been embarrassed when a constituent on the phone was the first to tell them what his or her own boss said on the radio. Everyone on the staff needs to know what the Member's external message is and what constituents are likely to be hearing in the media. If you send out a press release, email it to those who work with you.

The Webs We Weave

While you're at it, do everything in your power to lobby for the best website in Congress. As Harvard's Michael Porter has observed in *Strategy and the Internet*: "The key question is not whether to deploy Internet technology—companies (and governments) have no choice if they want to stay competitive—but how to deploy it."

By and large, Congress does not deploy it effectively. Although websites are where most people turn for "official" information about Members, most congressional websites are woefully inadequate. In its Gold Mouse Awards report for the 112th Congress, the non-partisan Congressional Management Foundation awarded "A"s to only 16 percent of all congressional websites. Nearly 60 percent got "C"s or worse. Here are some of Congressional Management Foundation's conclusions from the Gold Mouse Report:

- Forty-six percent lack information about the Member's voting record.

- Forty percent do not have links to sponsored or co-sponsored legislation.

- Only 53 percent have information about the legislative process.

- Only 33 percent tell visitors the best ways to communicate with the Member's office.

Many congressional websites are little more than online repositories for press releases, the Member's biography, some basic facts about the district and who to call for various congressional services. Offices historically have allocated little money to Internet communication. As a result, their websites tend to be little more than a personalized version of one of the dozen or so templates provided by House Information Resources, the Senate Sergeant at Arms office or an approved website vendor. They are a mere fraction of what they should be. In the vast realm of websites, they are equal to the lowest common denominator.

A study by the Congressional Institute, meanwhile, has revealed that constituents want useable information from which they can draw conclusions. They don't find it on most official websites. Few websites contain transcripts of the Member's floor speeches, and the vast majority of them do not include summaries of legislation or explanations of why a Member

Congressional Institute Communications Reports

Part of the Congressional Institute's mission is to help Members of Congress better serve their constituents, and to that end, it has commissioned a series of research projects on how legislators can improve their communications strategies. They place particular emphasis on how to harness new technologies, so any Member—perhaps long-serving incumbents especially—can benefit from their insights and recommendations. Topics covered include congressional websites, Facebook and other social media outlets, Web ads, and a host of others.

Rich Thau, President of Presentation Testing, Inc., and the lead researcher and author, has used the best sources available for these projects. He has interviewed both congressional staffers and voters from across the country and has supplemented their testimony with Internet surveys.

Each report is available for download at the Congressional Institute's website www.conginst.org.

2013
In the Eye of the Beholder: What Your Constituents *Actually See* When You Communicate Online and Via Franked Mail

2012
Putting a Premium on Pixels: Ways to Master Official Online Advertising

2011
You've Sent Mail: How Constituents Judge Their Representatives by the Snail Mail They Send

The Data-Driven Congressional Office: Evaluating E-Newsletter Readership Trends

2010
Helping a 221-Year-Old Institution Harness Cutting-Edge Communication Technologies

2009
The Facebook Effect: How Congress is Using Social Networks to Strengthen Ties to Constituents—and How It Could Be Doing It Better

2008
Transformational Effects of Tele-Townhall Meetings

2007
Congressional Websites and E-Newsletters

would vote for or against it. In tsk-tsking this sorry state of affairs, the report author discovered that the visitors assumed that the absence of such obvious information means Members are trying to obscure their voting records—that they've got something to hide.

And given the power of today's search engines, if your constituent wants to find out how your Member voted, they will find it—but there's an excellent chance they will find it on a hostile website that portrays that vote in the worse possible light.

Researchers pointed out to lawmakers that many of their sites do not have functioning search engines that can help visitors find information they're looking for: "Constituents go to a legislator's website to find a specific piece of information, and you need to make it easy for them to find it. If something is difficult to find they will assume it is not available."

There is no reason for an office not to have an online video of every floor speech the Member makes—they're inexpensive and easy to provide. Offices that rely on C-SPAN coverage to give the folks back home a glimpse of the boss in action are deluding themselves. The percentage of constituents watching C-SPAN when their Senator or Representative gives a two-minute speech is statistically insignificant.

Cable television offers on-demand programming so audiences can watch movies, children's shows and other offerings whenever they want. Members of Congress should be just as attentive to their constituents' needs and desires.

A website should also provide a blog that appears on the website and can also be subscribed to through access to an RSS (real simple syndication) news feed. Blog posts are less formal than press releases. They're more conversational and can be used to provide impressions gathered by a Member during a visit to soldiers at an overseas military base or the Member's thoughts on a major issue that has been receiving widespread attention in the media.

An e-newsletter is an unfiltered means of communicating directly with constituents. Not only is delivery immediate, but feedback is too. List-server software tells you if and when your email was opened, and even whether it has been forwarded. And of course, constituents can instantly reply.

Each Member should have a general e-newsletter that goes out once or twice a month, and offers constituents the option of receiving only those containing information they're interested in such as the budget, or defense, or energy, or the environment.

E-newsletters should not be massive rehashes of everything the Member has done, said or contemplated since the last time subscribers heard from your office. It should be a series of short teasers with links

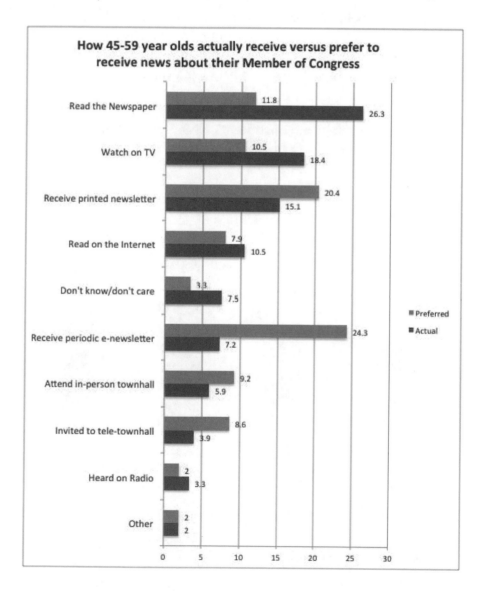

to items on the website that provide flesh and bone to whatever topics individual readers are interested in. For those who prefer to get such information in an audio format, a growing number of congressional offices have produced podcasts of floor speeches and audio versions of articles written by Members.

Getting names and addresses on your emailing list is somewhat more challenging.

Building a list of constituents who opt-in to receiving a Member's email communications should be a major priority for new offices. People generally see unsolicited emails as spam but tend to welcome emails they signed up for. The entire office should help sign people up: The website

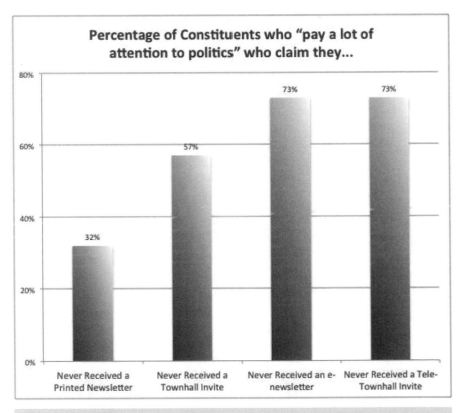

"Despite all the efforts to reach constituents, there are massive percentages of constituents—including those who say they "pay a lot of attention to politics"—who claim they never receive a printed newsletter, e-newsletter, or an invite to either an in- district town hall or tele-town hall," concludes the Congressional Institute's 2010 communications report.

STRATEGIC COMMUNICATION

should provide the opportunity; outreach staff in the district should collect email addresses in the district; and email signatures for the entire staff should include a link to opt-in to the Member's email list.

Conversely, every email communication, even to those who might have signed up for it, must include a way for the recipient to opt-out or be removed from the Member's distribution list. It doesn't pay to make a pest of yourself by sending material where it's not wanted.

The Congressional Institute (www.conginst.org) published a study in 2011, *The Data-Driven Congressional Office: Evaluating E-Newsletter Readership Trends to More Effectively Connect with Constituents* that details how an office can measure the success of its e-newsletter program. Download this from the website: http://conginst.org.

As with e-newsletters, social networking sites allow a Member to connect directly with constituents online.

Such sites, including Facebook, Twitter, and LinkedIn, are online communities where people discover and share common interests. The 2008 and 2012 Obama Presidential campaign combined this high-tech opportunity with the oldest form of political communication—word-of-mouth endorsement—to produce an invaluable campaign tool. The word of "friends" on Facebook carried more weight with some audiences than the same argument put forth by someone on radio or television. Though this approach is often referred to as *viral marketing,* it's actually nothing more than online word-of-mouth messaging—whose impact is exponentially increased by technology.

Through social networking, President Barack Obama's campaign not only motivated hundreds of thousands of young people to vote, but raised millions of dollars through small online campaign contributions—all for a fraction of the cost of traditional marketing and fundraising. In 2012, the President's supporters were able to flood Facebook with talking points provided by the campaign, taking personal advocacy a step further.

The 2010 Massachusetts Senate campaign of Scott Brown and the Virginia Gubernatorial campaign of Governor Bob McDonnell took new media to a higher level. In particular, Senator Scott Brown built a campaign that his opponents barely noticed until his momentum was too great to stop. New media allowed him to do that on a low-cost budget.

Unfortunately for him, he had no such element of surprise in 2012 and he was not reelected.

By the 2010 elections, a campaign would have a hard time explaining why they were not using Facebook, Twitter, Google Ads and a whole host of social media and smart phone apps. By 2012, it was impossible to campaign without them.

But while campaigns have showed success with new media, does it necessarily translate over to congressional offices and official government business?

A 2010 Congressional Institute study done by Rich Thau of Presentation Testing, Inc., found that there are three basic ways for a Member to maintain a presence on Facebook:

<u>Official Page</u>: Think of this as an extension of a Member's official website, operating in the Facebook environment. On an official page, Members engage "supporters." (Other types of celebrities engage "fans.")

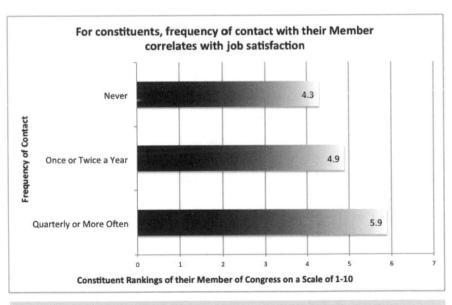

Why should offices reach out to constituents more frequently? Research sponsored by the Congressional Institute suggests that there is a strong positive correlation between the Members approval rating and the frequency of contact.

<u>Campaign Page</u>: Think of this as an extension of a Member's campaign website, operating in the Facebook environment. Similar to an official Facebook page, the campaign page also has "supporters." Importantly, Members cannot migrate supporters from an official page to a campaign page, or vice versa.

<u>Profile</u>: This is the kind of presence that the typical Facebook user maintains. These typical users don't have supporters; they have "friends." (It's a peer-to-peer relationship, rather than a celebrity-to-fan relationship or a Member-to-supporter relationship.) One reason some Members like to maintain their presence via the profile is that it causes the typical Facebook user to view the Member more informally—as someone who's approachable (and not on a pedestal). A shortcoming, however, is that Facebook limits the number of friends to 5,000 per account, and there are Members who have (or are about to) hit that limit. No such limit exists for the two other types of pages (official and campaign).

Additionally, the report "found that some Members maintained all three types of presence on Facebook. Others maintained two of the three, while others maintained just one (or none at all)."

Moreover, the report suggests that Facebook has great potential to reach a significant number of people, and interact with them in various ways:

While each office determines for itself how extensive a presence they should maintain on Facebook, what's important is that they view it as a tool that will have increasing value as the years pass. In an average Member's district, there are more than 200,000 constituents using Facebook. According to Facebook, half of these log on at least once on any given day. This is not an audience that Members can or should ignore—it would be like not having a telephone when 200,000+ constituents use one.

At the cutting edge, Members are using Facebook to:

- Build a relationship with the most informed and engaged constituents
- Alert constituents about upcoming votes, tele-town halls and physical town halls

- Encourage constituents to call the state's Senators in advance of a vote

- Create a Member-sponsored forum for discussion among supporters

- Recommend other media items for supporters to view (news articles, videos)

- Find constituents to act as the "face" of an issue for them.

Facebook has allowed Members to create elaborate personalities online, but Twitter, by contrast, has forced them to do more with less. Twitter, which was launched in 2006, allows users to create accounts from which they can publish 140 character posts, called "tweets" about any topic they choose. As with other social networking sites, users follow others' accounts, and those people's tweets show up in the follower's twitter feed. Following is not a reciprocal relationship, as "friending" is on Facebook, so even though you see someone's tweets does not mean they see yours.

Only a minority of adults uses Twitter, but some Members of Congress have nonetheless devoted much time and attention to it. Twitter allows Members to issue a near-constant stream of information to their constituents, colleagues, and journalists. For instance, Members can note where they are, whom they are meeting, how they have just voted on a piece of legislation, and what's for lunch. Because there is this torrent of tips, journalists particularly like this medium. They can use it to produce a news story about important events. And if any of the information proves inaccurate, they can excuse themselves by saying that they were just reporting in real time.

In addition to informing, pols tweet to tweak opponents. Shakespeare had Twitter in mind when he wrote, "Brevity is the soul of wit." Practically anything can be satirized. Following the BP's oil spill in the Gulf of Mexico in spring 2010, some wise guy created a genuinely humorous account called "BP Public Relations" pretending to be executives insensitive to the damage the disaster caused. Professional politicians, however, have tried to use it to more directly undermine their opponents. From time to time, President Barack Obama encouraged supporters to use the hashtag function to pump up his message with their own thoughts, and Republicans heeded that call to make their own points instead. In July 2011, the President also held his first "Twitter Town Hall" where he took questions from citizens, and Republican Speaker of the House John Boehner joined in on the action, asking him about job growth.

When tweeting for your boss—or advising him or her on what to do, if they elect to tweet for themselves—please remember that many posts don't communicate anything of value. Rise above the Web's detritus. Make your tweets either entertaining or informational. Better yet: Make them both.

Edelman Digital completed the most extensive study of the congressional use of Twitter, *Capitol Tweets: Yeas and Nays of the Congressional Twitterverse* in March 2012. The report contains a detailed chronology of the political use of Twitter, measurements of success, comparisons of how different groups of Members use the technology, and much more information besides. Perhaps most importantly, the study includes 10 best practices for congressional offices, including when to tweet (they suggest later in the week, when Congress is in session, and even over the weekend).

Politicians are now using Twitter's telephonic cousin, the text message, to communicate with targeted audiences. For instance, President Obama's campaign innovated the use of this technology in 2008 and perfected it in 2012. The campaign realized that younger voters tend to be enthusiastic text-messengers, so it began "capturing" cell phone numbers over which campaign messages could be sent. In 2008, a clever inducement was the announcement that those people who had signed up to receive text messages from the Obama campaign would be the first to know who his Vice Presidential running mate would be. Though the 3 a.m. delivery of this message drew some criticism, the effort enabled the campaign to accumulate hundreds of thousands of cell phone numbers that could be used to communicate everything from policy messages to information about the candidate's upcoming campaign stops.

Tele-town halls are a less well-known technology, but they are growing in popularity as well. These are nothing more than massive conference calls in which constituents participate from their homes. Organizers typically dial up random households in the district or state and invite constituents to take part and ask questions. Such events have proven to be an excellent alternative to traditional town hall meetings, which are more difficult to arrange and orchestrate. Most people, including

Members of the Congress, are too busy to squeeze another meeting into their schedules. In addition, traditional town hall meetings have become popular targets for agitators who do not foster dialogue, preferring instead to disrupt the gathering and play to the media.

The Congressional Institute has done two studies on tele-town hall meetings. The 2010 study finds:

> Members and their staffs are generally bullish on tele-town halls (TTHs). They are now an accepted part of Hill life, and offer the flexibility to call large numbers of constituents at a time that is most convenient for Members. Since they are not announced in advance, they can also be postponed due to last-minute votes without disappointing constituents who would otherwise be expecting a call.

> Yet, despite all their popularity on the Hill, tele-town halls occur at nowhere near the penetration and frequency rates that constituents indicate they should be. The survey found that only 16.8% of respondents said they'd been invited to join a tele-town hall in the past year; 48.6% of respondents said they had never been invited but would like to be invited onto future calls; and among those who have been called or would like to be called, 17.7% would like to participate monthly; 30.7% would like to do so quarterly; and 26.7% would like do so semi-annually.

> Looking at the big picture, the communications challenges remain great. "Despite all the efforts to reach constituents, there are massive percentages of constituents—including those who say they 'pay a lot of attention to politics'—who claim they never receive a printed newsletter, e-newsletter, or an invite to either an in- district town hall or tele-town hall," concludes the Congressional Institute's 2010 report.

It seems a communicator's work is never done.

Chapter Ten Summary

- Strategic communication involves the entire office.

- If the Member isn't comfortable with the strategy, the strategy won't work.

- A key element of strategic planning is the brand image the Member wishes to create.

- The introduction of legislation is an important opportunity to communicate an idea.

- There are many types of media and each has distinctive needs and objectives.

- Communications strategy involves many calculations.

- There are basic rules for talking with the press. The most important is to always be trustworthy. Another is that admitting ignorance is preferable to demonstrating stupidity.

- Communication is an outside and an inside exercise. Communicating is also listening and understanding how your audience listens and perceives.

- Strategy should incorporate the new technologies and new venues for communicating ideas.

For more than two centuries, new Members of Congress have grappled with the question of whether they were elected to make wise decisions based on their own good judgment or to vote the will of their constituents regardless of their own views. For Members from safe districts or states this is an interesting academic question. But for those who must wage competitive re-election campaigns, it is often a question of political survival.

Just as the Founding Fathers balanced republican and democratic principles of government in designing the Constitution, so must the Congress balance the priorities of the nation against the parochial interests of each constituency or balance the judgment of the elected and the will of the electors. When those needs and opinions mesh, life on the Hill can be very sweet indeed. When they don't, the skills—and sometimes the courage—of individual Members and their staffs can be tested to the limit.

When considering an issue, Members must carefully discern the extent to which the feedback they receive represents their constituents' deepest held beliefs or more fleeting attitudes. Social scientist Daniel Yankelovich, author of *Coming to Public Judgment: Making Democracy Work in a Complex World* has written extensively about public attitudes towards issues, and he makes a useful distinction between *public opinion* and *public judgment*. Public opinion reflects what voters are thinking about an issue at a given moment in time. By nature, it fluctuates, often quite frequently. It is not necessarily based on a thorough analysis of the facts and is susceptible to being influenced by people's emotions about an issue. Public judgment, on the other hand, is less liable to fluctuations. It is a far more mature consideration of an issue than public opinion is. When the public develops a "judgment" on an issue, it means they have thought through information on the topic, have examined various viewpoints, have assessed the issue in light of their values, and have reflected upon the consequences of their policies. The policies Congress enacts reflect— or ought to reflect—the public judgment on a matter, rather than the simple public opinion.

Public opinion is subject to change—and can shift with surprising speed. At the Presidential level, President George H.W. Bush trailed Governor Michael Dukakis by 17 points the day after the Democratic National Convention in 1988, but he went on to win a fairly comfortable victory just two months later. After the 2008 election, a writer for ABC News asked if the election meant "the veritable death of the Republican Party as they know it?" As *former* Speaker Nancy Pelosi would tell you, by 2010 the death of the Republican Party had been greatly exaggerated. (To be fair, the same thing was said about the Democratic Party after the 2000 election when President George W. Bush's victory gave the Republicans control of both the Congress and the Presidency for the first time since Dwight Eisenhower was first elected.)

At the outset of the 2012 Presidential and congressional campaigns, if a political prognosticator had predicted the Democrats would actually gain two seats in the Senate, he would have been laughed at. Yet the day after the elections, some were questioning the future strength of the Republican Party. Pronouncements of the deaths of political parties are as predictable as, well, elections themselves.

The point is that public opinion can change—and if the public feels threatened by a bad economy, terrorism or war, it can change in a hurry.

On the other hand, public judgment changes slowly, if at all. For example, for 60 years the Gallup Organization has asked Americans if they believed in God—and for 60 years 9 out of 10 Americans have said they do.

Public opinion is when people compare the facts—as they perceive them and as they continue to gather them—against their core beliefs or judgment. The core beliefs do not change—at least not quickly and easily—but how an individual perceives facts in light of those beliefs may change in the time it takes to view a 30-second commercial.

Over time, the challenge of distinguishing the two has increased as public opinion has become ever more readily accessible. The nation's population has become better informed and more technologically empowered. At the same time, a more opinionated public has created the need for even more sophisticated methods of gauging how that electorate feels about issues.

Polls have become an invaluable tool in trying to gauge public sentiment. So much so that some observers contend that political positions that once were solid as oaks now are more like the willow that bends and sways gracefully in the breeze. Public opinion surveys, and the poll results they produce, date to the 1920s. But as recently as the mid-20th century, the populations of congressional districts were small enough for the average Member to figure out for himself what his constituents were thinking.

When they were unable to do so, Representatives and Senators knew where to go. Society was less complicated and less nuanced then. Community leaders were easier to identify. Interest groups were fewer in number and less complex. The purveyors of news and information were just a few broadcasters and the local newspaper editor. Personal relationships were simpler and so was the economy. Members of Congress knew their constituents, who relied primarily on ingenuity, their neighbors and local government to resolve the issues that concerned them. A Member could learn much of what he or she needed to know merely by talking to local unions, church leaders, bankers, and local service organizations such as the Rotary and Kiwanis clubs and chambers of commerce.

As recently as 1950, the American Association of Retired People (AARP), the Semiconductor Industry Association (SIA), and Greenpeace did not exist. Nor did thousands of other trade groups, social and political associations, and global corporations employing thousands of lobbyists trying to steer the course of a multi-trillion dollar government that operates and manages hundreds of thousands of Federal programs with millions of rules and regulations.

America had about 135 million residents in 1950, compared to over 311 million today.

In the ensuing 50 years, the nation's population more than doubled, but the number of seats in the House of Representatives has remained constant. Despite improvements in transportation and communication, the challenge to keep up with constituent interests and needs has become immense. District size, demographics, social and educational diversity, the aging of the population, and a host of other factors have combined to make public opinion polls an essential source of information about the will of the electorate as well as national trends.

In addition to becoming a major source of information for politicians, polls have become an important part of the electoral process. When the late Senator Ted Kennedy died, practically everybody assumed that a Democrat would automatically win the seat in a special election, and very few people paid any attention to it. When a Rasmussen Poll showed the Republican candidate Scott Brown within striking distance a month before the election, the race suddenly became a national obsession. Senator Brown's victory fundamentally changed the political dynamic in Washington, DC, because it took away the filibuster-proof margin Senate Democratic leaders had and suddenly made President Obama seem politically vulnerable.

Not long after Senator Brown's victory in 2010, polls tried to measure the effect of a new political movement called the Tea Party and frequently underestimated their strength against established congressional incumbents—particularly in Republican primary elections. By October, a surge of Republican support in polls had leaders at the Democratic Congressional Campaign Committee (DCCC) "triaging" the electoral landscape—withdrawing campaign funding from incumbents whom the polls said could not win.

Similarly, in 2012 many top political pollsters were embarrassed because they underestimated the impressive voter identification and turnout effort President Obama's campaign achieved. Some pollsters did get it right when projecting who would actually vote, however, and they will be crowned king of the polling world—until the next election when someone else will figure out something that everyone else missed.

Polling variations during the 2012 campaign show how limited the instruments can be. While polls are ubiquitous on Capitol Hill, multiple pollsters frequently provide differing results to similar questions. If polling is a statistical science, how can this be?

Most professional pollsters freely admit that the biggest danger associated with surveys is that their results are subject to misinterpretation, and what they reveal can be easily exaggerated, over-dramatized and over-applied. Polls produce a snapshot of attitudes at a given moment prompted by a given question addressing an issue that has been simply defined. They require rigorous design, scientific analysis and an understanding of their limitations to be of any real value.

The challenge is to get the science right.

It All Depends How You Ask the Question

"Stand up if you want to go to heaven!" the preacher exhorted his congregation. The worshipers rose as one, with the exception of a man in the front pew. "Are you telling me you do not want to go to heaven when you die?" thundered the preacher. The man jumped to his feet, "When I die, yes. But I thought you were getting up a load right now."

Margin of Error

Many people are familiar with the term *margin of error,* which is a measure of a survey's accuracy. Generally speaking, the more people you survey, the more accurately the poll will reflect the entire group being studied. It's like the elementary school experiment where you flipped a coin 100 times to demonstrate that the closer you got to 100, the closer the heads-to-tails ratio was to 50-50.

Arriving at an acceptable margin of error, however, is the easy half of the science. Even more significant is what's known as the survey sample. In order for survey results to be accurate, this sample must reflect the demographics of the population whose opinion is being sought. Say, for example, 60 percent of your sample consists of women and 40 percent men, but the actual ratio of the population you survey is 53 percent women and 47 percent. The results are likely to be skewed because women will have been oversampled—that is, too many women were counted.

This is the cause of most variations in surveys asking essentially the same question. A survey will yield inaccurate results if it oversamples one of the political parties, ideologies, genders, generations, races, or any other number of variables. For instance, pollsters struggled to compare the historical data from the 2006 and 2008 elections with the enthusiasm gap between the two parties in 2010. The intensity of the anger independent voters felt about the 2010 healthcare bill and the government's economic policies was something that politicians could express anecdotally, but was difficult for pollsters to measure.

Successful pollsters must ensure samples accurately reflect the population considered relevant to the poll. In an election campaign, for instance, the sample ideally would consist exclusively of people who will be casting ballots. Those casting ballots often represent variables that were not expected to be a factor or voters representing the variables that were considered significant may decide to stay home. The challenge lies in figuring out who is going to vote. Pollsters must make educated guesses. Sometimes they guess wrong. For instance, in 2012, many pollsters assumed that the large turnout of minority and young voters in 2008 would not be duplicated. Oops. The survey samples based on the 2008 demographic turnout were the most accurate.

One of the greatest challenges in designing a poll is determining which respondents will actually vote. Even in the most highly contested Presidential elections, 20 percent of all registered voters don't vote. In an off year, when congressional elections take place but there's not a Presidential contest to be decided, fewer than 50 percent of registered voters may cast ballots. To address this problem, many pollsters insert a series of questions designed to identify *likely voters.* But even the best laid plans go astray, as they did in both 1998 and 2000, when the pollsters who didn't bother to distinguish between *likely* and *unlikely voters* were, ironically enough, more accurate than the ones who focused on so-called likely voters.

Identifying likely voters is not a pollster's only concern. They also must assess the validity of polls conducted through live interviews as opposed to automated polls where people respond to questions using their telephone keypads. Judging from the results of the last several elections, it seems both methods generate similar results, but the automated pollsters are able to contact more households.

Pollsters are also finding it difficult to survey significant sectors of the population. For one, an increasing percentage of the electorate has only a cell phone (and no landline telephone), so it is difficult to obtain phone numbers for such voters. Even if a pollster can reach a voter, the reality is that very many are not willing to participate. Both trends have driven canvassers to experiment with on-line polling, which in some cases has proven reliable and in others less so.

Still, whatever method is used, the competency and integrity of the pollster often determines the accuracy of the poll.

The Numbers Game

Polling anomalies aren't always random errors or the inability to forecast a certain demographic groups' participation level. The polling process can be easily manipulated by intentionally oversampling a key demographic. A partisan surveyor or one on the payroll of politicians can make a candidate appear stronger than the opposition—creating an impression of political strength or momentum—simply by oversampling members of the candidate's party.

Equally disturbing is a practice known as push polling, which isn't polling at all but an attempt to prostitute the process by asking a leading set of questions, intended not to measure voter opinion but to sway it. In his book *Playing to Win,* CBS news analyst Jeff Greenfield cites the infamous push-poll used by the 1950 campaign of George Smathers against then Florida Senator Claude Pepper. The question by the so-called pollster supporting Smathers was: "If you knew that Claude Pepper's brother is a practicing *Homo sapiens,* his sister is a known *thespian*, and that he openly *matriculated* when he was in college, would you still vote for him for Senate?" (There is some dispute as to whether or not this actually happened or if it is a political urban legend from the 1950s—nonetheless, it illustrates the point nicely).

Pepper lost that race by 60,000 votes, but was elected to the House in 1962 and served there for the next 26 years.

Today push-polls tend to be more sophisticated and more effectively disguised, but the objective is the same—to manipulate not only those who are polled but also those who are targets of the polling, including unsuspecting media.

Push-polls aren't the only problem for surveys that attract a great deal of undeserved attention. Ad surveys on specific Internet sites, for example. The results are nothing more than a reflection of attitudes shared by those people who frequent that website or who happened upon the questionnaire and took the time to answer it. The same can be said for Member polls conducted on their websites or in newsletters. Any similarity between those results and the opinions of the population as a whole is entirely coincidental.

Ad surveys and push-polls may lead a person to discount the practice altogether, but when conducted and interpreted properly, opinion polls taken over time and reflecting the same sample provide trends that allow sophisticated policy makers to perceive temporary and permanent changes in the public's mind. In the wrong hands, however, polls can produce interesting headlines and generate a great deal of heat—but very little light.

Public opinion instruments measure progress in the journey to public judgment. Public opinion is a weather vane, a means of telling which direction opinion is headed, a gauge of attitudes toward a range of issues that occupy the Congress. At the same time, they are far from infallible.

This is particularly true when a survey reveals only part of the equation—and why it is important to keep in mind that public opinion can appear to change without notice. It can be swayed by new information that exposes a conflict in values or by the day of the week when a survey is taken—those taken on a Friday night during football season, for example, always under-sample Republicans who are more likely than their Democratic counterparts to attend high school games.

Even if a poll is rigorously formed and impartially administered, its value will be limited if its significance is misinterpreted. One easy way of misinterpreting poll results is overestimating or underestimating the importance of a policy issue. Single-issue activists, particularly devotees of social and environmental causes, need to be especially honest with themselves about public opinion. For instance, gay marriage activists might be comforted by the support for their cause among younger voters. However, those same voters are not nearly as dutiful in exercising their franchise as older people. There is often a difference between a person's viewpoint on an issue and how intensely he or she is motivated to vote based on that issue above other issues.

In 2012, Democrats alleged that Republicans were waging a "war on women" and opposing policies the public broadly supported. And based on some public opinion surveys, it probably seemed like it would be a winning slogan. However, it turns out that economic issues that affected the health and prosperity of women's families were a far more important determiner of policy choices. In 2012 the Congressional Institute did a comprehensive survey on women's issues. Instead of seeking individuals' views on the latest issue or on candidates running for office, the survey sought to look at what long-term, underlying values inform women's decision making on public policy issues. The survey found the top 5 statements women believed reflected the most important outcomes in their lives:

1. Being able to have the health care you need.

2. Having a secure retirement.

3. Being able to effectively manage the cost of living.

4. Having job security.

5. Not having to worry about whether you can pay next month's bills.

Microeconomic issues were by far the most important, and access to birth control was sixteenth out of seventeen choices listed. In fact, women were skeptical of the sincerity of those who focused on social issues instead of economic ones. Three in four women agreed that "when *lawmakers talk about women's issues, they are just saying this to win the women's vote because they think this is what women want to hear*". Only 15 percent said that *"lawmakers are genuinely concerned about women's issues"*. Nearly 70 percent disagreed that there was a "war on women." The selective use of social issues with particular segments of the population may have been good politics, but the Congressional Institute survey demonstrated that many women thought that many in the media and in politics had a condescending view of what they felt was genuinely important in their lives.

The use of women's issues in 2012 is a prime example of the difficulty of using polling data in determining how to campaign and govern. Be cautious with polling. Always review a poll's source and design. Always ensure that your interpretations and analyses are appropriate and realistic and that you are not engaging in wishful thinking to see answers you want to see. If you use polling data wisely, surveys can be a useful means to come to understand both the short-term and long-term fluctuations in public sentiment, but keep in mind, a poll is just one tool of many in the policymaker's toolbox.

Impact Takes Time

Change occurs all the time in Washington, DC—that's one of the reasons the tax code and regulations take up more than 55,000 pages and is amended every year. Complex change, however, is rare. Even when it does occur, it can take years to understand how it occurred or what long-range effect it will have.

- In the 1960s, major change produced new laws on voting rights, desegregation and Medicare.

- In the 1980s, the United States economic policy underwent a dramatic change from a semi-Keynesian economy to a supply-side monetarist economy—where spending and inflation were replaced by tax reductions, tighter budgets and a money supply geared toward lower inflation.

187

- In the late 1990s, the social welfare infrastructure of President Lyndon Johnson's Great Society underwent dramatic reform that redefined entitlement to government assistance and reversed disincentives to work and marriage, greatly reducing welfare rolls across the country. Then came President Obama, and those polices were reversed.

The dawn of the new century also saw the first attack against the U.S. on American soil since the Japanese raid on Pearl Harbor. The September 11, 2001, terrorist assault caused changes in both opinion and judgment, permanently altering the way Americans viewed their own vulnerability and the way the country was viewed globally. The wars in Iraq and Afghanistan, which followed the attacks, also shaped new judgments about America at war and the human and financial resources required to fight those wars. President George W. Bush's presidency also produced change in the way seniors received prescription drug coverage, creating a massive new program based on free-market competition. The program went from cautious resistance and opposition to widespread acceptance and even popularity within a year of passage.

In 2008, the country elected our first black President. Many assumed that Barack Obama's election reflected transformational change in the country's political and ideological attitude, ushering in a new period of liberal government. It only took two short years, and the 2010 elections, to prove that expectation highly premature.

In 2010, health care reform passed, though it has not yet fully gone into effect. Given the lack of chronological distance, it is too early to make a judgment about the health care reform bill, but regardless of the controversy as to whether it was good or bad, there can be no doubt that the bill dubbed "Obamacare" represented transformational change.

As with Obamacare, it is also too early to tell if the Tea Party movement represents a historical tipping point, moving the country away from the ever-increasing size and scope of the Federal Government, or whether it is an ephemeral phenomenon. Have people, particularly middle-income voters, decided that the additional benefits they draw from the Federal Government are not worth the present economic damage to the economy and the long-range debt burden in the future? It is also too early to know the answer to this question as well.

The Science of Messaging

Not everyone is receptive to every message. That's because not all of us respond to stimuli in the same way. Research suggests that it is important to recognize how people process information in conversations and to recognize traits that can influence communication on a broader scale as well.

Around the outset of World War II, Isabel Briggs Myers and her mother, Katharine Cook Briggs, set out to find practical applications for Carl Jung's theory of psychological types. Their efforts have been perpetuated by the Myers-Briggs Foundation, whose research continues to identify distinguishing characteristics. To oversimplify, they suggest that four types of communication styles are among the most common: *Feelers, Sensors, Intuitors* and *Thinkers*.

None of these categories is necessarily absolute—individuals and groups will shift emphasis from one to another as they age, attain education and gain experiences, so it's helpful to know the clues to look for if you are trying to effectively communicate.

- **The Feeler** uses language to express emotion. He or she is what's referred to as an *empath*, someone who wants to connect, who wants to make you feel comfortable. Listen for signals that indicate frustration. The *Feeler* needs to know that you recognize he or she is having difficulties, something along the lines of, "high gas prices are making it harder to afford groceries...." The Feeler also needs to be recognized and appreciated: "You're good in situations like this one." Feelers judge political thought based on these emotive attributes and are not impressed with facts, charts, studies, etc.

- **The Sensor** thrives on deadlines and lives to get things done. A *Sensor* does everything—including communication—in spurts and can make "Good morning" feel like an intrusion. They respond most positively if they know you have a plan. Prepare ahead and communicate in easily digestible bites with Sensors. In the workplace, Sensors want to know what is going to happen next. The vast majority of voters perceive information from a Sensor perspective.

- **The Thinker** operates on logic. He or she loves organization and systems and likes to see projects through to the bitter end. They thrive on numbers and facts, are logical and realistic, and will reference projects that failed in order to deflate any plan that seems farfetched. *Thinkers* love problem solving. When you communicate, reassure them that you are grounded in reality and will get all the facts before coming up with a plan to deal with a problem. Thinkers constitute about half the population and have real trouble understanding the Feeler's perspective.

- **The Intuitor** is conceptual, a long-range planner, a problem solver—but not necessarily interested in doing the work that's necessary to implement the solution. He or she would rather move on to the next problem. They're likely to have big ideas that are difficult to understand but are presented as if you ought to have no trouble whatsoever grasping what they've said. They seldom provide context or last names when discussing an idea or a situation and become impatient if you interrupt with a question. *Intuitors* would prefer you let them talk out their ideas before you begin asking questions. Questions to them are best received if they are phrased in a way that indicates you like the Intuitor's ideas and simply need more information in order to get a clear picture. Intuitors are the least populous of the four styles, constitution only about 25 percent of the population.

Political leaders with the highly refined communication skills of Ronald Reagan, Bill Clinton and Newt Gingrich are able to embrace entire audiences—*Feelers, Sensors, Intuitors* and *Thinkers* alike.

Effective communicators think about the communication styles of their audience. A message intended for scientists would be skewed toward a Sensor/Thinker style while social workers would get a Sensor/Feeler message. The essence of the message should be consistent, but how it is delivered might be different for each audience.

For large audiences, emulate Clinton and Reagan and talk first to Sensors (who have the shorter attention spans) and then talk to Thinkers. This is particularly true for television where Sensor elements (who, what, when) combined with Feeler (empathy and sympathy) is best for interviews and 30-second sound bites.

In short, choose how you say something as carefully as you choose what to say. Delivering a speech on the floor of the House in an effort to persuade colleagues to vote in favor of a bill you co-sponsored isn't the same as delivering an emotional appeal on the floor of the House directly to constituents by means of CSPAN's cameras.

Following the 2012 elections, pundits started asking whether changing demographics had taken a hand in how public policy would be shaped. Have Hispanic Americans emerged as the fastest growing political demographic in the country? And does this really represent transformational change? Or, like other immigrant waves in U.S. history, will Hispanics constitute a statistical difference but not a behavioral difference in policy preferences?

Regardless of whether we agree with the major policy shifts that have occurred over many decades, the question is whether or not they reflect the complex and comprehensive shifts in thinking that are necessary to alter the public's approach to the fundamental issues of the time.

Stages of Public Opinion and Public Judgment

The many, even contradictory, changes in policy in the past few decades, described above, illustrate how public opinion can change dramatically. To some degree, that is to be expected. As Daniel Yankelovich once told a congressional audience, "People's opinions go through various stages as they gradually come to grips with an issue."

When we discuss complex change, we are talking about fundamental transformations to the way society approaches problems and institutes solutions. These are the "Big Issues," such as how we should reform Social Security, Medicare, and the immigration system; how we should use the military to promote democracy or fight terrorism in other countries; how we should use and generate energy; or whether we should pursue free trade or adopt a policy of protectionism.

In *Coming to Public Judgment,* Yankelovich defines a seven-step process that people go through in forming opinions on complex issues:

Awareness: *"This issue I keep hearing about is a problem."*

Through hearsay, the media, or public comments, individuals or groups become aware that change might be needed. They are aware, but not motivated to act.

Urgency: *"The problem must be solved soon."*

The public recognizes that a problem not only exists, but that it must be dealt with. A new revelation—perhaps something in the news or an event in one's personal life—gives the problem a sense of urgency.

Reviewing alternatives: *"What solutions exist?"*

People assess what can be done to confront the challenge: Can they avoid the change? Are there other options? Can someone else deal with it?

Wishful thinking: *"Maybe I can find a solution that doesn't require much change on my part."*

People latch onto options they hope will resolve the problem. This is where resistance to change becomes visible: "They can cut government spending, and they probably ought to—but not by cutting programs that benefit me. Something's gotta give, but why should I have to pay for it? Maybe they can tax the rich, or keep out the immigrants, or control Hollywood. . . ."

Weighing pros and cons: *"If I have to change, which alternative best fits my values?"*

People begin to calculate trade-offs and confront conflicts in personal or societal values: "Yes, I want better schools, but no, I don't want taxes raised to pay for it," or "No, I don't think we should bear the expense of inspecting every package, but I do think transportation must be made safer."

In every case, a conflict between at least two values must be resolved.

Consider, for example, flag-burning. When protestors abroad or at home burn a U.S. flag to show disgust or defiance over a U.S. policy, the majority of Americans are indignant. Activists in Congress move to outlaw such behavior, but when the value of patriotism is weighed against a value that's just as important—free speech—the majority reconsiders.

Members of the Congress and their staff must be attentive to real value conflicts and be able to frame them in such a way that they make a change in policy more valuable or more acceptable than existing policy.

Intellectual acceptance: *"I might not like the solution, but I can live with it."*

People have decided that change is the best course, even if, in their hearts, they still want to resist it. Public leaders are frequently undone at this juncture. They assume the decision of the affected individuals does not need reinforcement. Sometimes this is precisely when a Member and staff need to work overtime to keep acceptance firm.

191

Most truly contentious debates are over core values and therefore laden with emotion and ideology, defying logical resolution and pragmatic compromise. Even when the decibel level declines, care must be taken to determine whether the solution is durable enough to withstand changing perspectives or renewed opposition.

Institutionalized: *"Why revisit that issue when the new set-up works?"*

Institutionalization occurs when the acceptable solution is in place and becomes the status quo. Public judgment—which is far more stable than public opinion—has been attained. It is accepted both intellectually and emotionally. When true institutionalization exists, there is no need to consider change.

For purposes of clarity, the process described by Yankelovich has been presented here as a chronological progression, which it seldom is. New information or changes in circumstance often intrude, causing people to revert to earlier stages of thinking. A classic case occurred in 1988, when the Federal Government made a can't-miss leap in health care policy and fell flat on its face.

President Reagan and the Congress responded to concerns that catastrophic illnesses were bankrupting Americans on Medicare. Medicare covers the first 60 to 90 days of long-term care in a nursing home or comparable facility. Medicaid then picks up the slack—but only if most of the patient's life savings have been exhausted. The solution the Reagan administration came up with was a premium-based catastrophic insurance plan that would cover 100 percent of expenses after the patient ponied up the $2,000 deductible—and the coverage would cost only $59 a year.

The Congress decided to be even more generous and lowered the annual deductible, while tacking on additional benefits. By the time Reagan signed the bill just before the 1988 election, the new law was thought to be hugely popular—after all, the Congress had created peace of mind for the elderly without increasing taxes. The problem was that few people understood how the package would be paid for.

They didn't realize the Congress had decided that lower-income seniors couldn't afford the premiums that originally were proposed, so it provided a complex formula that exempted those who couldn't come up with $59 a year and required higher-income seniors to pay as much as $800 per year to make up the difference. Adding insult to perceived injury, the coverage duplicated what many retirees' union and Federal pension plans provided, in effect, forcing them to pay for coverage they not only didn't need but also couldn't use.

Retribution was unprecedented. As more and more interest groups railed against what they perceived as a *seniors-only tax,* popular opinion shifted from strong support to strong opposition. A massive letter writing campaign, punctuated by House Ways and Means Committee Chairman Dan Rostenkowski being mobbed by his own constituents on national television, resulted in the act being repealed before it could actually go into effect.

Supposedly painless reform, lean and clean, had become downright mean. The Congress had relied on logic and math without taking into consideration the resistance inherent in change. Public opinion in favor of the new Federal program had been undermined by failure to achieve public judgment.

Members and staff alike need to understand the limitations of public opinion and the impact of public judgment. Advocates of change must anticipate the resistance they will encounter and appreciate the conflicting values that are behind it. Opponents must expose the changes it will produce and reframe the debate to focus on values that are likely to be undermined. Reliable polling techniques can give both sides what they need to argue their point of view effectively.

Very little in the policymaking process had prepared millions of retirees to consider the tradeoffs in the catastrophic health insurance bill. Once they were informed that they had to pay the bill, their acceptance turned to rejection despite the fact that the change would have provided badly needed healthcare security, especially for less affluent seniors. As a result, valuable ground was lost in the effort to deliver catastrophic coverage for seniors. The issue reverted to the earliest stages of Yankelovich's progression—where people could grasp the importance but weren't prepared to seriously consider alternatives. The prospect of security in the face of potentially onerous health care costs had been weighed against having to pay for that peace of mind—and those who would have benefited decided they'd rather live with the comparatively long odds against being bankrupted by a catastrophic medical bill than pay to be protected against it.

Proponents of the catastrophic health care bill were undone by their failure to institutionalize the change. They did not anticipate opposition and failed to persuade, educate and consult with their constituents. But they did learn valuable lessons. When the Congress enacted prescription drug coverage 20 years later, Members spent enormous amounts of time explaining the new program to older constituents. In addition, the Federal Government launched a massive campaign to help people sort through any confusion. Opponents attacked various aspects of the program in an effort to derail it, but the education campaign won the day. By anticipating resistance, addressing it head on, measuring progress with public opinion surveys, and relentlessly educating the potential beneficiaries, Members turned the initial skepticism among older Americans into an 80 percent approval rate in less than one year, thus accomplishing a long-promised change.

By the end of the 113th Congress, we may be able to make a similar judgment about the health care reform bill passed in 2010. How will it be implemented? What controversies will arise as constituents begin to find out what is in the law? Will the polls turn around as voters gradually come to accept it?

One thing is for certain. There will not be a lack of professionals trying to find the answers.

Chapter Eleven Summary

- The Founders created a complex governing tension in establishing the United States as both a republic and a democracy.

- Because congressional districts are so large and conflicting views on public policy so rampant, Members have come to rely on public opinion tools as one way to gauge public attitudes.

- Public opinion polls are a great tool but they are insufficient to ascertain more complex public judgment, the values-based beliefs of the citizenry.

- Public opinion is subject to change—and can shift with surprising speed.

- Public judgment evolves much more slowly, if it shifts at all. Members who vote or act counter to public judgment will frequently find that a vote that looked reasonable the day it was cast will look unwise in coming months or years.

- Reading and using public opinion polls can be challenging for Members and staff. It is critical to understand the dynamics of sample size, margin of error and the nature of the survey sample.

- Because public judgment reflects core values the population holds, it both changes more slowly and at the same time is more reflective of the deepest attitudes of the populace.

- Public judgment on most significant attitudes is stable but it does move over time. When it does, it goes through a series of steps, at no specific timetable. It begins with an awareness of the need to examine an attitude. When awareness is motivated by urgency to act, it ignites a reexamination of the status quo.

- Once urgency to act has been acknowledged, the public looks for alternative solutions and is prone to focusing, initially, on those that appear to require the least amount of change or personal discomfort.

- The public, with the help of good leadership, weighs the ramifications of the alternatives against their own core beliefs. There is usually a contest between two or more values in evaluating alternate avenues for solving the problem.

- Once the public decides which core value is most critical to protect, they come to an intellectual decision on how the problem should be resolved.

- Finally, the decision becomes ingrained or institutionalized in the public attitude and the problem no longer dominates the public debate.

Enacting Major Legislative Change

Most of what we have discussed in preceding chapters has focused on the normal business of Congress: making corrections in the course of government, engaging in oversight of the executive and the judiciary, advocating and implementing change as mandated by the public in the last election or deemed warranted by political currents that will dictate the next election. Every so often, though, an opportunity to make major changes arises.

The 111th Congress (2009-2010) saw many changes. A dramatic change in the healthcare system, major bailouts of various companies, the exponential increase in spending and debt as a percentage of the gross domestic product to try to stimulate economic growth, the ratification of a nuclear arms reduction treaty, and new financial service industry regulations all represent a major shift in the governing philosophy of the country.

Prior to the Democrats' takeover in 2006, the Republican Congress that came in with the 1994 election had also made some important changes on policies such as welfare reform, education, homeland security, prescription drugs and other critical challenges facing the country. It had also passed the only balanced budgets (1998-2001) the nation had seen in the last half century.

It's not every day that Congress produces a major shift in the philosophies that drive congressional action or a major transformation in the country's social or economic life.

Most major legislative change that can alter the course of history takes time and an unusual synergy of energy, resources, and need. There is usually a good deal of adjustment that must take place politically, socially, and maybe culturally, before significant change is achieved and accepted. Bringing about such change requires deep commitments from those who seek it.

Our history offers other examples of what major legislative and cultural change requires: creation of a national bank, its dissolution, and creation again; westward expansion; industrialization; women's suffrage and equal access to education and employment; Prohibition and its repeal; the McKinley tariffs; the Sherman Antitrust Act; the Civil Service System, the designation of public lands and parks; trade protectionism; Social Security;

the Marshall Plan; welfare reforms; Medicare and Medicaid; space exploration; civil rights; and birth of the digital information age.

There are periods in our history when the times demanded change that would transform the way we live and the way we think. And most of the time, those changes took years, and sometimes decades, before they were realized. In some cases, legislation motivated the change, and in others, legislation codified a change made first in the culture.

In Congress, Members and staff have their hands full meeting routine constituent demands, satisfying their committee assignments, and focusing on a few of their own legislative priorities. That is the culture of Congress. As a result, there is little attention to critically needed long-term change. That may change; some would say, that must change.

This appears to be one of those times in American history when major change is desperately needed. Energy independence, accessible and affordable health care, retirement provisioning, international and domestic security, immigration, and safeguarding privacy from technological intrusion are just a few of the issues that are rapidly growing from problems into crises. They all are eclipsed by the pending economic disaster reflected in the nation's fiscal condition—high annual deficits and an exploding structural debt.

And, seldom have we had to wrestle with such an entangled array of threatening worldwide problems from terrorism to climate change, economic development and hunger, basic commodity consumption, globalization, and trade.

So how do Members of Congress and their staff rise to these challenges? How do they get beyond the weight of normal policy processes and constituent services into a whole other realm of big new ideas, complex public-policy decision-making, and harness the uncommon determination needed to legislatively attack the challenges? Where do they get the resources, the time, and the energy?

There is no manual that tells you how to do it, but there are some basic steps to enacting major legislative change that you can follow.

If your boss decides to take one of those rare opportunities to be a leader of change, the first priority is managing the process by adopting a sound strategic plan, creating a disciplined organization, and making the best use of resources such as time and personnel.

Other chapters in this book address legislative and communications strategies, public judgment, and parliamentary procedure. Those chapters contain valuable suggestions for navigating the political waters. We will try to avoid repetition here, but there are some observations and practices, some discussed previously and some not, that need to be emphasized when creating a strategic plan to achieve significant legislative change.

Let's divide this process into two components: (1) reaching consensus on what you want to accomplish, a discussion of which is partially borrowed from Yankelovich's research described in the previous chapter; and (2) organizing and managing the process.

First, you must determine what the Member wants to accomplish.

Defining the Mission

What does your boss seek to accomplish? Do you want to achieve energy independence in America through reliance on a private sector incentivized by government policy and enforced by government regulation? Do you want to create a retirement security system in America that emphasizes individual ownership and investment? Both questions imply a goal of enacting a specific policy outcome. Alternatively, you could ask: What problem is it we seek to solve? Do we want to reduce reliance on foreign imported oil? Do we want to stave off the "bankruptcy" of Social Security or reduce trade deficits with China by restructuring our relationship with them? Do we want to reduce traffic gridlock in urban areas by gradually reducing the use of automobiles?

What is the mission? Where do you want to end up when the initiative has run its course? If you are not absolutely clear on your intended goal before you begin, there is no telling how confused your project may become and how frustrated you colleagues will become.

Defining the Problem

In order to convince policymakers, the public and the media that drastic action is necessary, you must define a problem that is or has the potential to reach crisis proportions and therefore warrants drastic action. You must define a problem that has widespread implications for large blocs of people. You must define a problem that cannot be solved with small, incremental adjustments in public policy. You must define a problem with a sense of urgency. You must define a problem stark enough that risk is warranted.

Defining the problem is the beginning of the process of overcoming natural public resistance to change.

All major change encounters resistance. It is a natural human reaction that has served our species pretty well. People resist change because it requires them to modify their expectations and deal with the unknown. The status quo, even if undesirable, is predictable. Change is less so, and maybe not at all; something new may be worse.

A smoker knows the dangers of the habit, but puffs away until the coughing gets so bad it's hard to breathe, has a heart attack or gets cancer. It is amazing how fast most habitual smokers find the strength to change after a heart attack or cancer diagnosis.

In public policy, warning signs of danger are not as clear. A Federal program's failure may not be apparent or may be tolerated for years, despite wasted funds and unserved constituents. Traditional welfare in America went unchanged for decades despite clear and flagrant failure to assist the needy. It took new legislative leadership and new thinking to change the public policy. But even with new leadership and new ideas, resistance was strong, even from those who ultimately gained because of the changes.

Resistance is natural and structural, and too often when it arises, advocates of change shrink in the face of it, only because they do not understand it, do not anticipate it and don't know how to cope with it.

Breaking down resistance requires knowledge, appreciative under-standing and patience. You've got to understand why people are resisting and then devote the time to reframe the problem and convince them that the danger they are confronting is serious enough and broad enough in its effect that major change is required and that the risks of change are worth facing.

Identify The Affected

You can't even begin to overcome resistance until you identify those segments of society who are affected by the problem and would, therefore, have the largest stake in bringing about a solution.

Energy, for example, affects almost all of us in different ways, but before you can fashion an acceptable solution, you must know who is affected and how. Some of us—such as lower-income individuals and families, small businesses, and transportation-intensive industries—are hit harder by higher gasoline prices. Some are more affected by the residual effects of higher energy costs: for instance, families that face high heating and air conditioning bills and industries, such as food processing and distribution, that use large amounts of energy to produce their products or get them to market. Some place higher priority on the electricity grid that brings energy to us. The impact must be clearly understood, so you both understand why they resist and what policy alternatives can be considered and woven into a potential solution.

Developing Alternative Policy Solutions

The process of finding solutions means keeping an open mind to many alternatives. The more people invited to offer alternatives, the less likely they are to engage in opposition early in the process. And the more alternatives you consider, the more likely you are to arrive at the best and right solution. Some suggestions can and are taken off the table at the outset. Again, in the case of energy, few are going to tolerate any solution with the implication of public takeover of energy companies or energy rationing, two alternatives that violate basic national values. However, beyond the most radical solutions, most options should be reviewed.

Alternatives should be fully and widely aired, whether in media coverage; or in public hearings and discussions, such as town hall meetings; or through the activism of interested coalitions and organizations engaging in grassroots education and information programs.

Eventually, the public and the dynamics of political pressure will begin to point you in the right direction, toward a collection of alternatives that can be cobbled together into a workable, achievable solution. The process could take months. It could take years. Concluding it too early, which is to say, moving too quickly to one solution, may spell disaster. A classic example is President George W. Bush's proposed reform of Social Security. His solutions were on the table before the public was convinced there was a serious enough problem to demand a solution, and his solution was the only one on the table, other than doing nothing. It was a no-win formula.

Now reflect a moment on the points made earlier about clarifying your intent. If you started with a specific solution in mind, which is completely legitimate, you must realize, however, that you are going to significantly increase the challenges of overcoming resistance. President Bush's private accounts solution was three or more steps ahead of the public's thinking about Social Security and therefore it was easy for opponents to scare the public by attacking that specific element of his solution. Had he stated his intent as "saving Social Security" and not offered specific solutions, it would have been much harder for opponents to build resistance at an early stage.

Finding the Solution

Finding a solution requires the careful analysis of the alternatives that have been aired and building a strategy around one or more of them.

There is no easy way to settle on a solution. It lies somewhere between the mission you set out to accomplish at one end, and the reduction of resistance and acceptance by the people affected at the other. The terrain in the middle includes building the successful coalitions needed to win. But just enacting a law or laws to implement your goal is not the other end. Laws can be repealed. Policies can be reversed. The last step in the process is educating and convincing the public that the solutions are better than the risk of not changing existing policy. Once they come to that intellectual acceptance, you have achieved the change you intended. That is institutionalizing the outcome, making it as permanent as permanent can be.

There are a number of considerations in finding the right solution. Some of the more elemental are:

1. Making the case. All sides of your solution must be well thought out and highly defensible. Look at your solution, not from your perspective, but from that of the potential opposition. What elements need fortification? What elements need to be jettisoned? What elements

speak for themselves? What elements are so complex that they cannot be easily explained? If you find it difficult to convince yourself that one part of the solution is workable, maybe it isn't. Are you making your case to those who use logic to weigh pros and cons as well as those who rely more on emotion to evaluate your proposal?

2. Assess the elements of the solution in the context of achieving the mission. Which elements are essential? Which may be desirable, but not essential? What is negotiable? What isn't?

3. From which interest groups can you draw a majority coalition strong enough to win passage and enactment? What elements of the prospective solution bring which members of a prospective coalition? Are some potential members of the coalition more attractive than others? How important is bipartisanship? What do you give up to get it?

4. How will the media respond to each element of the prospective solution? As they say, are there dogs among your alternatives that just won't hunt? It is necessary to create a strategic media plan to support the effort.

Selling Your Solution

The second element we mentioned earlier is creating the organization and management infrastructure needed to achieve the change you want, winning acceptance of your solution by government and the public.

Some of the keys to success involve building out from the epicenter of the campaign:

- Building a team
- Developing a legislative strategy
- Communicating the message and a media strategy
- Dividing authority and identifying deliverables for each management team

Building the Team

Understanding the roles of key players is critical to success. Change is easier to lead in the private sector than in the public arena. In the private world, a clear hierarchy usually evolves, with a boss at the top and clear lines of authority and responsibilities underneath, making it easier to overcome resistance. Our Founders wanted no such concentration of power in our government. Public leaders, therefore, are required to follow a more complex course to success, and the roles they and their followers play are not always clear or well defined. But they should be as best as is possible.

There are four general roles and variations of the mix:

- In the business world, the *sponsor* is the individual or group with the power to bring about the change. The sponsor is the originator. In a democracy, the sponsor (not to be confused with the legislative term) is the institution or group of institutions able to enact change—the President and Legislature with the Judiciary looking over their shoulders. No one person in a democracy can accomplish political change by himself—the Framers of the Constitution established our Republic that way.

- An *advocate* recognizes that he or she does not have the personal or situational power to bring about the change and instead focuses efforts at influencing the process and working with other advocates to meet the objectives of the strategic plan. When the President sends a message to Congress, he is an advocate. When a Member drops a bill in the hopper, he or she is playing the role of an advocate. The media or lobbyists can be advocates but none of them have the independent power to force change.

- *Agents* often carry the main responsibility in shepherding the proposal to victory through the authority or empowerment afforded them by an advocate or sponsor. Staff will most often find themselves the agents of change promoted by their Member, committee or leadership. And this is where good staff work can actually change the country, perhaps the world, for the better.

- The final role is the beneficiary, or the *target*, of the change. Political change impacts citizens, Federal agency employees, or anyone whose behavior and expectations will be affected. Until the target accepts that the risks of change are preferable to the status quo, they have the power to resist. Unlike the private-sector worker who could be fired for too much resistance, the citizen has the power to fire the sponsor or advocate for disrupting their expectations. This reality makes leading change in the public world exceedingly complex and illustrates why most Members settle playing at the safer edges of policy.

To be successful, change requires that *all* the actors—sponsors, advocates, agents, and targets—display a commitment that is greater than an expression or feeling. It must become a life-altering reality. Enactment of major legislative change is an endurance contest. Your obstacles include rejection, exhaustion, criticism, doubt, division, abandonment, and numerous other dynamics that evolve from natural and synthetically created resistance. It is commitment that must be hard and fast.

Affecting Public Judgment

As was discussed in the previous chapter, effectively convincing the targets to embrace change is critical. It is usually assumed that if politicians advocate major legislative change that the public is already well enough aware of the problem for them to embark on such an endeavor. That is not necessarily true.

Many politicians don't champion policy changes unless there is public support behind them. That is the politically safer route. But, if the problem is real and the political leader is motivated to solve it, that leader must help shape the public's awareness of the risks involved with not changing. The actual process of making change requires a high degree of public awareness and public acceptance, first in concept and then in practice. People simply do not agree to solve problems they don't know exist. So making them aware of the problem is essential.

The next step is educating the public or targets to the urgency of solving the problem. Back to our smoker: It is easy to be aware that smoking can harm your lungs and you should stop. Panting after climbing a flight of stairs can convince some smokers that it is urgent to stop smoking.

The alternatives under consideration must be framed as both reasonable and necessary. The natural resistance to change will move the public mind to put off solutions with which they are not comfortable or feel may not be necessary. Wishful thinking enters the picture here and everyone faced with an urgent need to change will gravitate toward a solution that minimizes the change. Can I solve my breathing problem by cutting down to one pack a day? Wishful solutions don't solve problems; they just delay the day of reckoning.

Finally, the public must be convinced the adopted solution is consistent with their values and is the best course for them—and that it demands and deserves their support. Values are those basic beliefs we all hold about our country and society. A solution to solve governmental inefficiency by adopting a dictatorship would be rejected because it violates our basic democratic ideals or values.

Issues that are the subject of change initiatives must be framed and reframed by the proponents and not the opponents. If the opposition defines the issues, then defeat is likely. Those who resist change will make arguments for preservation of the status quo and highlight the risks of changing. The proponent able to claim consistency with the high value has a greater probability of winning. No doubt, half a century ago those who resisted school integration based their case on culture and tradition. But school integration was not simply about culture and tradition—nice values. It was about equal opportunity, justice, fairness and progress—higher values. If you engage the issues on the opponent's terms, you lose. If you engage the issues on your terms, defined to support higher values, you stand a better chance of winning. Frame the issues from the outset and reframe them as needed to meet the challenges of the opposition.

The Policy Strategy

Much of the strategic preparation for moving legislation through Congress and the executive branch are addressed in other chapters. However, here are some observations appropriate to major legislative change.

Designing a Process Specific to Your Mission

The policy process—the legislative strategy—must be developed to fit the proposed change like a well-tailored suit. Assuming the effort is not just for show but seriously intended to change policy, that means the initiative should be bipartisan and bicameral, and done in consultation with the executive branch. In other words, your potential supporters in both houses of Congress and the executive branch, along with the general public, must be convinced of the need for change and its urgency before the legislative process can be concluded.

That, of course, is a tall order, and the reason why conditioning the environment for change usually takes longer than the change itself.

The policy process should accommodate a sophisticated means of identifying policy options and vetting those alternatives among four critical groups: (1) the general public or targets, with emphasis on segments of the public that will be affected by the change being proposed; (2) the policy makers who must ultimately vote on the solution and sign the legislative act; (3) the interest groups that will have an impact on grassroots mobilization; and (4) the trade, Internet-based, and mainstream media.

While stakeholders in the process, particularly committee and subcommittee chairs, must have ample opportunity to air options, express opinions and influence the decision-making, no stakeholder can be allowed to hijack the initiative and turn the team away from its mission. The most effective way to avoid that happening is to keep the awareness and urgency of making a change highly visible.

Hijackers can also be found in the political organizations of both parties that are responsible for conducting and financing campaigns. National committees, congressional and senatorial committees, and tax-exempt political organizations all, for one reason or another, may decide that the best partisan advantage can be gained by exploiting, discrediting, or reframing the elemental issues involved in change. Their resistance is less likely if it is understood that tolerating the status quo is simply not acceptable.

The Timeframe

A timeframe for action and a timeline of specific benchmarks in the legislative process should be established so that alarm bells go off and tactical adjustments are made when the process is bogged down or threatened by opposition that is stronger than anticipated.

Decision-Makers and Decision-Making

The strategy should include a hierarchy for legislative and political decision-making, particularly as more and more individuals and organizations are empowered to influence the process.

Sometimes making a wrong decision is a better alternative than making no decision at all. Indecision leads to confusion and creates a political power vacuum that is usually filled quickly. The decision structure, however, must be accommodating enough to meet the needs of team leaders responsible for various phases of consideration, ranging from senior Members and staff in the subcommittees and full committees, to the primary spokespersons and political leaders.

The Communications Strategy: Creating The Brand

Framing the issues is part of creating a brand for your initiative that makes your team members comfortable and motivated. The brand is an easily recognizable and positive personality that gives your audience confidence they know what you are talking about and what you want to accomplish, whether those people are your closest teammates and advisors, the press, or the general public. That face might be a victim of the problem you are trying to solve or a Member. But, the face must be credible. It may sound a little too Madison Avenue to put branding among your top priorities, but the fact is that the inherent resistance to change must be offset by an incentive to change that feels natural and that begins with a familiar and friendly face for the initiative.

The communications strategy has three principle audiences: (1) the media that will carry the message to the public; (2) the supporters who will mobilize grassroots supporters behind the execution of your strategy; and (3) public officials who must enact laws to implement the change.

Creating the Messages

Messages define the brand a little more specifically. They should be few in number and give context and meaning to your mission and your brand. They must speak to what you have determined, through observation, discussion, and survey research, which elements of the problem are of greatest concern to your target audience. Message number one must be that the problem is serious enough to demand immediate and maybe drastic attention. Message number two could be that there are constructive alternatives available and that a solution can be achieved but it may take time and unity. The third message could be that the solution is dictated by certain values that are important to all of us. The fourth message is that it is better to adopt a solution than risk living any longer with the unworkable policy that exists.

Identifying the Messengers

It is important that the messages be delivered by skilled messengers and that they are disciplined to stick to the essential points without creating confusion or misunderstanding. They must all sing from the same hymnal.

The messengers should be trained in how to deliver the message and experienced in addressing questions intended to confuse the messages or distort the purpose.

The messengers must be convincing and persuasive public speakers. They should be directed to proactive outreach programs designed to get themselves in situations where the messages can be delivered to the targeted audience most effectively. The messengers should speak to and represent the various interest groups you consider important to ultimate victory, maybe including both political parties, both houses of Congress, and key members of the coalition.

The Venues for Message Delivery

Selecting the right venues for message delivery can be important. Some media outlets will probably be more productive and accessible than others. Some public forums may be more receptive. Some organizations may be more helpful in message delivery than others. There will be some media, some environments, and some venues that you should avoid.

Electronic communications, as discussed in other chapters, offer team members a wide variety of venues from which to choose. Each medium, from broadcast, to print, to cable, to cyberspace, has its own unique properties, constituencies and means of communication that requires its own individual treatment.

More often than not, communications should be done with a rifle and not a shotgun. Pick your targets. Pick your ammunition. Pick your territory. Pick your timing. Aim before you fire.

Tools of the Trade

Recall the earlier discussion in at the end of the previous chapter on communication style. Make sure that your messages fit your audience. They must be emotive if the audience is dominantly Feeler. If the audience is more Thinker oriented, be sure the messages are well written and backed up by solid research, but still easy-to-understand briefing papers and talking points that intellectually connect with the people you are trying to reach. In other words, we are not talking about an academic white paper for the American Political Science Association. The points you want to make must be clear. Your rebuttals of opposition arguments must be complete. Make sure your messengers and your supporters have what they need in order to do what you want them to do, whether that is a weekly update on activities, or drafting speeches, press releases, or graphics. Bring the best tools of the trade to the job.

When legislative proposals are drafted, they must be reinforced by both short and long summaries, talking points, briefs and background papers tailored to your messengers and your audiences.

Communication Timing

Each strategic move should be carefully timed, not only to accommodate media outlets and their deadlines, but also predictable events that may overshadow what you are doing. Communications activities have to be intimately coordinated with the timing of legislative activities.

Major Change in America: Examples from the Past

History offers excellent examples of Members of Congress, supported by good staff, who have been effective leaders of change. Some examples are more profound than others, but the examples to learn from abound: welfare reform (Representative Clay Shaw, then Representative Jim Talent and Senator Rick Santorum), the Base Realignment and Closure (BRAC) initiative (Representative Dick Armey), creation of Medicare and Medicaid (President Lyndon Johnson and Representative Wilbur Mills), and No Child Left Behind (President George W. Bush, Representative John Boehner, and the late Senator Edward Kennedy). Leadership of change can begin and end in Congress, but it takes a committed legislator with a skilled staff and enormous work.

The late Jack Kemp, a former Member from Buffalo, New York, was a tireless advocate of creating economic growth and prosperity by lowering tax rates. His effort became known as supply-side economics. Ronald Reagan adopted Kemp's position and made it his own when he became President. Yet it was Kemp who gave the hundreds of interviews and speeches necessary to build public support for the most dramatic tax cuts in American history, launching over 20 years of mostly unbroken economic growth and prosperity.

Before becoming Speaker, Representative Newt Gingrich woke up slumbering Republicans in the House who had grown accustomed to, and some suggested comfortable with, their condition after more than 40 years in the minority. His guerilla tactics on the House floor and confrontational use of issues and ideas launched the 1994 Republican Revolution that radically changed the balance between the political parties. At times Gingrich annoyed establishment Republicans almost as much as he afflicted the Democratic majority, but there can be no doubt he breathed new life into congressional Republicans and led them out of the political wilderness.

Former Representative Wilbur Mills, a Democrat from Arkansas, was one of the most successful leaders of legislative change, even though he came up short in his personal behavior. He probably owed his success more to intuitive understanding of how the world works than to disciplined study. Mills was largely responsible for the legislative success of Medicare, Medicaid, revenue sharing, significant trade legislation, and President John F. Kennedy's major tax reforms lowering marginal income tax rates and capital gains tax rates.

When once asked why he took two years to bring about adoption of a major change, Mills responded that the first year was devoted to getting the public and his colleagues to recognize the problem (awareness) and the need to act (urgency). Through a variety of public hearings and discussions, Mills got those audiences to look at a range of options that might solve the urgent need for change. After he had reframed their objections to various ideas, other policy makers would coalesce around his preferred solutions, and he would introduce a proposal. Once it was ready for prime time, he would move it through his committee allowing non-fundamental amendments and alterations, and fending off others.

Finally, he would take it to the floor of the House where it was always adopted. Mills only lost one floor battle in his career—the first bill he brought to the floor after becoming chairman of the House Ways and Means Committee—and that was the last time he brought a proposal to the floor without going through the process he later adopted and followed for the rest of his long career.

It must be acknowledged that Mills accomplished this in a much different time. There were no television cameras in committee rooms or the House floor. There were fewer media outlets and less scrutiny by reporters. There were dramatically fewer lobbyists and special interest groups attempting to influence the outcome of legislation, especially Ways and Means bills. Plus, Congress was used to working in a more bipartisan way. That, however, should not detract from the main point: To achieve great change requires a systematic approach that goes beyond Facebook posts and tweets on Twitter. In fact, today's more complex dynamics call for a more skillfully crafted and executed strategy.

Mills was one among many committee chairs, Speakers, majority and minority leaders, and rank-and-file Members, in both houses who had a capacity for achieving change. While many exercised power in different ways, the most successful understood the limitations of power and the need to cajole, compromise, convince, and sometimes confound, in order to overcome resistance and make people comfortable with their desired outcomes. All of them understood that enacting major legislative change requires the hands and minds of many—and in more recent years, particularly good, competent, professional, and in no small measure, humble, staff.

Chapter Twelve Summary

- Leading major legislative change takes time and an unusual combination of leadership, commitment, resources, and an understanding and application of established principles of change.

- Most Members and staff spend their time dealing with traditional congressional challenges, but certain times in history call for leadership of more important changes and we may be living in such a period.

- To be an effective leader of change, Members and staff must do more than simply introduce legislation. They must build a team that develops a vision and define the ultimate solution.

- Members and staff seeking to bring about a major change in policy must objectively identify the targets or beneficiaries of the change.

- Other key players in the dynamic of change include the sponsor or leader, and his or her agents and advocates.

- The process for implementing major change is well developed and practiced in the private sector but the Constitution makes leading public change harder.

- Understanding and defining roles are critical because no one in our divided form of government is an ultimate authority. In the private sector, top leaders can demand compliance, but in a democracy, more people must agree to change.

- Resistance is a natural reaction to all major change proposals. For that reason, creating public awareness of the problem is a critical task. There must be an urgency to change if there is any hope of overcoming resistance.

- Communications become the avenue through which resistance is confronted and objections reframed to conform to higher value attitudes.

- A communications strategy is much more than issuing one or even a multitude of news releases. An effective communications strategy has different stages of implementation. It initially builds awareness and urgency of the proposed change. Later it breaks down resistance. Finally, the communication strategy must advocate the solution.

- Successful change requires the commitment of leaders. Yet, day-to-day pressures of congressional offices undermine long-term commitment. Without sustained commitment and planning, major change is unlikely to succeed no matter how desirable the intended solution.

Playing By the Rules

Few professions are subject to as high an ethical standard or require as much transparency as that of an elected Federal official. They are under constant scrutiny, as they should be. Their every word and action is parsed and dissected by their constituents, the media and their rivals. The mere whiff of scandal can destroy a career, even if allegations later prove false. What taints one official has a tendency to taint the rest as well.

When it comes to trust, the American public tends to rank Members of Congress in close proximity, oddly enough, to journalists and used car salesmen. People have always been willing to believe the worst about their elected officials. American satirists from Will Rogers and Mark Twain to Johnny Carson and Jay Leno have made lucrative careers from the personal and professional woes of politicians.

Such satirists are fostering an American tradition, tied to our traditional disdain of government power, of casting a jaundiced eye towards anyone who would want to have power over us. Thomas Jefferson expressed this sentiment early, writing in a letter, "An honest man can feel no pleasure in the exercise of power over his fellow citizens."

Not all of the disdain has been without cause. In many respects the Congress is a microcosm of the country and its Members reflect behavior evident in the general population.

"It could probably be shown by facts and figures that there is no distinctly native American criminal class except Congress."
—Mark Twain

Members have, from the earliest days of the nation, produced their share of scandal. Some recent scandals have ranged from improper conduct towards pages and staff to tax evasion and bribery. These scandals stain the reputation of the entire institution and it's a wonder their colleagues don't tar and feather them before riding them out of town on a rail. Members, like most people, do not like to sit in judgment of their colleagues, but it is required by the Constitution.

The truth is, however, that the vast majority of Members of Congress have served with distinction and without a hint of impropriety.

But it is the scandals that people remember, and it is the magnification, and sometimes exaggeration, of the scandals by the media that lead to such exasperated expressions as, "Politicians are all corrupt. None of them are any good." The slightest innuendo makes good and decent Members guilty until proven innocent in the eyes of the public. And all too often, even if they're exonerated, the fact that they're not guilty seldom gets reported, leaving a lingering perception of wrongdoing. Politicians are also vulnerable to young, aggressive prosecutors who often rise to higher office on the reputations they build prosecuting public officials.

Public office today is a high-wire act performed before a live audience—but there is no net to catch someone who falls. One slip, one miscalculation can be fatal—and not just to the culprit, but his or her staff as well. It's why both the Senate and House have enacted and amended codes of ethics that govern the activities of Members, their families and their staffs.

Urban Legends and Congress

Public distrust is exemplified and exacerbated by the allegations contained in the statistical flight of fancy that appears below. It has been circulated by email and appeared on Internet posts that are taken as fact by both ends of the political spectrum, from ultra-conservatives to ultra-liberals. It has been living in cyberspace for more than a decade now, assuring anyone who will listen that:

- 29 Members of the Congress have been accused of spousal abuse.

- 7 have been arrested for fraud.

- 19 have been accused of writing bad checks.

- 117 have bankrupted at least two businesses.

- 3 have been arrested for assault.

- 71 have credit reports so bad they can't qualify for a credit card.

- 14 have been arrested on drug-related charges.

- 8 have been arrested for shoplifting.

- 21 are current defendants in lawsuits.

- And in 1998 alone, 84 were stopped for drunk driving but released after they claimed congressional immunity.

This so-called statistical analysis originated with the progressive on-line publication *Capitol Hill Blue* in 1999. It has since been the subject of comedy routines and cited as fact in television courtroom dramas. It has been retooled and passed off as a statistical breakdown of the NBA, as well as the NFL, and even gained international status by being transplanted to Canada, India and the United Kingdom, where these same figures are said to reflect the moral decay of those nations' parliaments.

The Urban Legends Reference Pages, more commonly known as Snopes.com, is a credible website that looks into Internet rumors and folklore of uncertain or questionable origin before providing evidence that either validates or debunks them. It expresses serious reservations when it comes to the numbers cited by *Capitol Hill Blue*.

You're likely to hear staff and even Members complain about the restrictions. Avoid the temptation to join in. It is each Chamber's constitutional obligation to *"determine the rules of its proceedings, punish its Members for disorderly behavior, and, with the concurrence of two thirds, expel a Member"* (Article I, Section 5).

Expulsion is typically reserved for Members who are convicted of crimes, but there are few precedents for other activities that might get you in hot water. The House couldn't even muster a two-thirds vote in favor of punishing South Carolina Representative Preston Smith after he caned Massachusetts Senator Charles Sumner so severely in 1856 that Sumner could not return to the Senate for several years. Beating another Member of the Congress may be considered bad form in some corners of society, but in the contentious days leading to the Civil War, it apparently didn't meet the disorderly behavior standard—in the House of Representatives, anyway. Don't bet your career that it wouldn't be frowned on in this day and age, however. A good deal of other activity is.

Short of expulsion, the Congress has also censured its members, and again, the record has been inconsistent. Representative Lovell H. Rousseau of Kentucky was censured for assaulting a fellow Congressman in 1866, a serious offense, but that same year, Representative John Chanler of New York was censured for proposing a resolution supporting a Presidential veto. Two years later, in 1896, Representative Fernando Wood of New York was censured for describing Reconstruction legislation as a "monstrosity." In 1979, Representative Charles Diggs of Michigan was censured for mail fraud and false statements. The most recent censure, that of Representative Charles Rangel of New York was for tax evasion and improper use of Federal offices. There are no clear lines of distinction in the degree of punishment.

In the years since Smith let actions speak louder than words, Congress has all too often adopted rules and procedures in reaction to scandal and the ensuing public outrage. But in its haste to meet public expectations, it often has issued rules that are confusing or absent of clear guidance for how they should be implemented. It often takes years of precedents to clarify their meaning and their application.

What is the logic that drives ethical standards in Congress?

217

It boils down to this: Members and their staffs are expected to obey the rules to the letter, and they are expected to avoid even the *appearance* of misconduct. The operative word is *appearance*. Most professions demand *adherence*—few judge their membership on the basis of how their actions might appear to others.

Congress does.

The problem is that judgments as to what constitute *appearance* change daily.

The appearance standard is critical. It expands the range of those who make and prosecute accusations from attorneys general, judges and juries to the press, blogs, political opponents and interest groups that make their living questioning the behavior of public officials. Anyone with access to the media or the web can allege wrongdoing and drum an adversary out of office without any charge ever being uttered in a courtroom. And the media can, and do, perform such exorcisms themselves without prompting or precedent.

The Role of the Media

The role of the media in prosecuting ethics violations has to be recognized and weighed carefully by those who must live by Congress' rules.

There are three basic roles the media might play:

- The media can serve as a straightforward purveyor of information regarding allegations of misconduct or a behavior that is simply suspect, without attempting to sway public opinion one way or the other, generate outrage or pass judgment.

- The media can serve as accuser, prosecutor, judge and jury in situations where a public figure has put himself or herself in a compromising position by engaging in behavior that invites criticism. The behavior may be an apparent violation of the rules, or it may be an activity that is not covered by the rules but the media think it ought to be—or it can be neither.

- The media can play the role of echo chamber for someone else's attempt to bring down a politician, beating the drums loudly and often enough that the accuser is able to orchestrate public demand for punitive action. That someone else might be an aggressive prosecutor who leaks damaging information, or any number of interest groups that make their living denigrating public officials, political parties or party organizations.

Sometimes the media perform these roles responsibly, and sometimes they do not. The choices they face are not fun, and those on the receiving end of the judgments they make will invariably credit them to prejudicial reporting, political bias or just plain cynicism.

You make your own judgments based on what facts you have and not on what emotions you feel. And you, like the rest of us, will draw conclusions about whether the press performs well, not so well, or even despicably in these circumstances.

We think there are a few general truths regarding media treatment of "scandal."

First, it is clear that media judgment and rules of engagement have changed dramatically since the administration of President Franklin Roosevelt when neither his infirmities nor his alleged liaisons were reported. The press protected Presidents in those days, as it did with the personal life of John Kennedy, whose use of painkillers and his supposed marital infidelities were not reported.

There was a different standard in place before Vietnam and Watergate and before the range of subjects and circumstances considered "off-limits" began to shrink until today, when it's impossible to think of a topic that's unlikely to be scrutinized.

It is safe to say that there are no general standards governing the activities of those individuals or enterprises that consider themselves media these days. Media cover or fail to cover what they will and each will justify its decisions to suit the circumstances – if it bothers to provide any justification at all. In 2008, for example, the mainstream media reported on an affair involving Senator John McCain– an allegation that was later debunked—but did not report an affair involving Senator John Edwards that it was aware of for a year before he admitted to it publicly.

Whether the subject is earmarks, relationships with lobbyists, personal behavior, the behavior of children and relatives, drinking or dalliances, some media go to great lengths to score points in the game of political "gotcha," making up new rules and drafting new standards of behavior to suit the situation.

Other media are less reckless and more circumspect in assessing how far to go before putting someone's reputation on the chopping block.

Irresponsible reporting isn't new. All of the Founding Fathers felt the sting of the pen—from Washington, who was accused of senility, to Andrew Jackson, who believed that published attacks on his wife led to her untimely death.

Today, however, the instantaneous and near-ubiquitous nature of information reported by competing and ever-changing outlets makes it more critical than ever for media to handle accusations responsibly—and more tempting than ever to do just the opposite.

Your career may depend on your ability to judge accurately how the rules of the institution tell you to behave, how Federal statutes require you to behave, and how critics will interpret your behavior. At the very least you must know enough to ask questions or seek advice when red flags are raised. Your knowledge of the rules will never be deep enough to guarantee safety in every situation. The rules are complex and confusing. They inevitably snare unsuspecting victims. And this always bears repeating: The rules are not the only determinant of right and wrong.

Responding to Allegations

When a Member or an employee stands accused of abusing the rules of the House or the Senate or violating Federal statutes, the accusation must be confronted directly and immediately. The only universally acknowledged rule of thumb is that stalling, covering up, and righteous indignation are losing tactics. Those who have been singled out must consider all options, but the overarching quandary can be reduced to this simple set of truths:

- The most basic principle of American jurisprudence is that we are all innocent until proven guilty.

- The surest reality of political life is that this basic principle doesn't apply. The unwritten but even more universal rule of political prudence holds that appearance of wrongdoing is as damaging as actual guilt.

Passing the Smell Test

The mere appearance of impropriety can be as devastating to a political career as actual malfeasance. It's why staff members sometimes lose jobs and Members lose elections even when they haven't done anything wrong or violated any rules.

Staffers refer to avoiding the appearance of impropriety as "passing the smell test"—an expression that refers to the way moms historically have gauged whether leftovers have been in the refrigerator too long. Regardless of how fresh they looked, they had to pass mom's smell test.

It's the same with the rules—even if activities are legal and allowed under the rules, the only reliable gauge of whether they're safe is to consider how the media, the public and political opponents will view them.

The first step in assessing the situation is to seek counsel you can bank on—legal counsel from an expert in the rules and the law. Get media advice from someone with expertise and experience in crisis management and communication. But get opinions as well from family, friends, counselors and anyone else whose judgment you value and whose discretion you can count on. Get political advice from trusted advisors, particularly individuals who know and understand your district or state. Finally, get the benefit of experience by seeking out those who've been through a similar crisis—and do it quietly.

There are no clear-cut guidelines for what to do once all that advice has been gathered. The decision rests with whoever is under the microscope, their conscience, their political judgment, their integrity and the tenor of the times.

You just have to hope that political expediency does not dictate punishing the alleged offender before guilt or innocence has even been determined—an action referred to in Washington, DC, as "being thrown under the bus."

Understanding the Ethics Process

The number one cause of *accidental* ethics violations is well-meaning staff trying to save money or time. Getting it right is worth the extra time and expense it might take. An example might be a big donor offering to discount rent on a district office space or a Member failing to properly report having hitched a ride on a corporate jet so he or she could attend the funeral of a community leader in the home district and get back to Washington, DC, in time to vote on an important bill. Both of these actions might save tax dollars and enable the Member to successfully perform the duties of office, but both would violate the rules.

Rules and regulations surrounding political campaigns can also blow up in your face, particularly those pertaining to campaign finance.

For a variety of reasons, including media costs, the size of districts and early primaries, campaigns have become sophisticated operations. They are expensive. On average, Representatives must raise $1 million for each two-year election cycle if they hope to remain in office. That's what a campaign costs. And that's just your common, run-of-the-mill campaign. A heavily contested, hard-fought campaign is likely to eat up much, much more.

The law requires a strict separation between campaigns and the duties of elected office. Members may not use the resources of their elected office for campaign purposes. They may not design or conduct fundraising appeals on official time or use official equipment. They can't mail campaign solicitations from congressional offices or use government postage. They absolutely can't ask for donations when lobbyists or others visit their offices.

These rules are—and should be—absolute.

All these prohibitions apply to staff as well.

Recent modifications do, however, permit a Member to designate one staff member as liaison between the campaign and the elected office, but only for specified purposes such as coordinating the Member's schedule. Like all other staff members, however, the liaison is prohibited from performing any campaign duties on government time or using government resources to do them.

Keeping an arm's length between campaigns and the elected offices is vital to the integrity of the Congress, but it does contribute to inefficiency and confusion. After all, in certain respects there is no distinction between serving constituents and running for re-election. The lines are sometimes very gray and narrow. Inconvenient or difficult as the rules sometimes might seem, it is foolish to skirt their edges and risk breaking one of them. The ability to keep track and make sense of the labyrinth that candidates, elected officials and their staffs must negotiate each day is why attorneys who specialize in election law are paid so much money.

Just as the Federal Election Commission, which enforces a variety of complex laws governing campaigns, regulates the actions and activities of candidates for Federal office, each Chamber's Ethics Committee governs the official actions and activities of its Members.

In 2009, the Congress added another layer to the ethics bureaucracy by creating the Office of Congressional Ethics (OCE). The OCE has the authority to examine the actions of House Members and staff and then refer cases to the Ethics Committee, indicating whether the OCE thought the cases should be dismissed or pursued. The OCE does not, however, recommend to the House that it take disciplinary action against Members and staff, as the Constitution permits only the House itself to do this.

The OCE is supposed to be strictly impartial. The board has six members, with two alternates. Both the Speaker of the House and the House minority leader are allowed to designate three board members and one alternate each. The Speaker must approve of the minority leader's choice and vice versa. Current Members of Congress and staff may not be on the board, nor can they for a year after they leave the service of the House. Nor may lobbyists serve. Former lobbyists may, but they must have left that profession for at least a year before being appointed. Additionally, the board members are limited in the types of activities—both political and otherwise—that they can engage in.

The House Ethics Committee has frequently clashed with the OCE for not operating according to established rules and for going beyond the limits set for it. In June 2010, The New York Times reported that some Members initiated legislation to reform the OCE. Representative Martha Fudge, a Congresswoman leading the initiative, implied that the board was unfair in its treatment of Members, saying, "OCE is currently the accuser, judge and jury."

The Ins and Outs of the Ethics Rules

Take the time to learn the rules and never act without certainty—if you don't know whether the action might be a violation, check it out with the House Committee on Ethics or the Senate Select Committee on Ethics. Both committees offer advice by phone and provide staff attorneys with whom you can confidentially discuss ethics questions. Take advantage of the one that serves the Chamber for which you work.

Ethical behavior cannot be legislated. Character cannot be fabricated. Scoundrels will break the rules. What follows isn't written with them in mind. This is written to help prevent good and decent public servants from making innocent and dumb mistakes. It is not written as legal advice, nor is it an excuse to avoid reading your Chamber's rules and ethics manual or asking questions.

Unless specifically stated, these rules apply to both Members and staff. In fact, the actions of the staff will be blamed on their boss, even if he or she had no knowledge of the staffer's violation.

In 2010 the House Ethics Committee stated: "Members are responsible for the knowledge and acts acquired or committed by their staff within the course and scope of their employment." While this does not appear in the Rules of the House, it is considered a precedent, established through the Ethics Committee's own previous investigations, that Members are responsible for actions of the staff even if they did not know their staffers were violating House rules.

Gifts

The rules prohibit staff and Members from accepting anything of value from a lobbyist or an entity that employs one. This is an important point. The manager of a plant in your district, for example, cannot take you to lunch if the company he or she works for employs a lobbyist.

If you are not sure whether a *venti latte* is going to get you in trouble, pay for it yourself or ask whether your acquaintance's company has a lobbyist on the payroll.

The same applies to tickets to sporting events and fancy pens—a former chief of staff was actually indicted for fraud against the House of Representatives after taking tickets to a Wiggles concert for his toddlers from a Jack Abramoff associate.

"Just say no" is a good rule of thumb even in situations that don't involve drugs.

A seemingly harmless violation can land you in hot water.

You can accept a gift or meal with a value under $50 as long as it's from someone who is not a lobbyist or a foreign representative. You can even accept two of them but not at the same time—and no more than two in a given year since there is an annual limit of $100.

You also may receive gifts from relatives, even if the relative is a lobbyist, but he or she has to be a relative before the gift is given. It used to be that a potential groom only needed the permission of a bride's father to give his love an engagement ring. Not anymore—at least not if he's a lobbyist and she works for Congress. The Ethics Committee must grant written permission for any gift from a lobbyist, even one you're going to marry. (No word on whether the committee will offer marriage counseling in the future.)

There are no limits on gifts from Federal, state and local governments, including sporting events at public universities. Informational materials such as books and DVDs, home-state products of "nominal" value and commemorative items such as inscribed plaques are also permitted.

It is always a violation, however, to ask or solicit a gift.

Remember, there's no such thing as a harmless violation.

Attending Events

You may go to a reception that offers food and refreshments of nominal value—milk and cookies, for example—but not if the food constitutes part of a meal.

As a staffer or a Member, you may attend an event where you are invited by the sponsor, but not if a lobbyist or someone other than the sponsor buys the ticket, and only if the event is deemed to be *widely attended*—which is an extremely important consideration. A *widely attended* event must have at least 25 non-Hill guests or participants and must either be open to the public or to individuals representing a range of characteristics and must be relevant to your official duties.

Sounds pretty vague, doesn't it?

Plan on spending a good deal of time conferring with the Ethics Committee to confirm that events you'd like to attend qualify.

If an event does qualify, you are permitted to accept transportation and a meal as long as the same meal is offered to everyone else who's there.

You may not accept a gift bag or souvenir.

You may attend a charity event if you are invited by the charity. A lobbyist cannot buy you a ticket to the Federated Cancer Fighter's ball, for example, but the FCF could.

Your spouse or dependent child may join you at such an event, but you must pay for a ticket for any other guest, including a sibling, parent or date.

If it is a campaign event, the Federal Election Commission also has a number of rules over and above what your Chamber might have. Always check with the Ethics Committee, and never make assumptions.

Confusing?

We don't make the rules; we just explain them.

Will Rogers on Government:

"I don't make jokes. I just watch the government and report the facts."

"Most people and actors appearing on the stage have some writers to write their material – but I don't do that. Congress is good enough for me. They have been writing my material for years and I am not ashamed of the material I have had. I am going to stick to them."

"All I know is just what I read in the *Congressional Record*. They have had some awful funny articles in there lately. As our government deteriorates, our humor increases."

Privately Sponsored Travel

Travel for which someone else foots the bill may be permitted under very strict circumstances. A trip sponsor must complete a multi-page certification form. The staff member who will be making the trip must then submit this form, along with a separate request for permission, to the Ethics Committee. Staff members also must have advance authorization from their boss.

At the conclusion of the trip, the traveler must file a disclosure form with details on exactly how much was spent on transportation, lodging and food. These disclosure reports become public record.

A U.S. college or university may sponsor trips up to four days domestically or seven days internationally, as can any group or other body that does not employ a lobbyist or foreign representative or agent. An organization that does employ a lobbyist can sponsor a one-day trip as long as the lobbyist is not involved in planning and does not travel with the participant on any leg of the event.

If all of these qualifications are met, the Member or staffer may accept coach- or business-class accommodations and meals that are reasonably priced—as defined by the Ethics Committee on a case-by-case basis—and served to everyone else making the trip.

The exceptions to these travel rules include official overseas travel by CODELs (congressional delegations), trips sponsored by state or local governments, travel paid for by foreign governments, and campaign travel, as long as the campaign committee reports the trip to the FEC as a campaign expense.

Campaign travel may not be on official time.

Campaign Work

Staff members may perform campaign work—paid or voluntary—on their own time but not on the congressional clock and only of their own volition. It is a felony for an office to compel an employee to perform campaign duties. In 2012, the House Ethics Committee formally reprimanded and fined Representative Laura Richardson for improperly pressuring her staff to work on her campaign and then trying to force them to lie about it to the Ethics Committee.

Campaign activities are prohibited in any congressional office—including district and state offices. Solicitation and acceptance of campaign contributions also are prohibited. If a contribution is inadvertently sent to the congressional office, it must be forwarded at the campaign's expense within seven days.

You may not make a campaign contribution to your boss—even if you want to and even if you contributed before you were employed on the Hill. With the exception of travel, an employee may not expend personal funds to cover a campaign expense even if it would be reimbursed. And if you aren't reimbursed the full amount of campaign travel, the difference will be considered an illegal campaign contribution.

Constituent Casework

On behalf of a constituent, you are permitted to inquire of Federal agencies about the status of inquiries or applications. You also may request full and prompt consideration.

You may not, however, ask an agency to make an exception to the law or the agency's regulations. You cannot threaten or make any promise to an agency official. You may not conduct communication with any official with decision-making authority in a legal or administrative proceeding. You may not contact an agency on a matter where you or your boss has a personal financial interest. Nor may you show preferential treatment to the Member's supporters, contributors or friends in casework matters. By the same token, however, you are not required to recuse yourselves from providing such assistance to supporters, contributors or friends.

What is demanded of them is simply that they treat everyone equally.

Offices are severely limited in the types of recommendations they can make for civil service positions. Study the rules carefully before making any recommendations.

Official Events

An office may not use outside resources to conduct official business. This means a Member may not jointly sponsor any kind of event with a private group or anyone else outside of government, for that matter. And you are not allowed to accept cash or in-kind support for an official event or meeting.

227

Allowances for the expenditure of campaign money in support of official events are limited—for example, food and beverage costs, room rental, printed materials and travel expenses for guest speakers are acceptable while most others are not. Nor can campaign funds be used to advertise an official event. Check with the Ethics Committee before using campaign funds for anything other than obvious campaign expenses.

The rules also limit how a Member's name can be used in conjunction with a private event. A Member can be listed as an honorary co-host, for example, but only if the invitation clearly identifies the sponsor of the event. Use of official letterhead or the official seal by an outside group is, however, prohibited. The same is true of the use of official resources, including the office's press release capability, its website or franking privileges, to promote an event sponsored by a private enterprise, no matter how local or how emotionally compelling the cause may be. A Member may send a Dear Colleague letter about a private group's event after the group has issued an invitation to those same colleagues, but only if the event is taking place in a House or Senate room.

Outside Employment and Financial Disclosure

Staff members may work or volunteer for an outside group or other entity—including charities and non-profits—but such activities are subject to strict guidelines. They cannot conflict with official duties. They cannot involve House or Senate resources, and no work on their behalf may be performed in congressional offices or while on the congressional clock. In addition, any staffer taking part in such activities must have his or her boss's approval to do so.

If you are considered senior staff—earning in the neighborhood of two-thirds the pay of a Member—the restrictions increase in number. How much you can earn moonlighting is limited to 15 percent of the Member's salary. Campaign pay is considered outside income and can be accepted for work done in your spare time, but there are strictly enforced limits.

Senior staff also are prohibited from working in or having an on-going affiliation with any profession that bears a fiduciary responsibility, including the law, real estate, insurance and financial planning. An outside firm cannot use your name and you cannot be a paid officer or board member of any such organization.

In addition, you are required to have advance written approval from the Ethics Committee before accepting any paid teaching position. There are strict limitations on outside royalty income, as well. No Member or senior staff may receive an honorarium—non-senior staff can but not for anything related to their official duties or if the source of the honorarium has interests before the Congress that the employee might in any way influence.

In other words, a non-senior staff member may be allowed to write a book on butterfly collecting—but only after the issue has been thoroughly vetted.

If you are a Member or senior-level staffer, you must file an annual financial disclosure report. Senior-level employees must also file a disclosure within 30 days of joining a staff and 30 days after leaving one. The report lists income, assets, liabilities, property and security transactions, certain types of gifts, travel expenses, outside positions and employment agreements. Financial information regarding spouses and children also must be disclosed.

In offices where no one earns enough to qualify as senior staff, the Member designates a staffer to file such a report. Usually it is the chief of staff, but it can be anybody who was on staff as of December 31 of the preceding year.

The Justice Department is authorized to take action on willfully erroneous information, so have your report reviewed by Ethics Committee staff prior to submitting it to make sure you got everything right.

There are fines for late filings.

There are also a number of post-employment restrictions for senior-level employees (those who earn 67 percent of a Member's salary), but considerably more for those who earn very senior staff salaries (75 percent of what the boss makes). Those leaving very senior staff positions in the House are prohibited from trying to influence formal activities in their former office for a full year. If they are committee staff, they are prohibited from lobbying their committee or its Members for a year, and leadership staff may not lobby leadership of either party in the House for a similar period of time. Very senior Senate employees can't lobby anyone in the Senate—Members or staff—for a year as well.

229

Very senior staff in both Chambers must disclose in writing any negotiation with a prospective employer within three days and recuse themselves from any issue where there might be a conflict of interest with a prospective employer.

Conflict of Interest

Common sense is all it takes to keep you from violating the host of conflict of interest rules. First and foremost among them is the prohibition against using your official position or any confidential information for personal gain. Any violation of the confidential information clause is the legislative equivalent of insider trading.

However, in a study of financial disclosure forms from 2008 and 2009, the *Wall Street Journal* concluded that at least 72 staffers traded shares of companies while they were employed by Members whose positions could have allowed the staffers special knowledge about matters that would affect the business' performances. As mentioned before, just because the media makes an accusation does not mean the staffers are guilty of anything.

Each Congress, however, passes numerous laws that regulate various aspects of the business world, and these laws have a significant impact upon the performance of these companies. It certainly would be quite possible for Members and their staffs to take advantage of this information in the stock market before the general public knows how legislation and other governmental activities will affect the business world. In the business world this is treated very seriously—just ask Martha Stewart.

In response to this, Congress passed the Stop Trading on Congressional Knowledge Act ("STOCK" Act) in 2012, which makes it a felony for Members or staff to profit from inside information they obtain through the course of performing their duties.

Nepotism is addressed in the rules as well. A Member is prohibited from hiring family members in his or her congressional office and cannot in their official capacity do any special favors for family.

And That's Not All

This is but a snapshot of the ethics rules that will guide your activities and those of your bosses in the Congress—and an idea of how serious and all encompassing they are. The manuals in which they are contained run to several hundred pages, and the Ethics Committees regularly add updates and guidance called "pink sheets" because of the color paper they are printed on. Mastering all the rules will take time. But even when you're confident you know the rules, it's still a good idea to confer with the umpire before setting foot on the playing field.

This is serious business. The penalties for making a mistake can be harsh. The whole experience can make you second-guess the attraction of public service. We hope not. We hope instead that by being aware of the rules and making a commitment to ethical behavior, that you might become the type of high-quality public servant that helps Congress restore its damaged reputation.

Chapter Thirteen Summary

- Few professions are subject to as high an ethical standard or as much transparency as elected Federal officials.

- The mere whiff of scandal can destroy a career, even if allegations later prove false. And what taints one official has a tendency to taint the rest as well.

- The truth is that the vast majority of Members of Congress have served with distinction and without any hint of impropriety.

- The Senate and House have codes of ethics that govern the activities of Members, their families and their staffs.

- Not only are Members and their staffs expected to obey rules to the letter, they are expected to avoid even the *appearance* of misconduct.

- The most basic principle of American jurisprudence is that we are all innocent until proven guilty. The surest reality of political life is that this basic principle doesn't apply.

- The number one cause of *accidental* ethics violations is well-meaning staff trying to save money or time.

- The law requires a separation between campaigns and the duties of elected office.

- The role of the media in the prosecution of ethics rules has to be recognized and weighed carefully by those who must live by them. There are three basic roles the media might play: a straightforward purveyor of information; litigator (accuser, prosecutor, judge and jury); or an echo chamber for someone else attempting to bring down a politician. Sometimes the media performs these roles responsibly and sometimes they do not.

- Take the time to learn the rules and never act without certainty—if you don't know whether an action might be a violation, check it out with the House Committee on Ethics or the Senate Select Committee on Ethics. Both committees offer advice by phone and provide staff attorneys with whom you can confidentially discuss ethics questions.

- Ethical behavior cannot be legislated. Character cannot be fabricated. Scoundrels will break the rules. This chapter is written to help prevent good and decent public servants from making innocent and dumb mistakes.

- The penalties for making a mistake can be harsh. We hope that by being aware of the rules and making a commitment to ethical behavior, that you might become the type of high-quality public servant that helps Congress restore its damaged reputation.

There are few terms in politics more derogatory than ... (Dare we say it aloud?) ... special interests. Special interests have probably played a role in every incident of influence peddling ever recorded. Even the words them-selves—*special* and *interests*—sound undemocratic.

Who are these evil interests?

And what makes them so special?

In point of fact, special interests are not evil—nor even undemocratic. Quite the contrary. We are all special interests. If you own a car or a refrigerator, travel on an airline, watch television, go to church, get sick, eat, fish, hunt, invest in a mutual fund or have a hard time breathing, you are a special interest, and there are associations and organizations representing you at both the state and the national level.

Few people realize, for instance, that AARP, one of the largest asso-ciations representing seniors, tops *Fortune* magazine's list of the most influential special interests in Washington, DC.

Boy Scouts of America is a special interest. So are barbers, bakers, basketball players, bird lovers, beauticians, bingo players, buglers, bureau-crats, bricklayers, bar owners, caterers, churchgoers, circus performers, car dealers, cartoonists, cab drivers, cooks, can manufacturers, cable operators, chaplains—and that doesn't even get us through the Cs. They are all represented in Washington and they all employ lobbyists. The fact is that a nearly $4-trillion government, with thousands of programs and millions of rules and regulations, affects just about everyone. At one time or another, we all need relief or assistance from the Federal Government or one of more than 87,000 state and local government agencies with over 513,000 elected officials all trying to be helpful, including counties, regional transportation authorities, cities, towns, townships, sanitary districts, school districts, water districts and the list goes on.

Generally speaking, *special interests* do not refer to concerns so much as to the groups representing them—in fact, the phrase typically is shorthand for *special interest groups.* They're also called single interest, public interest, advocacy, lobbying and even pressure groups. Their primary reason for being is to influence political decisions and public policy.

Special interest groups are a necessary component in a pluralist democratic republic. They provide lawmakers and executive agencies with valuable information that can help shape legislation and regulations. They also provide information on the political, economic, social and environmental impact that legislation or policies are likely to have. And they provide a barometer for how activities in the Congress are likely to affect the next election. And for each special interest advocating one position, there are other special interests advocating the opposite or another opinion, so, in terms of interest they tend to balance out each other.

There are four kinds of special interest groups:

Corporate: Thousands of companies and corporations of all varieties maintain a presence in the capital city, whether in the form of a Washington office with full-time employees or through a contractual relationship with one or more law firms, lobbying firms or trade associations. Private companies ranging from global conglomerates like General Electric to technology companies like Apple, Google and Facebook find a presence in Washington necessary to protect their interests or advance public policies that enhance their business opportunities and, in the process, make life better for their stockholders, their customers and their employees. Most present their case before the legislative and executive branches, regulatory agencies and quasi-governmental agencies.

While print and broadcast journalists often rail against special interests, the companies for which they work—*The Washington Post,* the *Wall Street Journal,* the *Chicago Tribune,* ABC, NBC, CBS, CNN and Fox—are represented by Washington lobbyists and trade associations advocating on their behalf over everything from content piracy to taxes and postal rates to protection of sources, and any issues that can have an impact on their ability to hire employees, produce a product and make a profit.

Associations and Organizations: These fall into two categories: Some, such as the National Association of Manufacturers, the Chamber of Commerce, the American Medical Association, the National Federation of Independent Businesses, and the Newspaper Publisher's Association, represent professions, occupations, industries, and even labor unions. Others, such as Common Cause, Citizens for a Responsive Politics, the American Heart Association and the National Rifle Association represent causes or issues and are self-perpetuating movements that rely on the loyalty and commitment of individual donors to fund their efforts. Theirs are among the literally thousands of lobbying efforts aimed at the same people and the same governmental agencies that corporations try to influence.

Associations represent the shared interests of their members—individuals and organizations that contribute financially to them, whether their contributions are in the form of union dues, annual membership fees or ad hoc contributions.

In most cases, associations do not exist for the sole purpose of lobbying. For many, lobbying isn't even their primary function. The Food Marketing Institute, for example, may lobby at the Federal, state and local levels, but its primary concerns are food packaging and food safety research, membership education programs, public opinion research and hosting conventions and conferences where members can exchange information.

Associations such as the National Federation of Independent Businesses and the National Association of Realtors provide a means for local mom and pop stores and one-person contractors to band together and have a voice equal to or greater than big corporations.

Some special interests attempt to wrap themselves in the cloak of altruism by contending that they're actually *public interest groups.* It's a slick branding strategy aimed at convincing outsiders that their objectives are more honorable—and by extension that the objectives of anyone who disagrees or has a commercial interest in the same issues are not. The motives of an organization whose mission is campaign finance reform, for example, are no purer than those of the Association of Can Manufacturers. They both advocate their own interests. People who run both organizations respond to the demands of those who pay their salaries.

The so-called public interest groups are particularly effective at influencing public opinion through the media. They have media access that few others do, making up for what they may lack in financial resources.

Single-Issue Organizations: These are similar to not-for-profit interests in terms of variables such as membership, financial support and tax status. They distinguish themselves by representing just one issue or set of related issues. While a labor union may have positions on a range of topics, including trade, minimum wage, health care and workplace conditions, the single-issue organization focuses all its energy on one, like abortion or gun ownership, a specific form of tax-reform or saving the whales. Single-issue organizations are less permanent. In theory, when their issue has been resolved to the satisfaction of the organization's backers, they often disband, or sometimes gravitate to another similar issue. One example of this phenomenon is the March of Dimes, which has been so successful in helping to wipe out polio—its original purpose—that it has been able to shift focus to preventing premature birth, birth defects, and infant mortality, and conducting maternal education programs promoting good health practices and care for unborn children and their pregnant mothers.

The reality is that few single-issue organizations ever disband. The issues that motivate them seldom get resolved to anyone's complete satisfaction.

Many organizations and associations have full-time employees representing their interests in the state capitals and Washington, DC, and even some foreign countries, but they also hire additional professional advocates or lobbyists to represent them. These professional advocates might be associated with law firms, with public affairs firms that specialize in both government and public relations, with large and small lobbying firms—or simply independent contractors.

Lobbying Companies, Multiple Advocacy or Consultant Organizations: There are over 2000 firms in Washington DC that lobby on behalf of their clients. These advocates are hired for a variety of reasons: The firm may have a particular expertise or an area of specialty—many employ former Members of Congress and committee staff with unique knowledge about pertinent issues and programs—or the client may find that hiring the lobbying firm is less expensive and faster to get started on its behalf than creating an in-house staff.

Some professional advocates have long-term contracts. In other cases, relationships are brief and involve a single, clearly defined task. If, for example, hedge-fund operators find their livelihood suddenly threatened by negative publicity that threatens punitive action in Congress, they may need the help of outside pros to improve their image and fight legislation that could have a negative impact on their livelihood.

Coalitions: Corporations, associations, foundations and single-interest lobbies will occasionally form coalitions to advocate an issue or action that is in their common interest. Coalitions are usually temporarily financed and structured to meet a specific mission or common goal. Normally a coalition will hire independent staff and solicit what might be referred to as *dues* even though contributions are actually based on what each member can afford or is willing to devote to the effort. An executive director who answers to a board of directors or board of advisors, usually made up of the biggest contributors, generally manages them. Coalitions sometimes operate out of the office of a consultant, lobbying firm, public relations firm or law firm that is hired to handle the campaign.

Governments: The world of special interests also is populated by state governments, public and private colleges and universities, regional governing authorities, cities, counties, townships, associations of governors and attorneys general and other bodies of elected officials or units of government. Governments also employ lobbyists and hire outside public affairs specialists. In addition, foreign governments have representation in Washington– most of which also depend on paid lobbyists to represent their interests.

By most estimates, there are from 15,000 to 20,000 lobbyists in Washington, DC, supported by staffs that take the advocacy community to 40,000 employees. There are more than 2,000 corporations, more than 8,000 non-profit and trade associations and thousands of government or quasi-governmental agencies with Washington representation.

All of these special interests realize that direct pressure may not be and often is not enough to solve their problems. If nothing else, there is strength in numbers and power in public opinion. That's why many, particularly when in trouble, will invest so much time, energy and money in indirect advocacy—grassroots or grasstops mobilization (or both), research, and public relations. All three forms of advocacy have evolved in recent years into highly sophisticated means of influencing public opinion and public policy.

An effective grassroots operation can educate thousands of people in a very short time and motivate them to write, email, tweet, or skype

---

Reasons Governments Lobby

- **Financial:** Governments often seek Federal grants to support services and infrastructure.

- **Corporate:** A government might participate in a corporate lobbying effort that affects the community's major employers.

- **Not-for-profit:** It might be associated with a not-for-profit such as one working to increase Federal aid for homeless programs.

- **Single-issue:** It might be involved in an effort to modify water-purity standards.

- **Coalition:** It might be part of an effort involving businesses and governmental bodies hoping to persuade the Congress to allocate funds for a comprehensive transportation program.

their Representatives and Senators; write letters to the editor of the local newspaper; participate in radio call-in shows; blog; show up at town hall meetings; dial into tele-town hall conference calls; and engage in other activities designed to influence the actions of their elected representatives and staffs.

The term grasstops describes campaigns that aim to educate and motivate public officials, opinion leaders and prominent local citizens. The goal is to motivate these individuals to call and put pressure on Congress to take a particular action, and begin word-of-mouth advocacy that gets those in their circle of influence involved in the campaign.

Intensive public relations campaigns can include paid and unpaid advertising, the creation of websites, pitches to journalists to encourage coverage of pertinent issues and development of a positive brand for an individual, an organization or an issue. In support of these initiatives, opinion polling and survey research provide data and themes for their messages.

An individual needing help with a problem usually can get it from an elected official. But the efforts of individuals rarely change laws or keep laws from being enacted. That takes many individuals working together. It takes a clearly defined strategy and a coordinated lobbying effort. No elected official has the time or the staff or the mental capacity to learn, retain and understand all that influences the lives of constituents, let alone all that influences the country as a whole.

The Founding Fathers may not have envisioned the level of sophistication that advocacy efforts have attained, but they codified the practice in the First Amendment of the Bill of Rights, which guarantees the right to petition government for redress of grievances. The Founders didn't go into a lot of detail about how such redress could be sought, but they made it clear that it was a right they wanted protected.

In the days before the volume became unmanageable, citizens were encouraged to actually submit written petitions directly to the Congress, where the House set aside time to address them. One of the first petition drives was led by Benjamin Franklin and advocated the abolition of slavery. It was the first real grassroots/grasstops lobbying effort.

Like every avenue to influence, the role of special interests is subject to abuse. Scandals have tainted special interests since the founding of the nation.

Take the dispute between Alexander Hamilton and James Madison that led to the formation of the Federalist and Republican parties. The Continental Congress was so poor throughout the Revolutionary War that it paid General George Washington's Continental Army with bonds, which were essentially IOUs. Believing the government would never redeem the bonds, most soldiers sold them to speculators at a fraction of their face value. These speculators held onto the bonds until 1787, when they began lobbying the new Federal Government for payment in full. Hamilton favored paying the face value to whoever held the bonds but Madison objected. Virginia had gone into debt redeeming bonds that had been paid out to soldiers from that state. Veterans deserved to be repaid, he argued, and should receive half the value of any bonds that were redeemed. Hamilton won out when, at a private dinner arranged by Thomas Jefferson, Madison dropped his demands in exchange for a commitment on the part of the Federal Government to pay off Virginia's debt and build the new capital on the Potomac River.

It was lobbying on behalf of multiple interests that resolved the issue and led to the designation of Washington, DC, as the capital.

The first efforts to regulate lobbying at the Federal level didn't occur until 1876 when a resolution approved by the House required lobbyists to register with the Clerk of the House.

The excesses of monopolists and the economic and societal impact of the Industrial Revolution led to exposés by muckrakers in the last decades of the 19th century—and those, in turn, led to a number of reforms with teeth and new regulatory agencies to give them bite. With each subsequent scandal in the interim—from Teapot Dome to Abscam to Jack Abramoff—have come calls for greater regulation.

In response to the Jack Abramoff scandal, in which several Members and staff were implicated in alleged influence peddling, Congress placed new restrictions on the activities of lobbyists. These dramatically increased disclosure requirements and the paperwork they must maintain and file, imposed harsh criminal sentences and fines for violations of the rules, and imposed new restrictions on Members and staff in their interaction with lobbyists.

The Congress considered but rejected provisions that would have restricted Members' ability to solicit political contributions from lobbyists.

What was enacted is a confusing set of restrictions that, on the one hand, prohibits a lobbyist from buying a Member lunch so they can discuss the merits of a legislative issue, but allows him to buy that same Member the same lunch if he brings a campaign contribution, not exceeding the $2,500 limit, of course.

Advice for Staff

A congressional staff member should take full advantage of the expertise and resources special interests have to offer—but do so with a clear understanding of the petitioner's intent and motivation and the restrictions limiting your interaction. Here are some simple rules to help guide you:

- Know who is financing, managing and controlling any special interest you encounter, particularly coalitions with noble-sounding monikers. A lobbyist may be paid by a corporation that is a wholly owned subsidiary of a larger one or a holding company that hopes to conceal its interest in the issue at hand. By the same token, a coalition calling itself the Energy Efficiency Organization may seem like an all-American enterprise if you neglect to take into consideration the fact that energy isn't a purely American concern—and that a coalition could have foreign interests. Know with whom you are doing business.

- Find out if the special interest or coalition is providing only its side of the issue or is willing to acknowledge contrary viewpoints and identify organizations that are advocating on behalf of the opposition.

- Don't reach a conclusion without examining all sides of an issue. If you hear from one side, make it a point to listen to the other side as well.

- Follow up: Ask questions, demand answers and additional information or verification of the information that has been presented.

- Maintain an arm's length relationship with special interests and coalitions—and make sure your activities are always within the rules of the House or Senate and comply with Federal statutes. But don't resist developing professional relationships with lobbyists through periodic contact. The system is, after all, still based on mutual trust and respect.

- Be cognizant of the appearances of impropriety that accompany association with special interest groups and campaign contributions from their respective members or political action committees. While many of the insinuations surrounding campaign contributions and their influence are bogus, some are valid and will stick to you.

- Don't be afraid to use trusted representatives of special interests as information resources when dealing with issues in which they have an expertise.

- Never make a commitment without a clear understanding of precisely what it is you're committing to. Lobbyists look at their meetings with you—whether in person, by email or by phone—as an action-producing mechanism. They want something to come of the contact. There's nothing wrong with taking action, but make sure you are comfortable taking the action you're being pressed to take.

- Be sure, as well, to understand the special interest's relationship to your interests—your district or your boss's committee assignments. Sometimes that connection can be professional and important to your Congressman or committee.

- Before you sit down with representatives of a special interest, understand not only the issues they're interested in, but also their relevance to your sphere of influence. Going into a meeting cold is disrespectful and unproductive. If you don't have time to prepare, let the meeting participants know so they can bring you up to speed, at least from their perspective.

Friendly Persuasion

Imagine that it's your first week on the job. Your boss took his oath of office yesterday and you're still trying to figure out which restroom you should be using. Out of the blue, the receptionist tells you a college buddy you haven't seen in years has stopped by to welcome you to DC.

You invite him in and after briefing one another on what's been going on in your lives since the last time you shared a pitcher of beer, he tells you he's a lobbyist for XYZ Corporation.

More out of politeness than interest, you ask what sort of issues he focuses on.

"Net neutrality," he replies.

"Never heard of it," you say with a laugh.

"It's pretty significant," he says and manages not to sound critical of your ignorance.

With little prodding, he does what a good lobbyist should not do: He provides you with a one-sided, subjective explanation claiming that existing regulations severely limit the Internet's usefulness, threaten to produce unfortunate precedents that will severely limit the nation's competitive telecommunications edge, discourage investment, deny providers the ability to offer services that distinguish them from one another and give other communication providers an unfair advantage.

Sounds downright un-American.

Exactly the kind of issue your boss is interested in.

You're leaning toward your friend's point of view when you stop yourself. Instead of committing to signing a letter or attending another meeting, you promise to look into the issue.

Wise decision.

When you do look into net neutrality, you'll discover it is among the most contentious issues facing the Congress. Like Churchill's description of Russia, it "is a riddle, wrapped in a mystery, inside an enigma...." Those opposing any change in the rules include content providers. They argue that allowing DSL (digital subscriber line) providers to charge for access would be tantamount to providing them with near-monopolistic authority over the Internet. By duplicating the content of providers and making it available free to their customers while charging the providers for delivering it, DSLs would be in a position to drive the competition out of the market, opponents say. And in the process, other opponents such as software manufacturers add that charges for DSL access would discourage innovation and development.

As one lawmaker said in sidestepping the controversy: "A lot of us believe that we don't have a problem, and we're not going to overly regulate a product that might stifle the entrepreneurship and the progress we want to make in the future."

What lesson do we learn from all this?

Do your homework, welcome advice but make your own judgment and understand that most issues have more sides than a cafeteria and all are so complex they are seldom fully understood by constituents or the media.

Chapter Fourteen Summary

- We all have special interests, and they are being represented on our behalf in the halls of Congress.

- The Founding Fathers may not have envisioned the level of sophistication that advocacy efforts have attained, but they codified the practice in the First Amendment of the Bill of Rights, which guarantees the right to petition government for redress of grievances.

- A nearly $4 trillion government, with thousands of programs and millions of rules and regulations, affects just about everyone. At one time or another, we all need relief or assistance from the Federal Government.

- Special interest groups are a necessary component in a pluralist democratic republic.

- There are four kinds of special interest groups: corporate, associations and organizations, single-issue organizations, and lobbying companies and consultants.

- Corporations, associations, foundations and single-interest lobbies will occasionally form coalitions to advocate an issue or action that is in their common interest. Coalitions are usually temporarily financed and structured to meet a specific mission or common goal.

- Public and private colleges and universities and state, local and foreign governments also populate the world of special interests.

- An effective grassroots operation can educate thousands of people in a very short time and motivate them to act.

- Intensive public relations campaigns can include paid and unpaid advertising, the creation of websites, and pitches to journalists to encourage coverage of pertinent issues and development of a positive brand for an individual, an organization or an issue.

- The first efforts to regulate lobbying at the Federal level didn't occur until 1876. With each subsequent scandal—from Teapot Dome to Abscam to Jack Abramoff—have come calls for greater regulation.

- Staff should know who is financing, managing and controlling any special interest they encounter, particularly coalitions with noble-sounding monikers.

- Do your homework and welcome advice, but make your own judgment.

Can't We All Just Get Along?

Throughout this book we have been referring to effects of political polarization on Congress. As a result, the authors believe the subject is worthy of greater discussion. Part of the modern culture of the Congress is the political polarization of the institution and, in a broader sense, the national body politic.

By partisan polarization we mean the increasing division between our political parties, particularly as those divisions are expressed in the legislatures of our nation. We're not against partisanship. Political parties are how we organize ourselves to elect those who govern us. The political parties offer us distinctions in the ideas and values that will be the basis for decisions in government. Excessive partisanship that degenerates into negativity, mean-spiritedness, distortions of truth, personal attacks and other forms of behavior based on the idea that the end justifies any means defeats the purpose of a party. The American people are becoming increasing intolerant of uncivil behavior and the extent to which it inhibits our ability to govern ourselves. The word "incivility" is derived from the Latin *incivilis*, meaning "not of a citizen," so the meaning is apropos in politics today. Incivility reflects the darker side of citizenship and threatens the fabric of our system of politics and government.

And let's be clear about another thing. Civility does not necessarily mean ideological moderation. Members of Congress, the media and policy advocates should be able to discuss profound differences with respect and in a way that encourages ideas to be fully discussed. It reflects the understanding that the right to express political viewpoints is only safe as long as your opponent's right to express their political viewpoints is protected.

The French writer Voltaire may have said, "I disapprove of what you say, but I will defend to the death your right to say it," but that statement neatly sums up the old traditional American ideal of tolerance and freedom of political speech.

Throughout most of American history, the Congress and our political system have reflected varying degrees of polarization and incivility.

Incivility even dates back to America's founding. Alexander Hamilton and Thomas Jefferson fought bitterly over the shape and form of the new federal government; their feuds spread among their supporters and detractors in the Congress and in the press of the day, a good share of which they controlled. Hamilton was also the victim of the ultimate act of incivility—he was shot by political rival Aaron Burr.

Incivility erupted periodically around scandals, one involving an accusation of spying and international intrigue with the French, another surrounding ethical transgressions related to our transition to a national currency, and more involving allegations of illicit sexual relationships. Incivility dominated some issues, including the impassioned disagreements over trade, banking, taxes, state nullification of federal laws and, of course, slavery. Ugly words were often exchanged and walkouts occurred. Incivility in the 19th century precipitated duels and a near-fatal beating on the Senate floor.

Despite its early contentions and rivalries, Congress has experienced periods in which bipartisan cooperation and civil behavior were more the norm than the exception. The period between World War II and the Kennedy Administration was a period of civil discourse and cooperative government. Yet even as society became more polarized in the 1960s, Members of Congress could disagree on policy but do so with respect and, indeed, in friendship. The friendship of Democrat Sam Rayburn and Republican Speaker Joseph Martin, as well as Democrat Tip O'Neill and Republican Bob Michel were examples of how Members could fight for their beliefs while respecting their colleagues. A high degree of civility was critical to the enactment of the Reagan agenda in a divided Congress during his first term.

Regrettably, Members of Congress and the President do not enjoy nearly the same comity as Reagan, O'Neill, Michel, and such great Senate leaders as Howard Baker and Mike Mansfield. Not surprisingly, Americans have become increasingly frustrated with the divisiveness of the past 25 years, and the result has been obvious in survey research that puts the esteem of Congress at an all-time low.

Research commissioned by the public relations firm Weber Shandwick in 2012 found that 63 percent of Americans think incivility is a major problem that complicates the resolution of major issues and deters qualified people from entering public service. Another survey by *U.S. News and World Report* found that 89 percent think civility is a serious problem. A majority of Americans expect it to get worse. Eighty percent think campaigns are uncivil. A *USA Today* study in 2010 found that 61 percent of Americans think TV news is pushing politics to be less civil.

What is occurring in American politics today is not new—nor does it approach the formative struggles of our new nation or the horror of the Civil War. In spite of that reality, it is occurring at a time when the country can ill-afford any more deterrents to governing.

The Rise of Modern Political Polarization

Multiple political events and demographic developments triggered today's polarization. Prior to 1994, the Democrats, with a few exceptions, had complete control over the Congress since the 1932 landslide election of Franklin Roosevelt. But the tumultuous 1960s began to drive wedges in the Democratic Party's coalition and change the face of both parties. Political realignment was still taking place in 2010, when the legislatures of North Carolina, Alabama and Tennessee had Republican majorities elected for the first time since Reconstruction.

The Democratic Party was especially fractured by the Vietnam War, the Civil Rights movement, the explosion in the size of government set off by Lyndon Johnson's Great Society, and the *Roe v. Wade* decision on abortion. These events affected the Republican Party as well, but there were fewer Republicans in the House and Senate, so the effect on the national political environment was less obvious.

The most dramatic change occurred in the South. With the exception of the election of war hero General Dwight Eisenhower, the South had monolithically voted Democratic since Reconstruction in the late 19th century. However, the Democratic control in the South began to wane in the second half of the 20th century. The Southern realignment first appeared nationally in the 1968 Presidential election when Republican Richard Nixon exploited the independent candidacy of the former Democratic Governor of Alabama, George Wallace. His candidacy divided the Democrats in the South and deprived Democrat Vice President Hubert Humphrey of a traditional source of electoral support. The South has been growing more and more Republican ever since.

The Southern realignment was not the only indication of a divide among Democrats; you could see this in Congress too. As part of the fissure in the Democratic ranks, party liberals rebelled against conservative Democratic committee chairs and forced through a series of rules changes that transferred power from the committees to party leaders.

The origins of the empowerment of congressional leaders can also be found in the Southern realignment. While Democrats did nominate a Southern Governor, Jimmy Carter in 1976, the shift in party allegiance continued through Reagan, who was probably the last American President to enter office with a clear and formidable public mandate. The realignment of the parties was reflected in the Congresses that enacted the Reagan agenda of tax and spending reductions and a stronger defense. Reagan and the minority Republican leadership in the House were able to win passage of major tax reductions in 1981 only with the help of more than 40 Democratic conservative Congressmen, mostly from the South.

In the face of those defections on the Democratic side of the aisle and the mid-term elections in 1982 that cost Reagan 26 Republican seats in the House, Speaker Thomas P. "Tip" O'Neill of Massachusetts began reasserting his control over the House and making it more difficult for conservative Democrats to flex their political muscle by moving power away from committees to the party leadership. O'Neill established tighter control over the committees and the floor by using the House Rules Committee to block Republicans from offering embarrassing amendments— particularly those offered by Representative Bob Walker of Pennsylvania, Representative Newt Gingrich of Georgia, and other young Turks, who were then insurgent backbenchers. Additionally, these changes included placing the Speaker in charge of the Democratic Steering and Policy Committee, giving him control over committee appointments (for the first time since 1911). The Speaker was given power to appoint all the Democratic Members of the Rules Committee, to refer bills to multiple committees, and to create ad hoc committees.

These changes had the effect of empowering the party leadership at the expense of the committee chairs. They allowed the party leadership to "stack" key committees with Members who would vote with the leadership. Additionally, the membership ratios on important committees were increased, giving the Democratic majority a disproportionately larger number of seats. The stacking of committees by the majority, and the use of proxy voting in committees, imposed a significant constraint on the minority's ability to participate in committee decision-making. The leadership further encouraged party discipline by rewarding Members who demonstrated party loyalty with additional power in the Congress and floor time for their legislation.

By depriving conservative Democrats of power if they did not toe the party line, many Southern Democrats found themselves caught between their leadership and their constituents. These Democrats found themselves casting votes to support the Speaker that angered their voters and cost them reelection.

Throughout the first term of the Reagan administration a limited degree of civility and mutual respect prevailed in much of the deliberations between the President, House and Senate Republicans and the Democratic leadership in Congress. Reagan and O'Neill were famous for working out legislative compromises over dinner and drinks. They were not necessarily the best of friends, and they both had strongly held ideological beliefs—but when the country needed answers they figured out a way to work out an agreement.

The environment steadily deteriorated as brash, young contingent of House Republicans chafed under autocratic rule that had gotten steadily worse over the course of, the long, uninterrupted Democratic reign. Republican young Turks launched their long struggle to win a Republican majority in the House, engaging in a form of guerilla warfare on the House floor. That movement received a huge electrical charge in 1985 when the Democratic majority insisted on seating Representative Frank McCloskey, of Indiana's Eighth Congressional District, whose election to the office was in serious dispute. The Democrats' handling of the matter led to a historic walkout by House Republicans.

The Reagan administration also suffered from politically debilitating events, including a recession, but most notably the Iran-Contra scandal. Additionally, a much more strident and—in the minds of Republicans—a more oppressive, partisan Texan named Jim Wright, who rose in the ranks of Democratic leadership and assumed the Speaker's chair in 1987.

The statistics tell the story. The number of conservative Democrats, mostly from the South, went from a high of 91 in the House to a low of 6 in the 104th Congress (1995-1996). At the same time, the number of moderate

Republicans, mostly from the North and Midwest, went from a high of 35 in the early 1970s to a low of 10 in the 103rd Congress (1993-1994).

In 1994, insurgent Republicans led by Newt Gingrich capitalized on the public frustration with a Democrat President and Congress (caused largely by President Clinton's health care proposal and crime legislation that increased regulations on certain firearms) and ultimately regained control of the House after 40 years in the minority. They accomplished this through a long-term strategy of political insurgency that proved profitable in restoring Republicans to the majority, but costly in terms of its effect on civility and polarization.

In recognition of all he had done to help the party succeed, the Republicans elected Gingrich Speaker and, he continued the consolidation of power in the hands of party leaders. In order to pass the Contract with America in the first 100 days of the 104th Congress, Gingrich created issue-specific *ad hoc* task forces (a power his Democratic predecessors established in the Reagan years) and used them to circumvent

Open rules are special rules passed by the Rules Committee that allow members to amend legislation under the "regular order" established by the rules of the House. By the 111th Congress, open rules had become non-existent.

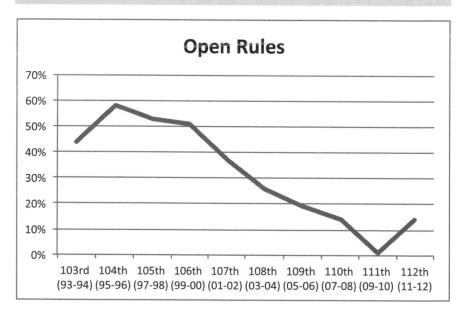

Open Rules

CAN'T WE ALL JUST GET ALONG?

committees and draft legislation, which he then referred to the committees with the expectation of rapid approval. This essentially bypassed the committee process, further weakening their autonomy and making it clear that they were subservient to the wishes of the party leadership.

By the time the 104th Congress convened, Speaker Gingrich had concentrated power at the expense of committees. Leadership-controlled agendas, fewer committee staff and reduced procedural powers for committee chairs, more open committee procedures and reduced protection on the floor, and the threat of being bypassed by a task force completed the neutering of the committees begun in 1980. Since then, power has remained in the hands of party leaders, even through the return to a Democratic majority in 2007 under Speaker Nancy Pelosi. Speaker John Boehner, who assumed the speakership in 2011, began reopening and re-empowering the committee process, but progress has been slow.

Two subsequent political events exacerbated polarization—the impeachment of President Clinton and the closeness of the 2000 election between George W. Bush and Al Gore. Since then, with the exception of a brief period following the September 11, 2001, terrorist attacks on the United States, the rhetorical excesses have rarely let up. For instance, the class warfare and character assassination tactics, particularly those of so-called "independent expenditure" groups, employed in the 2012 Presidential election will certainly leave lasting scars on the body politic.

Historians and partisans can point to numerous real and perceived slights—but the plain truth is that there is plenty of blame to go around, and no political party has a claim to purity when it comes to the coarsening of American politics.

Partisan polarization in the Congress is undeniable, and, from a historical perspective, it is an alarming new development. The parties have become ideologically homogenized to an extent that did not exist even a few years ago. According to *National Journal*, which tracks the party unity scores of individual Senators, the change has been dramatic and complete. In *National Journal's* 1982 vote ratings, 36 Senate Democrats had records at least as conservative as the most liberal Republican and 24 Senate Republicans had records as least as liberal as the most conservative Democrat—a majority of 58 Members falling between the Senate's ideological bookends. By 2010, there was no gap. Democrat Ben Nelson was the most conservative Democrat and Republican George Voinovich was the most liberal Republican, but Voinovich was still more conservative than Nelson. With both of these Members recently retired, the ideological stances of each party have moved further away from each other.

Gerrymandering

Population shifts from big cities and industrial states to the growing South and Southwest led to reapportionment that shifted congressional seats in a fashion more favorable to Republicans.

Gerrymandering, the process of redrawing congressional districts to suit partisan political interests, named after Elbridge Gerry of Massachusetts, has also played an important role in the polarization of the country. Congressional districts are redrawn every ten years, based on the census at the outset of each decade. The responsibility for reapportioning the districts rests with the state legislatures, in most cases. In redrawing district lines, they have often configured them not so much as to ensure rational and efficient districts, but to ensure the re-election of members of whichever party has control over the redistricting process at the time.

Skewing the boundaries of a congressional district to create "a safe seat" has a number of unhealthy results. First, it makes it easier for a Congressman to win re-election, so there is a tendency for the Congressman to be less responsive. Since gerrymandering creates districts that insulate Members from competition it reduces turnover in the House.

More important to polarization, however, is the fact that gerrymandered districts create an environment where a candidate seeking a congressional seat or running for re-election only has to be responsive to one part of the electorate in the district. In a heavily Republican district, for example, a candidate only has to solicit support from the Republican base, a base that is usually more conservative than the district as a whole. The same logic applies in districts that are drawn to heavily favor a Democrat. In those districts, the candidate only has to appeal to a strong Democratic base and can be, therefore, more liberal than the district as a whole. This gerrymandering scheme has been applied all over the country through many decades and has resulted in a Congress that, arguably, is more conservative on one side and more liberal on the other than the population in general, resulting in polarization.

Another variation is the creation of "majority-minority" districts, areas where most of the voters are from minority ethnic or racial groups, which help ensure that such groups have representation in Congress. Following the 1990 census, some states have used highly precise computer software to draw majority-minority districts, to comply with the Voting Rights Act and related court decisions that promote minority representation in Congress. These map-making initiatives have created a *de facto* alliance between Southern Republicans and minorities, because both groups find their electoral odds improved in their respective districts. They dilute Democratic strength in non-minority districts, resulting in the election of more Republicans there and more liberal Democrats in the minority-majority districts. Conservative Democrats in the South have been left out in the cold.

When the dust had settled after 1994, the remaining Democrats in the House were more liberal and more loyal to the party leadership. At the same time, Republicans became a majority in the Congress for the first time in 40 years largely because of their increased numbers in the South. Republicans comprised less than 10 percent of Southern representation in the 1960s—in fact, it wasn't until 1964 that the Republicans elected their first post-Reconstruction House Member from the states comprising the old Confederacy. By the 1990s, Republicans held more than half of Southern districts.

SOUTHERN CHIVALRY — ARGUMENT versus CLUB'S.

In the time before the American Civil War, polarization sometimes became violent, as when Senator Charles Sumner of Massachusetts was nearly beaten to death by Representative Preston Butler of South Carolina.

Another trend that does not bode well for fixing this problem is the trend towards one-party state government. *The New York Times* wrote that following the 2012 elections there are 37 states where one party controls the governor's mansion and both chambers of the legislature—24 Republican and 13 Democrat. If this pattern persists through 2020, it makes it nearly impossible for the minority party to check the redistricting plans of the incumbent majorities.

The Media's Role in Polarization

Another major contributor to polarization in government and society is the media. While Republicans had long complained of a liberal bias in the major network news bureaus, cable news; the Internet's social networks; and the new media, particularly blogs, have turned our system of information gathering and dissemination upside down, making a mockery of balance, objectivity, factual accuracy and the idea of putting public interest over profit (to the extent it actually existed in the mainstream media).

There are no longer clear lines between information and entertainment and news and commentary. Many sources of information are unedited. And there are no longer clear distinctions between information and knowledge. The public is being told less and less about issues and serious policy considerations and more and more about sex scandals, dance contests, gossip, and innuendo. Public policy is now treated much like sporting events with a focus on winning moves and scoring points. The media are more divisive, pitting one politician against the other, inciting emotions and anger, focusing on the extremes and the absurd. Voters can easily find websites that conform to their views, essentially self-selecting the news they want to receive. To compete, newspapers and other media polarize their news coverage to obtain or preserve viewership. For instance, MSNBC is seen as appealing to the left and Fox News to the right. Neither news organization could become more centrist without the risk of losing viewers.

The media leave voters without the knowledge they need about critical issues to make intelligent decisions at the polls. Worse yet, the choices the voters have are diminished by what seems to be the growing disinclination of good people to run for office, in part because they simply do not want to put themselves and their families through the injurious media gauntlet they must endure for two years or more.

What has media behavior done to civil discourse? It has created an environment in which stridency, polarization, drama, exaggeration and hyperbole get attention and civil, honest behavior doesn't. It has created an environment in which civil discourse about complex issues can no longer break through the noise and negativity.

Partisanship

Polarization is also the result of excessive partisanship, the degree of control the political parties exercise not only over the elective process, but also the governing process. The practical effect of this polarization has been to damage the institution of Congress, and make legislating—already difficult under the Constitution—more difficult. Real damage has been done by the obstacles to open debate and compromise through the increased use of closed special rules in the House and the use of the filibuster in the Senate.

The restriction of debate and the obstruction of legislation through manipulation of the rules is where polarization has dramatically damaged the functioning of the national legislature. When strong party leadership in the House blocks amendments and stymies debate it makes compromise nearly impossible—punishing moderates on both sides and fostering polarization. If the majority takes away the voice of the minority and makes it impossible for them to constructively participate in the crafting of legislation, the minority has no alternative but to obstruct the process that deprives them of their voice.

In the Senate, when a strong minority (or a stubborn majority) can simply block legislation rather than try to get the "best deal" possible, the filibuster strengthens the extremes and weakens the center. Some experts like former Senate Parliamentarian Robert Dove argue that this is what makes the Senate the Senate, and that the filibuster is designed to kill legislation.

In the past, the threat of filibuster was actually something that encouraged compromise—a Senate majority could not pass legislation unless it had the support of at least a handful of Senators from the other party. However, in the absence of a majority willing to work with at least some colleagues in the minority, the filibuster changes from a tool to promote bipartisan consensus to a bludgeon the excluded minority uses to grind the Senate to a halt.

The evidence is apparent in the increasing dysfunction of the Congress. By 2010, the House, for the first time since the 1974 Budget Act passed, was unable to even vote on a budget for the Federal Government, much less finalize, a plan with the Senate a streak that continued through 2012. The 111th and the 112th Congresses (2009-2013) adjourned without sending even one of the twelve required appropriation bills to the President for his signature.

259

Highly partisan votes also suggest Congress is becoming increasingly dysfunctional. Major legislation such as healthcare reform and the nearly trillion dollar economic stimulus were passed without bipartisan support.

Such partisan votes for major transformative legislation are unprecedented in the modern political era. Compare the passage of healthcare reform and the economic stimulus package to three of the most transformative pieces of legislation from the last century, the Social Security Act, Medicare, and the Civil Rights Act. They all passed with bipartisan majorities: the Social Security Act with a vote of 372-33 in the House and 77-6 in the Senate; Medicare with a vote of 313-115 in the House and 68-21 in the Senate; and the Civil Rights Act with a vote of 290-130 in the House and 73-27 in the Senate. With the exception of the Medicare Act when Senate Republicans narrowly voted against it 13-17, each of those bills had a majority of support from both parties.

Legislating Polarization Away: Empower Committees, Decrease Polarization

Polarization cripples the political process. Not only does the Congress fail to enact legislation, polarization empowers the extremes and disempowers the middle. In fact, the middle of the political spectrum, where compromise is normally found, becomes downright politically dangerous, as consensus builders arouse suspicion and animosity among ideological extremists. There are serious issues facing the country: stubbornly high unemployment and sluggish economic growth, massive budget deficits and government debt that threaten the stability of our economy, the reform of Social Security and Medicare, energy independence, the financial system's disarray, globalization, and the global war on terror. A polarized Congress cannot solve these problems. No serious observer of the Congress can believe any of these issues stand a chance of resolution in today's highly charged atmosphere. There is no better example than the negotiations over deficit and debt reduction, which began in 2011, continued for the rest of the 112th Congress and stretched into the 113th. This ongoing saga produced little more than what was called the fiscal cliff, the expiration of the Bush tax cuts and the payroll tax holiday and the enactment of $109 billion in automatic cuts to discretionary spending—all on January, 1, 2013.

If problems can't be resolved, is it any wonder the congressional approval rating is at an all time low? In an interview with *National Journal* shortly before assuming the speakership, Representative John Boehner provided a suggestion that will significantly increase the Legislature's effectiveness:

> We need to stop writing bills in the Speaker's office and let members of Congress be legislators again. Too often in the House right now we don't have legislators; we just have voters. Under Speaker Pelosi, 430 out of the 435 members are just here to vote and raise money. That's it. That's not right. We were each elected to uphold the Constitution and represent 600,000-odd people in our districts. We need to open this place up, let some air in. We have nothing to fear from letting the House work its will—nothing to fear from the battle of ideas. That starts with the committees. The result will be more scrutiny and better legislation…The House is the body closest to people. That's by design. We're the ... the crucible, the testing ground for new ideas and new policies. And the institutions of the House that have grown up over 200 years of trial and error are the best way to test those ideas and policies. We don't need five members sitting behind a closed-door writing a bill, like they did with the "stimulus" or "Obamacare." It's nuts…. this is a serious commitment. I know it's going to be a pain in the neck, but we're going to do it.

No doubt his philosophy comes from his own experience: Boehner is the first person to become Speaker who also served as a committee chairman since Tom Foley in 1989, and the first Republican Speaker to have also chaired a committee since Joe Cannon in 1911.

One element of the problem for Members of Congress is procedural. The procedural solutions are not that complicated—what is required is the political will to restore "regular order" in the Congress. The challenge for the House leadership is how to protect the rights of individual Members and generate greater participation in the legislative process without committing procedural suicide. Shifting power back to committees will help accomplish this.

Shifting power back to the committees would lessen the degree of polarization both in Congress and in the country as a whole. Empowering committees would improve congressional decision-making; as Speaker Boehner said in his *National Journal* interview, more people could scrutinize legislation. Strong committees promote civility because Members of both parties have opportunities to participate. They can advance personal goals whether they are in the majority or minority. Also, committee decision-making allows Members to fulfill their multiple roles as both representatives of their local constituents and members of a national legislature. Members can specialize on committees important to their districts and participate in bipartisan drafting of bills. Additionally, another consequence of shifting power back to committees is that lawmakers can form coalitions along non-party lines, such as regional and issue-specific (agriculture, transportation, energy, etc.) interests.

A strong committee system promotes a healthy political atmosphere, but dominant party leadership destroys civility. The ability to participate in lawmaking channels Members' efforts in positive ways. If a minority has no ability to participate in the legislative process, its only power is to obstruct the majority through dilatory, sometimes uncivil tactics. A minority has no choice but to be negative. Similarly, strong party leadership promotes hyper-partisanship, because allowing minority members to work with majority members hurts the minority party's cohesion. In other words, leadership breaks bipartisan coalitions—the party decides what the Member supports. Under strong party leadership, Congress behaves like a parliament with one party supporting legislation and the other simply opposing it. A genius of our Constitution is that each of the three branches of the Federal government checks the power of the others; a strong committee system continues that tradition by establishing a check on party power within the Congress itself.

Voters and Polarization

Although Congress can reverse excessive polarization by taking such steps as reinvigorating committees, the public can reshape the institution as well. The Gallup Poll, the Pew Foundation poll and pollster David Winston have shown that the public is, overall, slightly center-right, yet its Congress is increasingly polarized. By the end of 2010, the United States had seen three "tidal-wave elections" in a row where voters chased incumbents out of office. The public is telling their elected leaders that they are not interested in party politics and that they insist on being listened to. In our system, the voters should remember that they are the bosses, and have the right to fire a Member of Congress every two years if they believe he or she is not listening.

Simply put, when politicians are rewarded by the voters for uncivil behaviors, they will continue those behaviors. But when politicians are punished by the voters for dividing the country and polarizing the Congress, their leaders will begin to change behavior. Most Members want to be reelected. They respond very quickly to cues from their constituents.

As Ecclesiastes tells us, there is "nothing new under the sun." On our Nation's 100th birthday, President James Garfield stated as much in his centennial address:

> "Now more than ever before, the people are responsible for the character of their Congress. If that body be ignorant, reckless, and corrupt, it is because the people tolerate ignorance, recklessness, and corruption. If it be intelligent, brave and pure, it is because the people demand those high qualities to represent them in the national legislature."

But the issues are bigger than the politicians. Winston Churchill once famously proclaimed that "democracy is the worst form of government except all the others that have been tried." Once again, democracy is competing against a wide range of different ideologies and forms of government—from totalitarian capitalism to radical Islam. American legislators should ask themselves if the champion of democracy is modeling a legislative decision-making process that other peoples would want to emulate.

What is needed, and what was envisioned by the signers of the Constitution, is not that the people's representatives should be moderating their views or compromising their principles. Rather, they should be able to engage in a battle of ideas in a civil and peaceful manner on the floor of Congress, where all elected representatives may be heard and all ideas weighed against each other, and where decisions on legislation are informed by a broad range of opinions expressed by people representing a diverse population, confirmed or rejected every two years at the ballot box.

Chapter Fifteen Summary

- Throughout most of American history, the Congress and our political system have reflected varying degrees of polarization and incivility. While today's polarization does not approach the formative struggles of our new nation or the horror of the Civil War, Americans have become increasingly frustrated with the divisiveness of the past 25 years; public opinion of Congress is at an all-time low.

- The practical effect of this polarization has been to damage the institution of Congress, and make legislating—already difficult under the Constitution—more difficult.

- Prior to 1994, the Democrats, with a few exceptions, had complete control over the Congress since 1932. But the tumultuous 1960s began to drive wedges in the Democratic Party's coalition and change the face of both parties. The most dramatic changes occurred in the South, which has gradually transitioned from a Democratic to a Republican stronghold.

- Under Democrat Speaker Tip O'Neill, committee chairmen were weakened, and some of their powers were transferred to party leaders, concentrated in the Speaker. This allowed him and subsequent Speakers—continuing to the present day—to exert much control over legislation that is passed. This has the effect of thwarting not only the minority, but also dissenters within the majority party.

- Gerrymandering, the process of drawing congressional districts to ensure that a given party retains control over a congressional seat, also fosters polarization. When a district is configured to benefit one party, to get elected, a candidate needs only to appeal to the base of that party and survive the primary election. As a result, he or she is often more conservative or liberal than the district as a whole.

- Another major contributor to polarization in government and society is the media. Voters can easily find websites that conform to their views; to compete, newspapers and other media polarize their news coverage to obtain or preserve viewership.

- Shifting power back to the committees would lessen the degree of polarization both in Congress and in the country as a whole. Powerful committees would enable more Members of Congress to participate and fulfill their legislative goals, making polarization unnecessary.

This book provides a glimpse into the complexity of challenges you're likely to help grapple with during your stay on Capitol Hill. Keep in mind the enormity of the impact that even seemingly innocuous contributions can have. Take pride in everything you do, no matter how insignificant it might appear to be.

Remember that you are a citizen of Capitol Hill, a small city with just two employers—the House and the Senate—which coexist, compete and cooperate to conduct the nation's business. The 40,000 or so staff members working for Congress represent a cross-section of America. They come from every state, every race, every religion and every socio-economic background. They're mostly young people—ambitious, patriotic, intelligent, driven. They hold political views every bit as diverse as their bosses', but there is a common bond that generally fosters mutual respect and a kind of pride that comes with public service. Regardless of what opinion polls may say about attitudes toward the Congress, you'll rarely see a Hill employee bashful about saying where he or she works.

Working on Capitol Hill is one of those rare experiences that will never be forgotten and will make each employee better at whatever else they decide to do.

Epilogue

INTRODUCTION

Learn the rules and understand the precedents and procedures of the House. The congressman who knows how the House operates will soon be recognized for his parliamentary skills—and his prestige will rise among his colleagues, no matter what his party.

House Speaker John W. McCormack (1962–1971) of Massachusetts, giving advice to new House Members

I. HOUSE IS CALLED TO ORDER BY THE SPEAKER

Time of Meeting:

The daily hour of meeting is set by a House Resolution adopted on the first day of each session. On January 5, 2011, the House adopted H. Res. 10, which established the following House meeting times before February 1, 2011:

- 2:00 p.m. on Monday;
- 12:00 p.m. on Tuesday;
- 10:00 a.m. on Wednesdays and Thursdays; and
- 9:00 a.m. on all other days of the week.

Beginning February 1, 2011 until the end of the first session:

- 2:00 p.m. on Monday;
- 12:00 p.m. on Tuesday (or 2:00 pm, if no legislative business was conducted on the preceding Monday);
- 12:00 p.m. Wednesday and Thursday; and
- 9:00 a.m. on all other days of the week.

The hour of meeting can be changed by order of the House at any time, usually by unanimous consent after consultation between both party leaderships.

A Member's office is notified of any time changes by the Whip's office, usually by electronic mail. If in doubt, a Member's office should check with the Republican Cloakroom at 225-7350 or the Democratic Cloakroom at 225-7330.

Three-Day Adjournment Limit:

Article I, section 5 of the U.S. Constitution prevents either house from adjourning for more than three days (not including Sundays) unless the other house concurs. Such adjournment authority for more than three days is accomplished through the adoption by both houses of a concurrent resolution, which does not require the signature of the President.

In the case of an emergency in which the House may be under immediate danger, the Speaker may declare an emergency recess under clause 12 of Rule I. If during a recess or adjournment of not more than three days the Speaker is notified by the Sergeant at Arms of an imminent danger to the place of reconvening, the Speaker may postpone the time for reconvening the House. The Speaker may also reconvene the House under those circumstances before the time previously appointed to declare the House in recess again. These circumstances require the Speaker to notify Members accordingly. At the outset of the 112th Congress, the House agreed to H. Con. Res. 1, which permits the Speaker and the majority leader of the Senate to assemble at a place outside the District of Columbia whenever, in their opinion, the public interest shall warrant it (the Senate has yet to take action on H. Con. Res. 1).

Furthermore, the House has a rule which allows it to deal with the consequences of a terrorist attack or other catastrophe that may incapacitate large numbers of Members. The rule (clause 5(c) of Rule XX) allows the House to act if a roll call vote is required following a catastrophe and a quorum cannot be achieved. Quorum is the majority of the whole number of the House and is calculated from those Members who are chosen, sworn and living. Thus, if all Members of the House are alive, quorum is the majority of 435, or 218 Members. Incapacitated Members, though unable to vote, are nonetheless counted for purposes of quorum. If more than a majority of the House is incapacitated, the House would be unable to take a roll call vote because of a lack of quorum. The rule change allows for the House to conduct business with less than a majority of a fully constituted House—but only in times of catastrophe and subject to a number of procedural protections. This smaller number is called the provisional quorum. Operating with a provisional quorum lasts only until enough Members are revived for a regular quorum. Any legislation considered with a provisional quorum would be subject to the bicameral and presentment to the President requirements, and any votes adopted could be ratified or repudiated at a later time by a fully constituted House.

Legislative Schedule:

The scheduling of legislation for House Floor action is the prerogative of the majority leadership. However, the following table is useful in determining the time it takes to prepare legislation for Floor consideration under regular order:

Tuesday Committee orders a bill reported; views requested
Wednesday Day #1 for filing views.
Thursday Day #2 for filing views.
Friday Committee files report. (May be Day #1 of report availability if report is filed the day before.)
Monday Day #1 that report is available to the House.
Tuesday Day #2 that report is available to the House.
Wednesday Day #3 that report is available to the House. Floor consideration is possible.
Thursday Rules Committee meets to grant rule.
Friday Rule and bill may be considered on House Floor.

Usually on the last legislative day of the week, a representative of the minority leadership seeks unanimous consent to speak out of order for one-minute to address the House for the purpose of asking the majority leader about the legislative schedule for the upcoming week. Following the announcement, the Whip offices will send Members "Whip Notices" for the next week listing the specific bills to be considered including how each bill will receive Floor consideration (for example, suspension of the rules, a rule from the Rules Committee, unanimous consent, etc.). Offices will receive publications electronically from the Republican Conference or the Democratic Caucus with summaries of the upcoming legislation. Finally, if the bill is to be considered under a rule from the Rules Committee, information about the amendment process, debate time, etc., is available on the majority's Rules Committee website at www.rules.house.gov or the minority's Rules Committee website at http://democrats.rules.house.gov.

Even though the majority leadership announces a program for the coming week, it is possible for the schedule to change. Therefore, it is to a Member's benefit to follow any updates. The Republican Cloakroom provides recorded information for the week's program at 225-2020 and 225-7430 for the Floor program for that specific day. The Democratic Cloakroom provides recorded information for the week's program at 225-1600 and 225-7400 for the Floor program for that specific day.

In addition to the announced schedule of major bills, legislative matters may be called up for consideration by "unanimous consent." In keeping with the Speaker's announced policy, unanimous consent requests of that type must be cleared by the majority and minority leaderships as well as the bipartisan leadership of the committee(s) of jurisdiction.

Following clearance, these matters may come up with little notice except to the Members managing the request (i.e., the chairman and ranking minority member of the committee(s) of jurisdiction). If Members have a specific interest in something that might come up by unanimous consent, they should contact the appropriate committees and leadership representatives as early as possible. A Member might also ask the floor staff to be on the lookout for the matter of interest.

In addition to the normal order of business as presented here, there are several "special legislative days." Bills may be brought up under "suspension of the rules" on Mondays, Tuesdays, and Wednesdays of each week, although this process is separate and apart from the calendar system. There is no "suspension calendar." Suspension of the rules will be discussed in detail later in Section VIII of this manual. Private Bills may be considered on the first and third Tuesdays of each month.

Powers of the Speaker:
The Speaker traditionally opens the session each day, but may designate a "Speaker pro tempore," who is a Member of the majority party, to serve in this capacity for up to three legislative days. The Speaker or Speaker pro tempore may preside through one-minute speeches and other House business (such

as debate on special rules) until the House resolves itself into the Committee of the Whole House on the State of the Union, at which time the Speaker appoints a majority Member to preside as the Chairman of the Committee of the Whole. The Speaker or Speaker pro tempore returns to the Chair when the Committee of the Whole rises to come back into the whole House.

NOTE: House Rule I details the numerous duties of the Speaker, many of which directly affect Members. It is also important to understand the Speaker's power of recognition under clause 2 of Rule XVII. In most cases, it is the Chair's prerogative to recognize a Member. The power of recognition cannot be appealed.

Morning Hour:

By agreement of both the majority and minority leadership, the House has instituted a "morning- hour" period for special order speeches on legislative days of Monday and Tuesday of each week. On those days the House may convene two hours earlier than normal for morning-hour debate.

Beginning on February 1, 2011, on the legislative days of Wednesday or Thursday, the House will convene two hours earlier for morning-hour debate.

Morning-hour special order speeches are equally divided and rotated between majority and minority party Members. Members designated by the leaders may speak for up to five minutes on any subject of their choice (except for the majority and minority leaders and minority Whip, who may speak for longer blocks of time). If a Member wishes to participate, he or she must sign up for the time in their respective Cloakroom.

II. PRAYER IS OFFERED BY THE CHAPLAIN

The House Chaplain is the Reverend Patrick J. Conroy, S.J. Guest Chaplains are permitted in the Chamber and each Member may consider inviting a clergyman from his or her district to offer the daily prayer. Members should contact Father Conroy for further information at 225-2509.

III. APPROVAL OF THE JOURNAL

Article I, section 5 of the U.S. Constitution requires that the House keep a Journal of its proceedings, which is a summary of the day's actions. The Speaker is responsible for examining and approving the Journal of the previous day. The Speaker announces approval to the House immediately after the prayer is offered by the Chaplain. Following the announcement of approval by the Speaker, any Member may demand a vote on the question of the Speaker's approval. However, the Speaker has the authority to postpone a vote on agreeing to the Speaker's approval of the Journal until a later time on the same legislative day.

NOTE: The Journal is not the *Congressional Record*.

IV. VOTING BY ELECTRONIC DEVICE

When the Speaker or the Chair announces that the yeas and nays are ordered and a recorded vote is ordered or announces that a quorum is not present and the yeas and nays are automatic, the vote is taken by electronic device. A Member casts a vote by electronic device by inserting a voting card into the nearest voting station and pressing the appropriate button: "yea," "nay" or "present." It is advised that Members go to another voting station and reinsert their voting card until the light comes on and verifies the vote cast at the first station. Members should also visually check the voting board to make sure that the light next to their name reflects their intended vote.

Members that do not have their voting card should go to the table in the well and obtain an appropriate voting card from the boxes placed there (green card for yea, red card for nay, orange card for present). The Member should sign the card and give it to the tally clerk who will be standing on the first level of the rostrum. The clerk will then register the vote into the computer, but the Member should visually check the board to make sure the vote is recorded correctly.

Members deciding to change their vote may do so by reinserting their card into a voting station and pressing the appropriate button during the first 10 minutes of a 15-minute vote, or at any time during a 5- or 2-minute vote. However, during the last 5 minutes of a 15-minute vote, a change in a Member's vote can only be made by going to the well, taking a card from the table, signing it, and handing it to the tally clerk on the rostrum. The clerk then registers the change and a statement will appear in the *Congressional Record* indicating that the Member changed his or her vote. Members using this procedure to change their vote should be sure to check the board to see that it reflects the change. Also, Members may change their vote during a five or two-minute vote by machine and no statement about the change will appear in the *Congressional Record* unless it comes after the voting stations are closed and before the result of the vote is announced.

NOTE: Once the record vote ends (by the Chair announcing the result), and the motion to reconsider is laid on the table, the vote is final—no further voting or changing is permitted. However, if a Member has missed the vote he or she may submit a statement declaring how he or she would have voted had he or she been present. Such an explanatory statement containing the Member's original signature will be inserted in the *Congressional Record* at the point immediately after the vote. A suggested script for such an explanatory statement on missed or mistaken votes may be obtained from the floor staff. It is important to remember that this statement does not affect whether or how the Member is recorded on the vote.

Clause 2 of Rule III specifically prohibits Members from allowing another person to cast their vote and from casting the vote of another Member. This unethical action was banned at the beginning of the 97th Congress.

The allotted time for a quorum call or recorded vote under the Rules of the House is not less than 15 minutes (clause 2 of Rule XX). It is the prerogative of the Speaker or presiding officer to allow additional time beyond the 15 minutes. Often one will hear Members calling "regular order" when an electronic vote extends beyond 15 minutes under the mistaken impression that recorded votes are limited to 15 minutes—they are not limited. The regular order is to allow more time on recorded votes if the Chair desires.

In the 110th Congress, clause 2 of Rule XX was amended to prohibit a vote from being held open for the sole purpose of reversing the outcome of the vote. This provision was not included in the 111th Congress rules package on the recommendation of a bipartisan select committee because it was found to be unworkable in practice.

It has been the custom of the House since the 104th Congress to attempt to "limit" these 15-minute votes to 17 minutes. The Chair should allow all Members who are on the floor before the final announcement to be recorded, but is not obliged to hold the vote open to accommodate requests through the Cloakrooms for Members "on their way" to the House floor. In the 112th Congress, clause 6 of Rule XVIII, was modified to allow for two-minute voting. Two-minute voting is only permissible in the Committee of the Whole.

V. PLEDGE OF ALLEGIANCE TO THE FLAG

After approval of the Journal, the Speaker recognizes a designated Member to lead the House in the Pledge of Allegiance to the American flag. The Member designated alternates between the majority and minority party on a daily basis. The Member is usually informed in advance if he or she is the designated Member.

> *I pledge Allegiance to the flag of the*
> *United States of America and to the*
> *Republic for which it stands, one nation*
> *Under God, indivisible, with Liberty and*
> *Justice for all.*

VI. ONE-MINUTE SPEECHES

These short speeches (300 words or less) may be made by Members before legislative business each day. If the speech given at the beginning of the day is longer than 300 words or includes extraneous materials, it will appear in the Extension of Remarks section of the *Congressional Record*. Any Member may seek recognition to give a speech on a subject of his or her choice not exceeding one minute in duration. One-minute speeches are often coordinated by the majority and minority leaderships to focus on particular topics, but the speeches are not limited to such topics. Participants in these coordinated efforts usually receive priority seating and recognition.

The one-minute speech period is granted at the discretion of the Speaker, as are the number of such speeches. Some days 1-minute speeches may be limited to 10 or 15 speeches per side. On other days, they may be unlimited. On occasion, this period is postponed until the end of the day if the business of the House is heavy and time is short. In this case, a Member may address the House for one minute at the end of legislative business for the day.

To give a one-minute speech, a Member should go to the front row of seats on their party's side of the floor and sit down. The Speaker will recognize Members in turn, alternating between the majority and minority sides. At the appropriate point, the Member should stand to seek recognition and address the Chair by saying: **"Mr. Speaker, I ask unanimous consent to address the House for one minute and to revise and extend my remarks."**

The Speaker will respond by saying: "Without objection, so ordered." The Member may then proceed to the podium in the well to give the speech. The Chair will tell the Member when the one minute has expired at which time the Member may finish the sentence, but no more.

NOTE: Members are strongly encouraged to read House Rule XVII, Decorum and Debate (especially clause 1), as well as section XVII of the Jefferson's *Manual*, Order and Debate. See also Conduct During Debate under Part XI of this manual, "General Debate in the Committee of the Whole."

It is not proper at any time for a Member to refer to the television audience. Rule XVII states that a Member must always address the Chair and only the Chair.

Furthermore, clause 7 of Rule XVII states specifically that Members may not introduce or otherwise make reference to people in the Visitors or Press Gallery.

It is acceptable to refer to actions taken by the Senate. House rules allow for references on the House Floor to the Senate or its Members. However, these remarks must be limited to the question under debate and may not include personalities. (See clause 1 of Rule XVII).

Not only is it inappropriate to address the President of the United States directly (Members must always address the Chair), but it is also improper to refer to the President in a personally offensive manner.

NOTE: A Member does not actually have to deliver a one-minute speech. He or she can simply ask unanimous consent that it be placed in the *Congressional Record* and yield back his or her time. The speech will be inserted at that point, but it will appear in different type to indicate that it was not delivered in person. Also, if extraneous materials are inserted with a one-minute speech, the entire speech will appear at the end of the *Congressional Record* just prior to special order speeches.

VII. UNANIMOUS CONSENT REQUESTS

The House does much of its non-controversial work by "unanimous consent" procedure, whereby a Member stands up and asks that something be done by or permitted by unanimous consent and no other Member objects to the request. These requests may involve debate time (similar to the language of a special rule) in order to consider a measure or conference report, or waive points of order against a measure. Before the Chair will recognize a Member for a unanimous consent request, it must be cleared by both the majority and minority leadership and relevant committee leadership.

In most cases, the Chair, hearing no objection, replies: "Without objection, so ordered."

If a Member is unfamiliar with the request or its motives, the best way to find out what is behind the request is to "reserve the right to object." This gives the Member the floor and the opportunity to inquire about the request.

If the discussion during the "reservation of the right to object" proceeds for too long, any Member can demand "the regular order," which means that the Member reserving the right to object should stop talking and either object or withdraw the reservation. The Member reserving the right to object may yield to another Member on the subject of the objection.

VIII. SUSPENSION OF THE RULES

Under clause 1 of Rule XV, it is in order on Monday, Tuesday, and Wednesday of each week, and during the last six days of a session, for the Speaker to entertain motions to suspend the rules and pass legislation.

Bills brought up under suspension of the rules are spoken of as "suspensions" in floor terminology. There is no suspension calendar. The purpose of considering bills under suspension is to dispose of non-controversial measures expeditiously. Consideration of legislation under suspension of the rules on other days of the week is possible by unanimous consent or a special rule.

A motion to suspend the rules requires a vote of two-thirds of the Members present and voting. No amendments are in order unless submitted with the bill by its manager as part of the motion to suspend the rules.

Debate on a bill brought up under suspension of the rules is limited to 40 minutes, 20 minutes controlled by a Member who supports the bill and 20 minutes controlled by a Member in opposition, a division that does not always follow party lines. It is typical for the chairman or Member of the committee of jurisdiction to manage the time. For control of the opposition time, priority is given to a minority Member of the committee that has jurisdiction over the bill. Often the 20 minutes "in opposition" is controlled by the ranking minority member of the committee or subcommittee who may not be opposed to the measure because no one rises in opposition.

However, he or she may be challenged for control of the opposition time by another Member who qualifies as being opposed to the measure.

The majority leadership usually schedules several bills under suspension of the rules on the same day and the Chair often exercises its authority under clause 8 of Rule XX to announce beforehand that recorded votes on passage of each suspension, if ordered, will be postponed until the debate is concluded on all such suspensions (or up to two legislative days).

At the conclusion of debate, the postponed votes may be "clustered" and put before the House. If several votes have been ordered and the Chair has announced that the time for voting will be reduced, the first vote in the series will consume not less than 15 minutes and all subsequent record votes will take not less than 5 minutes each. It is important for Members to be mindful of when a five-minute vote is expected, so that it will not be missed.

In the event of a series of two or more votes in which any votes after the first one will be reduced to not less than five minutes, the Member will be summoned to the floor by two bells followed by five bells.

IX. SPECIAL RULES FOR MAJOR BILLS

Each major piece of legislation, except privileged matters (such as appropriations bills, budget resolutions and conference reports) not in violation of any rule of the House, normally needs a "special rule" to be adopted before the measure can be considered. A special rule, also known as an "order of business resolution," is a House resolution that sets the terms for debate and amendment. A special rule is highly important because it controls what the House can and cannot do regarding the bill itself. Special rules are reported to the House by the Rules Committee, acting as an arm of the majority leadership. They require adoption by the full House by a simple majority vote in order to take effect. Bills considered under suspension of the rules or on other special procedural days do not require a special rule in order to be considered on the House Floor.

Special rules should not be confused with the established procedures of the House. Generally speaking, special rules provide exceptions to, or departures from, the established procedures of the House. Those procedures are found in the Constitution of the United States, applicable provisions of Jefferson's *Manual*, Rules of the House adopted on the opening day of each Congress, provisions of law and resolutions having the force of rules of the House, and established precedents by Speakers and other presiding officers of the House and Committee of the Whole.

Among the various types of special rules considered in the House, the most common are:

Open rules, which permit general debate for a certain period of time (typically one hour) and allow any Member to offer an amendment that complies with the Rules of the House and the Congressional Budget Act during consideration of the bill for amendment under the five-minute rule.

Modified open rules, which permit general debate and allow any Member to offer an amendment which complies with the Rules of the House under the five-minute rule subject only to a requirement that the amendment be pre-printed in the *Congressional Record*. Modified open rules may also allow for any amendment that complies with the Rules of the House to be offered without pre-printing in the *Congressional Record*, but the rule may place an overall time cap on consideration of the bill for amendment.

Structured rules, which permit general debate for a certain period of time, but limit the amendments that may be offered to only those designated in the special rule or the Rules Committee report to accompany the special rule, or preclude amendments to a particular portion of a bill, even though the rest of the bill may be completely open to amendment.

Closed rules, which permit debate for a certain period of time, but do not allow amendments to be offered to the bill.

NOTE: To encourage Members to pre-print their amendments in the *Congressional Record* in advance of their consideration, the Rules Committee routinely includes a provision in open rules allowing the Chair to give priority in recognition to such Members. This common provision encouraging pre-printing should not be confused with the provision in modified open rules requiring the pre-printing of amendments.

One of the most important features of a special rule is what it designates as the base text for purposes of amendment. This often may be the text of the committee-reported amendment in the nature of a substitute, an amendment in the nature of a substitute as modified by another amendment, the text of the bill as introduced, or a completely new text printed in the *Congressional Record*, or in the report of the Committee on Rules accompanying the rule, or consisting of the text of another introduced bill, or consisting of the text of a Committee Print of the Committee on Rules.

When a special rule waives points of order, it means that some rule of the House (such as germaneness or a provision of the Congressional Budget Act) is being set aside to permit the bill to be called up for consideration, or to permit certain amendments to be offered to the bill in question. Without such waivers, a point of order would lie against consideration of the bill or amendment and any Member could make that point of order, thereby preventing consideration of the bill or amendment.

Before a special rule is considered by the House, it is the subject of a hearing by the Rules Committee during which Members testify as to the type of rule and amendments they support. Members are usually notified by the Committee, in the form of a "Dear Colleague" letter and a Floor announcement by the Rules Committee Chairman, in advance of a meeting if a rule structuring the amendment process is anticipated. After a hearing is held, the Rules Committee will consider a motion to grant a special rule, and will then vote to report the rule to the House. The rule and accompanying report are usually filed on the same day.

A special rule may not be considered on the same day it is reported, except by a two-thirds vote of the House (unless it is within the last three days of the session). This prohibition (clause 6(a) of Rule XIII) is sometimes waived by the adoption of another special rule reported by the Rules Committee.

The process for considering a rule in the House is as follows:

- The rule is called up for consideration in the House by a majority Member (manager) of the Rules Committee.

- One hour of debate is permitted and the majority manager customarily yields one half of the time to the minority manager for the purposes of debate only.

- Amendments to special rules are very rare. Special rules can be altered by unanimous consent or the manager may offer an amendment. It is also possible but unlikely that the majority manager will yield for the purpose of amendment, or that the previous question will be defeated (see subsection E).

- The previous question is moved and put to the House by the Chair for a vote.

- Once the previous question is ordered, the House then votes on the rule. Upon adoption of the rule, the House may proceed to consider the legislation.

The previous question is a motion made in order under clause 1 of Rule XIX and is the major parliamentary device in the House used for closing debate and preventing further amendment. The effect of adopting the previous question is to bring the resolution to an immediate, final vote. The motion is most often made at the conclusion of debate on a rule, motion or legislation considered in the House prior to final passage. A Member might think about ordering the previous question in terms of answering the question: Is the House ready to vote on the rule, bill or amendment before it?

NOTE: The previous question is not in order under a motion to suspend the rules.

In order to amend a special rule (other than by using those procedures previously mentioned), the House must vote against ordering the previous question. If the previous question is defeated, the Speaker then recognizes the Member who led the opposition to the previous question (usually a Member of the minority party) to control an additional hour of debate during which a germane amendment may be offered to the rule. The Member controlling the floor then moves the previous question on the amendment and the rule. If the previous question is ordered, the next vote occurs on the opposition's amendment followed by a vote on the rule as amended.

Adoption of the rule occurs after the previous question is agreed to. When the previous question is not a subject of controversy, it is simply disposed of "without objection." Next, the question of adopting the rule is put to the House, and the rule is either adopted or defeated. The underlying bill is not prejudiced for future consideration if the rule providing for its consideration is defeated. The Rules Committee can report another rule providing for consideration of that initial underlying bill.

X. RESOLVING INTO THE COMMITTEE OF THE WHOLE

The Committee of the Whole is a parliamentary device, derived from the practice of the English House of Commons, used to expedite the work of the House during the debate and amendment process. It involves several less formal arrangements to conduct business, including a lesser number of Members required for a quorum (100 as compared to 218 in the full House). It also has a different procedure required to obtain a recorded vote (25 Members standing in support as compared to the requirement of one-fifth of those present standing or a lack of a quorum in the full House). Certain motions allowed in the House are prohibited in the Committee of the Whole, such as motions for the previous question, to adjourn, to reconsider a vote, or to refer or recommit.

The Speaker does not preside in the Committee of the Whole, but appoints a Member of the majority party to preside with the full authority to keep order, rule on questions, recognize Members, and order votes. The Member designated to preside is addressed as "Mr. Chairman" or in the case of a female Member as "Madam Chairman." On entering the House Chamber and facing the Chair, an easy way to determine whether the House is in the Committee of the Whole or in the full House is to note the position of the Mace to the left of the Chair. If it is in the lower position, the House is in the Committee of the Whole.

XI. GENERAL DEBATE IN THE COMMITTEE OF THE WHOLE

There are two ways for the House to be resolved into the Committee of the Whole. Normally the House is resolved into the Committee of the Whole when, pursuant to a special rule, the Speaker declares the House resolved into the Committee of the Whole, in which case the resolving action is automatic and no vote is put to the Members. The second less common way is when the manager of the bill moves that the House resolve itself into the Committee of the Whole (by authority of the standing Rules in the case of a privileged matter such as an appropriations bill), in which case the motion is put to the Members.

Once the House has resolved into the Committee of the Whole, pursuant to a special rule, to consider a particular measure, the parliamentary conduct of the Committee is dictated by the special rule (refer to this manual's Section IX, "Special Rules For Major Bills") as well as general House Rules.

The "first reading" of the bill is normally dispensed with by the specific provisions of the special rule governing consideration of the bill. The Clerk reads the title and then the Chairman recognizes a majority and minority party Member to manage the debate. This is usually the chairman and ranking member of the committee or subcommittee with jurisdiction over the pending bill.

One half of the general debate time is customarily allotted by the special rule to the minority and that time is usually managed by the ranking minority member of the committee or subcommittee.

Speaking During General Debate:
The time for general debate is controlled by the majority and minority floor managers of a bill and a Member should ask the majority or minority manager at the committee table for time to speak. Normally, Members of the committee with jurisdiction over the bill speak first, and those not on the committee speak later. The first speech is given by the majority and the order of speakers then informally rotates back and forth across the aisle.

If Members need additional time to speak, they must ask the floor manager to yield more time. It is not in order to ask unanimous consent for additional time during general debate because the time is "controlled." A Member may instead wish to speak briefly about the bill and ask unanimous consent to revise and extend their remarks and insert a much longer statement into the *Congressional Record* to cover all the points the Member wants to make. (NOTE: Different typeface will appear in the *Congressional Record* to distinguish unspoken words.)

How a Member Obtains Time to Speak:
The floor manager will yield time to a Member and the Chairman of the Committee of the Whole will recognize him or her for the allotted time. Once at a microphone, a Member's remarks may be prefaced by saying, **"Mr. Chairman (or Madam Chairman), I ask unanimous consent to revise and extend my remarks."** Then he or she may proceed to speak for the time yielded. The floor manager may yield extra time to Members to complete their statements if requested and the time is available.

If a Member would like to ask a question of another Member who is speaking or make a comment, he or she should address the Chair and say, **"Mr. Chairman (or Madam Chairman), will the gentleman (or gentlewoman) from (STATE) yield to me?"** If the Member wishes to yield, he or she may do so at his or her discretion and must remain standing while the other Member speaks. The Member who has yielded may at any time "reclaim" his or her time and then the other Member must stop speaking and allow him or her to continue. A Member to whom time has been yielded can yield time to another Member as long as he or she remains standing, unless he or she is the Member controlling the debate time.

Conduct During Debate:

Words Taken Down: A Member should avoid impugning the motives of another Member, the Senate or a Member of the Senate, the Vice President or the President, as well as using offensive language or uttering words that are otherwise deemed unparliamentary. These actions violate the Rules of the House and are subject to a point of order. A point of order may be made by a Member "demanding that the gentleman's (or gentlewoman's) words be taken down." If this happens in the Committee of the Whole, the Committee of the Whole rises and the Speaker must return to the Chair and rule on the propriety of the words used. In the case of remarks regarding the Senate and the President, the Chair may take the initiative and admonish Members for unparliamentary references.

Often the offending Member obtains unanimous consent to withdraw the inappropriate words or the demand is withdrawn before the Speaker rules and then the Member proceeds in order. However, if the Member's words are ruled out of order, they may be stricken from the *Congressional Record* by motion or unanimous consent, and the Member will not be allowed to speak again on that day, except by motion or unanimous consent (clause 4 of Rule XVII).

Relevancy: A Member may get carried away in debate and stray from the subject under discussion. If so, he or she may be subject to a point of order that their remarks are not relevant to the debate (clause 1(b) of Rule XVII).

Speaking Out of Order: If a Member has to make an important announcement to the House that is not relevant to the debate, the Member may ask unanimous consent to "speak out of order" for a period of time (usually one minute). If granted, the Member may then speak on the desired subject for the allotted time.

Addressing the Chair: A Member must be standing while speaking. If not, the Member may be subject to a point of order because of unparliamentary posture (clause 1(a) of Rule XVII).

<u>Walking in the Well</u>: Members should avoid walking between the Chair and any Member who is addressing the House. In addition, Members should not walk through the well of the House when Members are speaking (clause 5 of Rule XVII).

<u>Dress Code</u>: Members should dress appropriately, which traditionally means male Members should wear a coat and tie and female Members should wear business attire. Members should not wear overcoats or hats on the Floor while the House is in session. Eating, drinking, and smoking are not permitted. The use of a mobile electronic device that impairs decorum, such as the use of a cellular phone, including the taking of pictures or recording proceedings, is strictly prohibited on the floor of the House (clause 5 of Rule XVII).

<u>Forms of Address</u>: Members should not address their colleagues by their first name on the House floor. They should be addressed as "the gentleman or gentlewoman from (State)."

NOTE: All of the same cautions and prohibitions mentioned above with respect to conduct during debate in the Committee of the Whole also apply to conduct during debate in the House.

<u>Quorum and Vote in the Committee of the Whole:</u>
A quorum in the Committee of the Whole consists of 100 Members. However, during general debate the Chairman has the discretion to refuse to entertain a point of order that a quorum is not present. If the Chair does permit a quorum call at this point and orders the call by electronic device, Members will be summoned by three bells to the House floor to record their presence.

The Chairman must entertain a point of no quorum during consideration of a measure under the five-minute rule (the regular amendment process) if a quorum has not yet been established in the Committee of the Whole on the bill on that day. However, if a quorum has been established in Committee, the Chairman may not later entertain a point of no quorum during consideration under the five-minute rule unless and until the question is put on a pending amendment or motion. Whenever such a question is put before the Committee, any Member may rise and say: **"On that question I request a recorded vote, and pending that, I make a point of order that a quorum is not present."**

If less than 100 Members are present, the Chair will direct that Members record their presence by electronic device. The Chair at his or her discretion may order either a "live" or "notice" quorum call. For a live quorum call, Members must respond by recording their presence. A Member's absence will be noted in the *Congressional Record*. In the case of a "live" quorum call where a five-minute vote on an amendment is expected following the quorum call, Members are summoned by three bells followed by five bells.

Alternatively, in the absence of a quorum, the Chair may order a "notice" quorum call and vacate the quorum call at any time when 100 Members appear. The Committee then continues its business, and no indication of who responded to the call will appear in the *Congressional Record*. In the case of a "notice" quorum call, Members are summoned by one long bell followed by three short bells. In current practice, notice quorum calls are very rare.

XII. AMENDMENTS UNDER THE FIVE-MINUTE RULE

After all of the general debate has concluded, either by all time having been consumed or both sides yielding back the balance of their unused time, the Chairman of the Committee of the Whole will direct the reading clerk to read the bill for amendment. This is the so-called "second reading" of the bill. Under the standing Rules of the House, a bill is read for amendment by section (or by paragraph in the case of an appropriations bill), although a special rule may provide that it be read by title for amendment, or that it be considered as read and open for amendment at any point. A special rule may also specify the order in which amendments must be offered.

The special rule frequently provides for each section (or paragraph or title) to be considered as read. In that case, the reading clerk only designates each section as it is reached.

Offering an Amendment:
If a Member wants to offer an amendment, he or she must be on the floor when the clerk reads to the point at which the amendment is in order. At that point, the Member asks for recognition to offer the amendment. If a Member misses the opportunity to offer the amendment at the proper time, he or she may not be able to offer the amendment at all unless unanimous consent is granted to return to the appropriate place in the bill or the Member is able to redraft it to amend a subsequent section of the bill that has not yet been read for amendment. In general, Members should be sure that their amendments comply with the Rules of the House.

Amendments must be "germane" to the bill and to the section to which it is offered. (See clause 7 of Rule XVI for an explanation of germaneness.) Failure to comply with this Rule means that the amendment may be ruled out of order if a point of order is made against it. Amendments should be reviewed by the office of the Parliamentarian well in advance of the debate to ensure its germaneness and compliance with House rules.

Members are also advised to have the Congressional Budget Office review their amendment and consult with the Committee on the Budget in order to ensure their amendment complies with budget enforcement rules.

Amendments should be shared with the appropriate Members of the committee of jurisdiction unless the element of surprise is desired. Review by the committee of jurisdiction, which may recommend alternative language to make an amendment more acceptable, will enhance the prospects for passage.

Members should also provide sufficient copies of their amendment (a minimum of 10) to the reading clerk on the rostrum. The Member may either take the copies to the clerk in advance or may send the amendment to the desk as the Member offers it from the floor.

Members should make sure the floor and Cloakroom staffs have information about their amendments so they can communicate them to the membership by posting them at the leadership desk on the floor and in the Cloakroom, and by informing Members over their pagers if record vote(s) are ordered.

Time Limits Under the Five-Minute Rule:
Under the normal process of debate during consideration of amendments, the author of an amendment is recognized for five minutes, followed by recognition of a Member who wishes to speak in opposition for five minutes. Other Members may speak for five minutes by standing to seek recognition and saying, **"Mr. Chairman (or Madam Chairman), I move to strike the last word."**

This pro forma amendment is simply a device to get time without having to offer an actual amendment. Once a Member is finished speaking on a pro forma amendment, it is considered to have been automatically withdrawn and no vote is required on it.

When speaking under the five-minute rule, a Member may be able to obtain additional time by asking unanimous consent to proceed for the additional time desired. If an objection is heard, the Member may not proceed with additional debate time. Unlike general debate, time under the five-minute rule is not allocated to any specific Member, unless specifically provided for in a special rule. Additional time can be obtained by unanimous consent or by asking other Members who have not consumed all of their five minutes to yield time. When all Members who wish to be heard on an amendment are finished, the Chair puts the question to a vote.

In addition to time limitations that may be imposed by special rules governing consideration of bills, clause 8 of Rule XVIII outlines the manner in which the time for debate may be limited—either for tactical advantage or because all parties agree that enough debate has occurred. Such limits are proposed by a Member, usually the manager of the bill, asking unanimous consent that all time on an amendment and all amendments thereto be limited to a specified amount of time. A Member may ask that all debate on an amendment (or section) and all amendments thereto end at a certain time. These requests may be granted "without objection" or, if an objection is heard, they may be offered as a motion and be subject to a vote.

Protecting an Amendment:

It is advisable for Members to have their amendments printed in the *Congressional Record* (where they will be numbered accordingly) before their consideration. There are occasions in which a special rule governing a bill will require amendments to be printed in the *Congressional Record* prior to their consideration. Normally, however, such special rules, if open, will provide preferential treatment for pre-printed amendments. There is a special box for such amendments on the lower tier of the rostrum. If the Member submits an amendment for printing, it must be signed in the upper right-hand corner. Facsimile copies are not acceptable. Once printed in the *Congressional Record*, the Member is assured five minutes to speak on the amendment under an open rule, as will one opponent, even if a time limit is imposed by the Committee of the Whole. However, this protection will not apply if the special rule governing the bill adopted by the House includes a time limitation or the rule does not include the Member's amendment in the list of amendments that are to be made in order. The time for consideration of amendments may be limited overall by a rule, or the rule may specify time limits for each amendment made in order.

<u>How to Get a Vote on an Amendment:</u>
Once all debate has concluded on an amendment, the Chair will state, "The question occurs on the amendment offered by the Gentleman (or Gentlewoman) from (State). All those in favor will say, 'Aye.' Those opposed will say, 'No.'" Then the Chair will announce the outcome of the voice vote. Typically, if any Member is dissatisfied with the outcome of the voice vote, he or she may demand a recorded vote on the amendment.

NOTE: Rarely will a Member demand a "division" vote before requesting a recorded vote. Under this little-used procedure, the Chair will first ask those in favor to rise, then those opposed. The Chair will count the Members and announce the total. If the Member is still unsatisfied with the outcome, a record vote may be requested.

In order to obtain a record vote in the Committee of the Whole, 25 Members must rise to be counted by the Chair. As noted earlier, a point of no quorum can be made pending the request for a record vote in order to get more Members to the floor to support the request. If so, the Member should say: **"Mr. Chairman (or Madam Chairman), I request a record vote and, pending that, I make a point of order that a quorum is not present."** If a sufficient number of Members stand, the point of no quorum should be withdrawn and the request for a record vote restated.

XIII. CONCLUSION OF A BILL'S CONSIDERATION

<u>Committee of the Whole Rises:</u>
Usually a special rule will provide that, automatically following the disposition of all amendments, the Committee of the Whole rises and reports the bill back to the House with the recommendation that the bill, as amended, does pass. If the rule does not include this provision, the majority manager of the bill will be recognized to make such a motion. The Committee of the Whole then rises and the Speaker or a Speaker pro tempore resumes the Chair.

<u>Separate Votes on Amendments Adopted in the Committee of the Whole:</u>
The Chair, now the Speaker, asks the House: "Is a separate vote demanded on any amendment adopted in the Committee of the Whole?" Separate votes may be demanded only on amendments adopted by the Committee. Amendments that were defeated may not be voted on again. If there is no request for any separate votes, the amendments adopted are put before the House en bloc and adopted without objection. On the other hand, if an

amendment has been adopted by a narrow margin or a voice vote in the Committee of the Whole, at this point, the opponents may try to reverse the outcome by demanding a separate vote on it in the House.

Previous Question:

Under a special rule, the ordering of the previous question is typically automatic to ensure that the measure makes it to final passage; therefore, no vote on the previous question is allowed. In the absence of such a provision (such as on appropriations bills considered without a special rule), the Speaker will move that the previous question be ordered "without objection." If an objection is heard, the motion for the previous question must be voted on.

At the beginning of the 111th Congress the Rules were changed to allow the Speaker to indefinitely postpone consideration of a measure, if that measure is being considered pursuant to a rule or special order of the House, regardless of the operation of the previous question (Rule XIX, clause 1(c)).

Engrossment and Third Reading of the Bill:

This is a routine motion that orders the Clerk to prepare the measure for transmission to the Senate and read its title (the "third reading").

Motion to Recommit:

After the engrossment and third reading of a bill or joint resolution (but not simple resolutions, concurrent resolutions and conference reports), a Member opposed to the measure is given preference in recognition to offer a motion to recommit the measure, with or without instructions, to a committee that originally reported the measure. This motion is traditionally the right of the minority and gives them one last chance to return the measure to committee or have its version voted on. The Rules Committee may not report a special rule on a bill or joint resolution that denies a motion to recommit with instructions if offered by the minority leader or a designee.

If the motion to recommit is without instructions it is not debatable and has the effect of sending the bill back to a committee until such time the committee decides to take further action on the bill or joint resolution.

Usually the instructions are for the committee to "report the bill back to the House forthwith with the following amendment...." The text of the amendment is then read in full. The motion to recommit with instructions is debatable for 10 minutes, equally divided, but not controlled, which means neither side may yield or reserve time, between the proponent and the opponent, although the time may be extended to 1 hour at the request of the majority floor manager.

If the motion is adopted, the bill is recommitted with such "forthwith" instructions. The bill is immediately reported back to the House on the spot with the amendment, the amendment is voted on, and the House proceeds to final passage of the bill.

At the beginning of the 111th Congress the Rules were changed to deny the minority the option of recommitting a bill or joint resolution with any instructions other than "forthwith" instructions. Prior to the 111th Congress, motions to recommit could include instructions directing a committee to report back to the House "promptly" rather than "forthwith." Such instructions generally required the committee to examine and report back a specific amendment. The rule change also prohibits motions instructing a committee to hold further hearings, or that an investigation be conducted and that a report of that investigation be made to the House.

In order of priority, the minority leader and then minority party Members on the committee handling the bill, by seniority, have the right to offer the motion. This does not preclude Members of the majority party from offering the motion to recommit. They "qualify" to offer the motion if they state that they oppose the bill. The Member who qualifies and offers the motion usually votes against final passage of the bill if the motion to recommit fails.

XIV. FINAL PASSAGE OF A BILL

In bringing a measure to a final passage vote, the Speaker is required under House rules to first put the question to a voice vote by stating, "As many as are in favor (as the question may be), say, 'Aye.' As many as are opposed, say, 'No.'" The Speaker then makes the "call" on which side prevails. The only remedy available to any Member that disagrees with the Speaker's announcement on the voice vote is to demand a division or recorded vote.

<u>Obtaining a Recorded Vote in the House:</u>
Because the Constitution requires a quorum to be present to do business, whenever a quorum (218 Members) is not present, a recorded vote can be obtained by addressing the Chair and declaring: **"Mr. Speaker, I object to the vote on the grounds that a quorum is not present and I make a point of order that a quorum is not present."**

An alternate means of obtaining a recorded vote when a quorum is not present is to request the "yeas and nays," which requires that one-fifth of those Members present stand up to order the vote. This could be as many as 87 if all 435 Members are present, or as few as 1 if less than 5 Members are on the floor. Once the Chair determines that one-fifth of those present support the demand for the yeas and nays, the vote is ordered.

A Member can obtain a recorded vote when a quorum (218 Members or more) is present by addressing the Chair and declaring: **"Mr. Speaker, on that I demand a recorded vote."** A "recorded vote" under these circumstances requires only one-fifth of a quorum (44 Members) to stand and support the request.

General Leave:
It is customary, either just before or after consideration of a bill, for the majority floor manager to ask unanimous consent that all Members have five legislative days in which to revise and extend their remarks and to include extraneous material on the subject of the bill. Once this request is granted, Members may insert remarks on the bill without having to ask permission personally. The remarks should be labeled "General Leave." If the material is submitted rather than actually spoken on the floor, it will appear in different type in the *Congressional Record*.

Revising and Extending Remarks:
Once a Member has requested to see his or her remarks before they are printed in the *Congressional Record*, especially those made during debate when other Members are involved, certain rules of courtesy should be followed. As soon as the Official Reporter gives the transcript to the Member, it should be corrected for grammatical errors and immediately returned so that other Members may do the same.

The substance of a Member's remarks should not be changed—only grammatical corrections are allowed to be made. If elaboration is desired with tables or other "extraneous material," and permission has not been granted under general leave, specific permission must be obtained in the House and not in the Committee of the Whole. It will take approximately one hour between the time a speech is given and the time the transcribed remarks will be available on the floor.

Motion to Reconsider:

The motion to reconsider is available to any Member who votes on the prevailing side of a question and who wishes to move reconsideration on the same or succeeding legislative day. This often occurs when Members (usually minority Members) determine there is a need to slow down the legislative process. After final passage, it is the common practice in the House for the Speaker to declare, "Without objection, the motion to reconsider is laid upon the table." If no objection is raised, this has the parliamentary effect of ending any possibility that another vote on the bill can take place.

Postponement of Votes:

The Speaker has the discretion to postpone votes for up to two legislative days on a number of questions, including final passage of bills. Other questions that can be postponed by the Speaker include adoption of resolutions, motions to instruct, agreements to conference reports, previous question votes on any of the above matters, suspensions, motions to reconsider (and motions to table reconsideration), and agreements to amendments reported from the Committee of the Whole. The Chairman of the Committee of the Whole has the authority to postpone and cluster votes on amendments.

Clustering of Votes:

The Speaker may reduce the voting time to 5 minutes for electronic voting on certain questions after a 15-minute record vote has been taken. Votes can only be clustered by the Chair when there has not been intervening business between the votes in question.

Vote Pairs and Missed Votes:

The practice of announcing "general pairs" or the "pairing" of votes was eliminated in the 106th Congress. While "general pairs" are no longer announced, "live pairs" are still permitted. A "live pair" is an informal agreement between one Member present and voting and another on the opposite side of the question who is absent. By agreement, the voting Member withdraws his or her vote and records his or her self as "present." If the present Member wishes to announce the "pair," they must do so prior to the announcement of the final vote total.

If a Member misses a vote, they may have their position on the missed vote made part of the public record by inserting a brief statement in the *Congressional Record* at the proper point indicating how the Member would have voted. Such statements appear in the *Congressional Record* under the heading "Personal Explanation." For more information about this practice, contact the floor staff.

Conflicts of Interest:

Each Member must be present in the Hall of the House during its sessions "unless excused or necessarily prevented" and "shall vote on each question put, unless he or she has a direct personal or pecuniary interest in the event of such question." It has been ruled that only the Member can decide whether such a conflict exists and not even the Speaker will question his or her judgment, nor can any other Member challenge his or her vote on such grounds. Members should let their consciences be their guide. If Members believe they have such a conflict, they can vote "present" on the record vote and include an explanation in the *Congressional Record*.

XV. CONFERENCE REPORTS

In order for a bill to be presented to the President for signature, it must pass both the House and Senate in the exact same form. The device used for reaching agreement between the two houses is often, but not always, a conference committee. Sometimes differences between the two bodies are resolved by amendment—e.g., the House will agree to the bill as passed by the Senate with an amendment and the Senate will subsequently concur with that amendment.

A bill may be sent to conference by special rule or unanimous consent. If objection is heard, the bill may be sent to conference by motion or suspension. A motion to request or agree to a conference with the Senate is in order if offered by direction of the primary committee and of all reporting committees of initial referral. If such a motion has not been authorized by the committee, a special rule may be required to go to conference. The 109th Rules of the House included a change that gave committees the option to adopt a rule directing the chairman of the committee to offer a privileged motion to go to conference at any time the chairman deems it appropriate during a Congress.

Following the motion to go to conference, but prior to the appointment of conferees, the Speaker will recognize a minority Member, with preference given to the minority floor manager (if recognition is sought) to offer a motion to instruct House conferees. The motion is debatable for one hour, divided between the majority and the minority managers. If both support the motion, however, a third Member may demand time in opposition. All three Members are then recognized for one-third of the time. The motion to instruct conferees is not amendable unless the previous question is defeated. The instructions are not binding and they may not propose to do what the conferees could not otherwise do under the Rules of the House (e.g., exceed the scope of the conference). Additional opportunities to instruct occur when a conference report is recommitted or after 20 calendar days and 10 legislative days if the conference has failed to report. A Member who wishes to offer a motion to instruct conferees after 20-and-10 days must notify the House 1 day in advance of offering the motion.

Conferees are named by the Speaker and usually include Members of the committee(s) of jurisdiction and principal proponents of the legislation's major provisions.

When a conference agreement is reached, it comes back to the House in the form of a "conference report" that the House must consider and approve. Unless waived, the Rules of the House require that a conference report be filed at least three calendar days (excluding Saturdays, Sundays, and legal holidays) before it can be called up for consideration. The Rules also require that a majority of the conferees sign the conference report. After that time, it becomes privileged and can be called up at any time. If the conference report violates a rule of the House, it may be subject to a point of order that would prevent its consideration.

Debate on a conference report is limited to one hour, the time divided between the majority and the minority, unless the majority party manager and the minority party manager both support the conference report. In that case, one-third of the debate time will be given to an opponent of the conference report who makes such a demand.

Before adoption of the conference report, a motion may be in order to recommit the conference report to the committee on conference, either with instructions (that must be within the authority of the conferees and comply with the Rules of the House) or without instructions, although separate debate time is not allowed on either motion. Such a motion is only in order if the Senate has not yet acted on the conference report, thereby discharging its conferees, and the instructions in the motion to recommit are not binding because the House cannot bind Senate conferees. A Member qualifies to offer the motion if he or she opposes the conference report and states that fact.

If the House is first to act and the motion to recommit is adopted, the conference must meet again and a new conference report must be filed prior to consideration of the measure again. The rule requiring a three-day layover of conference reports still applies unless waived by special rule.

Following debate on the conference report and in the absence of a motion to recommit or upon the defeat of such a motion, a vote then occurs on adoption of the conference report, which may not be amended on the floor.

When dealing with appropriations conference reports, there may be times when conferees cannot reach agreement on all the amendments in disagreement. Also, there may be times when conferees must report provisions outside the conference report. For example, conferees may not exceed the scope of the conference or include legislative or unauthorized provisions in an appropriations bill. In those cases, the conferees will present a conference report to the House and Senate that includes all amendments on which agreement has been reached but excludes the amendments that remain in real or technical disagreement. The conference report is considered first and, assuming adoption of the conference report, the amendments in disagreement are then considered and disposed of individually.

XVI. DISCHARGE PETITIONS

After a bill has been introduced and referred to committee for 30 legislative days or more, any Member may file a motion with the Clerk of the House to discharge the committee from further consideration of the bill. A Member may also file a motion to discharge the Rules Committee from consideration of a special rule after the rule has been pending before the Rules Committee for at least 7 legislative days and the bill has been reported by a standing committee or has been referred to a standing committee for 30 legislative days.

Discharge petitions may cover only a single introduced measure, not multiple bills. A motion to discharge must only provide for the consideration of similar subject matter. In other words, a discharge motion cannot waive the germaneness rule.

If a Member is successful in convincing a majority of the total membership of the House (218 Members) to sign a discharge petition, the petition becomes eligible for consideration on the second or fourth Monday of the month after a 7 legislative day layover (except during the last 6 days of any session when the layover is waived). The discharge motion is debatable for 20 minutes, equally divided between the proponents and an opponent. If the motion to discharge a bill is adopted, it is in order to move that the House immediately consider the bill itself. If the motion to discharge a rule is adopted, the House turns immediately to consideration of the rule.

NOTE: Signatures on a discharge petition must be made available to the public by the Clerk and are made available on the Internet. The names of new signatories are printed in the *Congressional Record* on the last legislative day of each week.

XVII. END OF LEGISLATIVE BUSINESS FOR THE DAY

After completion of the scheduled legislative business, it is customary at the end of the day for the House to consider miscellaneous unanimous consent requests that were not made earlier in the day, including personal requests of individual Members.

Personal Requests:
Such requests can only be made by the Member benefiting from the request. These include to:

- Make a correction in the *Congressional Record*;

- Have a Member's name removed as a cosponsor of a bill or resolution (this request may also be made by the original sponsor of the measure);

- Include extraneous material exceeding two pages in the *Congressional Record*, which must be accompanied by a cost estimate from Government Printing Office.

Official Leave:
Members are allowed to be absent and excused on grounds of necessity which can include a death in the family, illness or official business. A request for a leave of absence should be made through the Cloakroom and signed by the appropriate party leader. Such requests are laid before the House each evening and made a part of the *Congressional Record*.

Extension of Remarks:
Members may insert comments in the section of the *Congressional Record* entitled "Extension of Remarks" by submitting to the Cloakroom such remarks with the Member's original signature. It is no longer necessary to obtain "permission" to include extensions in the *Congressional Record*. All

material submitted must bear an original Member's signature in the upper right-hand corner of the front page—facsimiles are not permitted—and the Member's typed name to be sure of identification. Members must be sure clerks will title the extension themselves.

If the extraneous material to be inserted will exceed two pages of the *Congressional Record*, it must be submitted to the Government Printing Office in advance for a cost estimate. When the estimate is received, the Member must ask leave of the House in person that it be printed, notwithstanding the cost. At the beginning or the end of the day, the Member must ask unanimous consent to extend his or her remarks in the *Congressional Record* and to include therein extraneous material notwithstanding the fact that it exceeds two pages. As part of the unanimous consent request, the Member also should include a cost estimate by the GPO. (As of February 2011, it is estimated that each page of the *Congressional Record* costs $380.00.)

Extensions should be delivered to the Cloakroom, handed to the *Congressional Record* clerks who sit at the bottom tier of the rostrum during session, or delivered to the Office of the Official Reports of Debates in Room HT-60 of the Capitol by 5 p.m. or 15 minutes after the House adjourns, whichever is later.

Special Orders:

Special order speeches are given after legislative business is completed for the day. They may be on any topic, and may either be given orally or submitted in writing (as with extensions of remarks). Members are recognized first for five-minute special orders, alternating between the majority and minority. At the conclusion of five-minute special orders, the Chair will recognize Members who wish to speak for longer periods of time, also alternating between the majority and minority. Special orders cannot be requested more than one week in advance.

Pursuant to the Speaker's announced policy of January 5, 2011, the Chair may recognize Members for special order speeches for up to four hours. Special order speeches may not go beyond 10 p.m. The four-hour limitation is divided between the majority and minority parties. Each party is entitled to reserve its first hour for respective leaderships or their designees. The second hour reserved to each party is divided into two 30-minute periods.

Any questions concerning special orders should be directed to the Cloakrooms.

Adjournment:
A motion to adjourn closes the business of the day.

XVIII. EARMARK RULES

At the beginning of the 110th Congress the House adopted new rules concerning the consideration of Member-directed projects or "earmarks," specifically clause 9 of Rule XXI and clause 17 of Rule XXIII (the Code of Official Conduct). These rules followed efforts in the 109th Congress to provide greater transparency in the earmarking process.

The rules are intended to prohibit the consideration of legislation that does not identify individual earmarks and the Members who sponsored them. The rules also require the distribution of the information in a way that makes it readily available before the legislation is considered, and certification by earmark sponsors that neither they nor their spouses have a financial interest in the earmark.

Point of Order:
Clause 9 of Rule XXI requires the chairman of the committee of initial referral to either disclose all earmarks contained in a bill, joint resolution, or conference report, or certify that the bill, joint resolution, or conference report contain no earmarks, and provide that information either in the accompanying report or printed in the *Congressional Record*. If the chairman of the committee of initial referral does not fulfill either of these requirements prior to the consideration of the measure, a point of order would lie against the consideration of the measure. This requirement also applies to unreported measures (in which case the information must be printed in the *Congressional Record*).

Clause 9(c) of Rule XXI prohibits the Rules Committee from waiving those disclosure requirements. If the Rules Committee reports a rule waiving clause 9 of Rule XXI, it would then be in order to raise a point of order against consideration of the rule. Disposition of the point of order raised against the rule would be determined by the Chair putting the question of consideration after 20 minutes of debate on the point of order equally divided and controlled by the Member initiating the point of order and a Member opposed. At the conclusion of debate on the point of order the Chair will put the question as follows: "Notwithstanding the assertion of the gentleman (or gentlewoman) from (STATE), that House Resolution ___ violates clause 9(c) of Rule XXI, shall the House now consider House Resolution ___?"

Members should also be aware that clause 9(a)(3) of Rule XXI applies the point of order to the initial amendment made in order under a special rule from the Rules Committee if that amendment is authored by a Member of the committee of initial referral. Clause 9(a)(3) requires the sponsor of the amendment to comply with the same disclosure requirements by having a statement printed in the *Congressional Record* either disclosing earmarks contained in their amendment or certifying that there are no earmarks in their amendment.

The point of order is also applicable to conference reports accompanying general appropriations bills (debatable as a question of consideration) for the failure to include a list of "air dropped" earmarks in the joint statement of managers. Unlike other points of order raised under clause 9 of Rule XXI, this point of order does not have a congnizability standard, allowing Members to question the accuracy or completeness of the list.

Clause 17 of Rule XXIII (the Code of Official Conduct) imposes a disclosure requirement on a Member who requests a congressional earmark, a limited tax benefit, or a limited tariff benefit in any bill or joint resolution or in any conference report on a bill or joint resolution. The committee of primary jurisdiction over the bill shall determine, using the definitions of "earmark," "limited tax benefit," and "limited tariff benefit" provided in clauses 9(e), (f), and (g) of Rule XXI, whether any particular spending provision constitutes an earmark or a request for an earmark.

A Member can raise the point of order at the point the manager calls up the conference report by saying: **"Mr. Speaker (or Madam Speaker), I raise a point of order under clause 9(b) of Rule XXI against the conference report for the failure to include a [complete/accurate] list of congressional earmarks."**

If the rule providing for consideration of the conference report waives all points of order, the point of order automatically moves to the rule. The form of that point of order is: **"Mr. Speaker (or Madam Speaker), I raise a point of order against H. Res. ____ under clause 9(b) of Rule XXI, because the resolution contains a waiver of all points of order against the conference report and its consideration."**

The point of order would then be debated as if raised under clause 9(c) of Rule XXI.

<u>Earmark Certification:</u>

A Member who requests an earmark or other provision must provide a written statement to the chairman and ranking member of the committee of jurisdiction of the bill, resolution, or report that contains the following information:

- The name of the Member;

- In the case of an earmark, the name and address of the intended recipient or if there is no intended recipient, the location of the activity;

- In the case of a limited tax or tariff benefit, the name of the beneficiary;

- The purpose of the earmark or limited tax or tariff benefit; and

- A certification that both the Member and the Member's spouse have no "financial interest" in the earmark or limited tax or tariff benefit.

Clause 17(a)(5) of Rule XXIII (the Code of Official Conduct) requires a Member who requests an earmark to certify that the Member and his or her spouse have "no financial interest in such congressional earmark." In the great majority of cases, Members should readily be able to determine whether they have a financial interest in an earmark by simply determining whether or not it would be reasonable to conclude that the provisions would have a direct and foreseeable effect on the pecuniary interests of the Member or the Member's spouse. However, Members are strongly encouraged to consult the Ethics Committee for guidance with any fact specific questions they have.

Additionally, various committees and the Republican Conference have their own standards for certifications and disclosures regarding earmarks, limited tax benefits, and limited tariff benefits. Members are strongly encouraged to check with the committee of jurisdiction before requesting an earmark to ensure that they are complying with all applicable standards.

XIX. CUT-AS-YOU-GO (CUTGO)

At the beginning of the 112th Congress, the House adopted changes in the Rules of the House concerning budget enforcement, specifically clause 10 of Rule XXI. Previously, clause 10 of Rule XXI was known as the "Pay-As-You-Go (PAYGO)" rule and required mandatory spending increases to be offset with either an equal decrease in mandatory spending or increase in revenue. The new "Cut-As-You-Go (CUTGO)" rule changes the emphasis of the rule, requiring that increases in mandatory spending be offset only with equal or greater decreases in mandatory spending. Like the PAYGO rule, CUTGO requires provisions be compliant in the current year, the budget year, and over the 5 and 10 year budget windows.

The rule is intended to stop growth in the size and scope of the Federal government and prioritize spending cuts over revenue increases.

XX. SPENDING REDUCTION AMENDMENTS IN APPROPRIATIONS BILLS

At the beginning of the 112th Congress, the House adopted a new standing order intended to assist Members seeking to use the amendment process to reduce discretionary spending in general appropriations bills. Prior to this standing order, if the House adopted an amendment to a general appropriations bill reducing the funds appropriated to a particular program, the amount of that reduction became "headroom" under the overall spending limit for the bill. The effect was to provide another Member with the ability to offer an amendment increasing spending later in the bill, making it nearly impossible to reduce the overall spending in a particular appropriations measure.

Under the new standing order, general appropriations bills must contain a "spending reduction account" which allows a Member offering an amendment to reduce the spending level in one part of the bill and increase the level allocated to the spending reduction account. Further, it is not in order to consider an amendment which reduces the level in the spending reduction account, or an amendment proposing to increase net budget authority in the bill, meaning that if spending is reduced in one part of the bill, another Member cannot offer an amendment to utilize the "headroom" created by the earlier adopted reduction. While this provision does not change the actual budget allocations for the bill, it does protect spending reductions through House consideration and provides a marker for the Appropriations Committee as it conferences the bill with the Senate.

Adjournment to a Day Certain —Adjournment under a motion or resolution that fixes the next time of meeting. Under the Constitution, both houses must agree to a concurrent resolution for either house to adjourn for more than three days. A session of Congress is not ended by adjournment to a day certain.

Adjournment Sine Die —Adjournment without definitely fixing a day for reconvening; literally "adjournment without a day." Usually used to connote the final adjournment of a session of Congress. A session can continue until noon, January 3, of the following year, when, under the 20th Amendment to the Constitution, it automatically terminates.

Amendments (Types of) —A proposal of a Member of Congress to alter the text of a bill or another amendment. An amendment usually is voted on in the same manner as a bill.

> **Amendment in the Nature of a Substitute** —An amendment that seeks to replace the entire text of an underlying bill. The adoption of such an amendment precludes any further amendment to that bill under the regular process (also, see Substitute Amendment).

> **Pro Forma Amendment** —A motion whereby a Member secures 5 minutes to speak on an amendment under debate in the Committee of the Whole. The Member gains recognition from the Chair by moving to "strike the last word." The motion requires no vote, does not change the amendment under debate, and is deemed automatically withdrawn at the expiration of the 5 minutes of debate.

> **Second Degree Amendment** —An amendment that substitutes or modifies the text of a pending amendment.

> **Substitute Amendment** —An amendment that replaces the entire text of a pending amendment.

Bills Introduced —In both the House and Senate, any number of Members may join in introducing a single bill or resolution. The first Member listed is the sponsor of the bill, and all Members' names following the sponsor's are the bill's cosponsors. When introduced, a bill is referred to the committee or committees that have jurisdiction over the subject with which the bill is concerned. Under the standing Rules of the House and Senate, bills are referred by the Speaker in the House and by the presiding officer in the

Senate. In practice, the House and Senate Parliamentarians act for these officials and refer the bills.

Budget Authority —Authority provided by law to incur into financial obligations that normally result in the outlay of funds. The main forms of budget authority are appropriations, borrowing authority, contract authority, and entitlement authority.

Budget Outlay —Payments made (generally through the issuance of checks or disbursement of cash) to liquidate obligations. Outlays during a fiscal year may be for payment of obligations incurred in prior years or in the same year.

Budget Resolution —A concurrent resolution which outlines in broad parameters the levels of spending and revenues for the next fiscal year. The concurrent resolution, which is not signed by the President, contains allocations of spending authority for House and Senate committees which serve as constraints on their consideration of legislation. The Appropriations Committee gets an allocation for discretionary spending.

Calendar —An agenda or list of business awaiting possible action by the House or Senate. The House has four calendars (the Discharge Calendar, the House Calendar, the Private Calendar, and the Union Calendar).

Chaplain of the House or Senate —He or she opens the legislative session with a formal prayer, a custom since the First Congress. The Chaplain provides pastoral counseling to Members, their families, and staff. Guest Chaplains of various denominations regularly offer the prayer.

Chief Administrative Officer (CAO) —He or she is responsible for certain administrative and financial activities that support the operations of the House, including the finance office, Members' accounts, information resources, human resources, office systems management, furniture, office supplies, postal operations, food services, and various media services.

Clerk of the House —As the chief legislative officer, he or she directs administrative activities that support the legislative process including keeping the Journal, recording all votes, certifying bill passage, and processing all legislation.

Committee —A panel of Members elected or appointed to perform some service or function for its parent body. Congress has three types of committees: standing, special or select, and joint. Committees conduct investigations, make studies, issue reports and recommendations, and, in the case of standing committees, review and prepare measures on their assigned subjects for action by their respective houses. Most committees divide their work among several subcommittees or, in some cases, task forces, but only the full committee may submit reports or measures to its house or to Congress. With rare exceptions, the majority party in a house holds a majority of the seats on its committees, and their chairmen are also from that party.

Committee Allocation —The distribution, pursuant to section 302 of the Congressional Budget Act, of new budget authority and outlays to House and Senate committees. The allocation, which may not exceed the relevant amounts in the budget resolution, usually is made in the joint explanatory statement that accompanies the conference report on the budget resolution.

Committee of the Whole —A committee composed of all House Members created to expedite the consideration of bills, other measures, and amendments on the floor of the House. In the Committee of the Whole, a quorum is 100 Members (as compared to 218 in a fully populated House) and debate on amendments is conducted under the 5-minute rule (as compared to the hour rule in the House). In addition, certain motions allowed in the House are prohibited in the Committee of the Whole including, but not limited to, motions for the previous question, to table, to adjourn, to reconsider a vote, and to refer or recommit.

Desk —The presiding officer's desk. In parliamentary parlance, a Member may send an amendment or a written motion to "the desk," or a measure may be "held at the desk."

En Bloc —Several amendments offered and considered as a group. Because Members normally may offer one amendment at a time for consideration, they must obtain unanimous consent to offer amendments en bloc, or a rule providing for consideration of a measure may provide authority for a Member to offer amendments en bloc.

Engrossed Bill —The official copy of a bill or joint resolution as passed by one Chamber, including the text as amended by floor action, and certified by the Clerk of the House or the Secretary of the Senate (as appropriate). Amendments by one house to a measure or amendments of the other also are engrossed. House-engrossed documents are printed on blue paper while the Senate's are printed on white paper.

Enrolled Bill —The final official copy of a bill or joint resolution that both houses have passed in identical form. An enrolled bill is printed on parchment. After it is certified by the chief officer of the house in which it originated and signed by the House Speaker and the Senate President pro tempore, the measure is sent to the President for his signature.

Expedited Procedures —Procedures that provide a special process for the accelerated congressional consideration of legislation. This accelerated process usually includes consideration in committee and on the floor of the House and Senate. Furthermore, these procedures often involve a departure from the regular order of the House. Expedited procedures are provided by law, as opposed to by a special rule.

Five-Minute Rule —A debate-limiting rule of the House used when the House sits as the Committee of the Whole. A Member offering an amendment is allowed to speak for five minutes in support of each amendment and an opponent is allowed to speak for five minutes in opposition. Other Members may rise to "strike the last word" and receive five minutes to speak in favor or opposition. Additional time for speaking can be obtained through a unanimous consent request.

Free-Trade Agreements —The establishment of bilateral or multilateral trade agreements establishing free-trade areas (FTAs) require changes in U.S. trade legislation. Trade law sets out procedures for the enactment of such legislation and its implementation. This law provides for expedited congressional consideration of the relevant measure and, as a rule, prohibits any amendments to it. The expedited consideration, originally called "fast track" procedure, but recently also named "trade authorities procedures (TAPs)," provides for mandatory consideration of the measure by Congress once introduced, with specific deadlines for each legislative phase and a final up-or-down vote.

Germaneness —A rule requiring amendments pertain to the same subject as the matter under consideration. Questions of germaneness, both in committee and on the House floor, are determined by the Chair and/or the Speaker subject to appeal to the House or the Committee.

Hopper —A box on the Clerk's desk in the House Chamber into which Members deposit bills and resolutions to introduce them. To "drop a bill in the hopper" is to introduce it.

House Bill (H.R.) —H.R. stands for "House of Representatives" and designates a measure as a bill, followed by a number assigned in the order in which bills are introduced during a two-year Congress. A bill becomes a law if passed in identical form by both houses and signed by the President, or passed over the President's veto, or if the President fails to sign it within 10 days after receiving it while Congress is in session.

House Concurrent Resolution (H. Con. Res.) —H. Con. Res. stands for "House Concurrent Resolution." This is a resolution that requires approval by both houses, but is not sent to the President for his signature and therefore cannot have the force of law. Concurrent resolutions deal with the prerogatives or internal affairs of Congress as a whole. For example, they serve as the vehicles for agreeing to congressional budget decisions, fixing the time of congressional adjournments, agreeing to a joint session, expressing the sense of Congress on domestic and foreign issues, correcting errors in enrolled bills, authorizing the printing of documents of interest to both houses, and creating temporary joint committees.

House Joint Resolution (H. J. Res.) —H. J. Res. stands for "House Joint Resolution." This is a legislative measure that Congress usually uses for purposes other than general legislation. Like a bill, it has the force of law when passed by both houses and either approved by the President or passed over the President's veto. Unlike a bill, a joint resolution enacted into law is not called an act; it retains its original title. Most often, joint resolutions deal with such relatively limited matters, such as the correction of errors in existing law, continuing appropriations, a single appropriation, or the establishment of permanent joint committees. Unlike bills, joint resolutions are also used to propose constitutional amendments, which do not require the President's signature and become effective only when ratified by three-fourths of the states. While a preamble is not considered appropriate in a bill, it may be included in a joint resolution to set forth the events or facts that prompted the measure, for example, a declaration of war.

House Resolution (H. Res.) —H. Res. stands for "House Resolution." This type of measure is a simple resolution; that is, a non-legislative measure that is effective only in the House and does not require concurrence with the Senate or approval by the President. Simple resolutions express nonbinding opinions on policies or issues or deal with the internal affairs or prerogatives of the House. They are used to establish select and special committees, appoint the Members of standing committees, and amend the standing Rules. In the House, the Rules Committee reports its special rules in the form of simple resolutions.

Lay on the Table —A motion to "lay on the table" is not debatable and is usually a method of making a final, adverse determination of a matter.

Legislative History —The documents that accompanied a bill throughout the legislative process comprise its legislative history. These include the committee report, the conference committee report and the statement of managers (if applicable), and the text of the floor debate in both chambers. Legislative history is used by federal agencies to clarify vague provisions in the laws they are required to implement.

Marking Up a Bill —The process by which a committee or subcommittee moves through the contents of a measure, debating and voting on amendments to its provisions by revising, adding, or subtracting language prior to ordering the measure reported.

Motion to Recommit —A motion made on the floor after the engrossment and third reading of a bill or resolution, but prior to the Chair posing the question on final passage. Preference is given to a Member who is opposed to the bill and is reserved by tradition to the minority party. The Speaker usually gives priority recognition to the bill's minority floor manager. The motion to recommit may be without instructions, which is non-debatable and has the effect of killing the bill, or with instructions (subject to 10 minutes of debate split between a proponent and opponent, and usually directs the reporting committee to amend "forthwith," meaning immediately, or rewrite the bill in a specified way). The Rules Committee's responsibility on the motion to recommit is different for simple resolutions or concurrent resolutions, but may apply to conference reports where the House acts first.

Office of the Parliamentarian —An office managed, supervised, and administered by a non-partisan Parliamentarian appointed by the Speaker. This office is responsible for advising the presiding officer, Members, and staff on the Rules and procedures of the House, as well as for compiling and preparing the precedents of the House. All consultation with this office is confidential (if requested).

Official Reporters —Official Reporters are responsible for collecting material for printing in the *Congressional Record*. These Clerks sit in the center of the first tier of the rostrum on the House floor. All submissions for the *Record*, for example, extensions of remarks, corrections to Member's floor statements, and extraneous material, are given to the Official Reporters.

Parliamentary Inquiry —A Member's question, posed to the presiding officer, about a pending procedural situation. The Chair is not required to answer such questions, but usually does if they are proper inquiries and properly made. A proper inquiry deals only with questions of procedure on a pending matter, not with hypothetical situations or the interpretation or consistency of amendments.

Point of Order —An objection that the pending proposal (bill, amendment, motion, etc.) is in violation of a rule of the House. The validity of points of order is determined by the presiding officer, and if held valid, the offending bill, amendment, or provision is ineligible for consideration. Points of order may be waived by special rules.

Privilege —A status relating to the rights of the House and its Members and the priority of motions and actions on the Floor of the House. "Privileged questions" relate to the order of legislative business, while "questions of privilege" relate to matters affecting the safety, dignity, or integrity of the House, or the rights, reputation or conduct of a Member acting as a Representative.

Privileged Matters —House rules give certain House committees a "green light" to bring certain categories of legislation to the House Floor for immediate debate. The Speaker must recognize any chairman for the purpose of calling up a privileged matter reported from his or her committee. Examples of privileged matter include special rules from the Rules Committee, conference reports from any conference committee, congressional budget resolutions from the Budget Committee, censure or expulsion resolutions from the Ethics Committee, and general appropriations bills from the Appropriations Committee.

Previous Question —A motion offered in the House to end debate and preclude further amendments from being offered. In effect, it asks, "Are we ready to vote on the issue before us?" If the previous question is ordered in the House, all debate ends and usually the House immediately votes on the pending bill or amendment. If the previous question is defeated, control of debate shifts to the leading opposition Member (usually the minority floor manager) who then manages an hour of debate and may offer a germane amendment to the pending business. The effect of defeating the previous question is to turn over control of the floor to the minority or opposition.

Quorum —The number of Members whose presence is required for the House to conduct business. A quorum in the House is a majority of the Members (218). A quorum in the Committee of the Whole is 100 Members. A quorum is presumed to be present until its absence is demonstrated. If a quorum is not present when the question is put, a point of order can be made that a quorum is not present, at which time the Speaker (or Chair) counts for a quorum. If the Speaker (or Chair) determines that a quorum is not present, Members may be summoned to the Floor. If a quorum fails to respond to the call, the only business in order is a motion to adjourn or a motion to direct the Sergeant at Arms to request the attendance of absentees.

Ramseyer Rule —A House rule requiring that committee reports contain a comparative print showing, through typographical devices such as italic print, the changes in existing law made by the proposed committee language (the "Cordon Rule" is a parallel rule of the Senate).

Reading for Amendment —In the Committee of the Whole, after a clerk has read or designated a section or paragraph of a measure, it is a House practice to complete action on all amendments to that section or paragraph before moving on to the next section or paragraph. A full reading of a section's text is often waived by unanimous consent or by a special rule from the Rules Committee, in which case the clerk reads only the section's number or designates the paragraph. Sometimes, by unanimous consent or special rule, a measure is read or designated by title rather than by section or paragraph.

Recognition —Permission by the presiding officer for a Member to speak or propose a procedural action. A Member seeking recognition must rise and address the Chair, but may not do so while another Member holds the floor unless that Member has violated a rule. Generally, recognition in the House is within the Chair's discretion. Under some circumstances, the Chair's discretion is absolute; under others, the Chair may be required to recognize a Member eventually, but not necessarily the first time the Member seeks recognition. Under still other circumstances, the Chair is required to recognize certain Members for specific purposes. However, the Speaker must recognize Members for privileged business and motions, but when several Members seek recognition on business of equal privilege, the Speaker has discretion in deciding whom to recognize first. By tradition and practice, both the Speaker and the Chairman of the Committee of the Whole follow certain priorities of recognition during debate. In both houses, the Chair's recognition authority is not subject to appeal.

Reconsideration —A motion to reconsider the vote by which an action was taken has, until it is disposed of, the effect of putting the action in abeyance. In essence, it is a motion to vote again on that which was just agreed to.

Re-Referral —The assignment of a measure to a committee different from the committee to which the measure was initially referred. Usually used to correct erroneous initial referrals.

Rules (Types of) —There are two specific types of Rules.

> **Standing Rules** —These are the standing Rules governing the normal order of business in the House or in a committee. These Rules are adopted by the full House and by each committee at the beginning of each Congress. These Rules generally govern such matters as the duties of officers, the code of conduct, the order of business, admission to the floor, parliamentary procedures on handling amendments and voting, and jurisdictions of committees.

> **Special Rules** —These involve a departure from the standing Rules of the House for the consideration of specified House action. They are resolutions reported by the Rules Committee, most of which govern the handling of a particular bill on the House floor.

Senate Bill (S.) —S. stands for "Senate" and designates a measure introduced in the Senate as a bill, followed by a number assigned in the order in which bills are introduced during a two-year Congress. A bill becomes a law if passed in identical form by both houses and signed by the President, or passed over the President's veto, or if the President fails to sign it within 10 days after receiving it while Congress is in session.

Senate Concurrent Resolution (S. Con. Res.) —S. Con. Res. is an abbreviation for "Senate Concurrent Resolution." This is a resolution that requires approval by both houses, but is not sent to the President for his signature and therefore cannot have the force of law. Concurrent resolutions deal with the prerogatives or internal affairs of Congress as a whole. For example, they serve as the vehicles for agreeing to congressional budget decisions, fixing the time of congressional adjournments, agreeing to a joint session, expressing the sense of Congress on domestic and foreign issues, correcting errors in enrolled bills, authorizing the printing of documents of interest to both houses, and creating temporary joint committees.

Senate Joint Resolution (S. J. Res.) —S. J. Res. is an abbreviation for "Senate Joint Resolution." This is a legislative measure that Congress usually uses for purposes other than general legislation. Like a bill, it has the force of law when passed by both houses and either approved by the President or passed over the President's veto. Unlike a bill, a joint resolution enacted into law is not called an act; it retains its original title. Most often, joint resolutions deal with such relatively limited matters, such as the correction of errors in existing law, continuing appropriations, a single appropriation, or the establishment of permanent joint committees. Unlike bills, joint resolutions also are used to propose constitutional amendments, which do not require the President's signature and become effective only when ratified by three-fourths of the states. While a preamble is not considered appropriate in a bill, it may be included in a joint resolution to set forth the events or facts that prompted the measure (for example, a declaration of war).

Senate Resolution (S. Res.) —S. Res. stands for "Senate Resolution." This type of measure is a simple resolution; that is, a non-legislative measure that is effective only in the Senate and does not require concurrence with the House or approval by the President. Simple resolutions express nonbinding opinions on policies or issues or deal with the internal affairs or prerogatives of the Senate. They are used to establish select and special committees, appoint the Members of standing committees, and amend the standing Rules.

Sergeant at Arms —The Sergeant at Arms is the chief law enforcement officer for the House of Representatives. The officer is responsible for maintaining security, order, and decorum in the House Chamber, House wing of the Capitol, and the House office buildings.

Standing Committees —These permanent House panels are identified in House Rule X, which also lists the jurisdiction of each committee. Because they have legislative jurisdiction, standing committees consider bills and issues and recommend measures for consideration by the full House. They also have oversight responsibility to monitor agencies, programs, and activities within their jurisdictions, and, in some cases, in areas that cut across committee jurisdictions.

Suspension of the Rules —A timesaving method used to consider legislation. By suspending the rules and passing a measure, this procedure has the effect of preventing any points of order from being raised against a measure for violation of a rule. Under this procedure, the bill is un-amendable (except for 1 amendment by the floor manager if offered as part of the motion) and debate on the motion and the measure is limited to 40 minutes equally divided between a proponent and an opponent. A motion to recommit is not in order under this procedure. However, a favorable vote of two-thirds of those present is necessary for passage. This procedure is in order every Monday, Tuesday, and Wednesday and is intended to be reserved for relatively non-controversial bills. Both the Republican Conference and Democratic Caucus have their own internal rules for determining whether legislation is eligible for suspension consideration.

Unanimous Consent —A method used to expedite consideration of non-controversial measures on the House floor. Proceedings of the House or actions on legislation often take place by unanimous consent of the House (i.e., without objection by any Member), whether or not a rule of the House is being violated.

Unanimous Consent Agreements—Agreements negotiated among Senators by the majority and minority leaders to limit debate on a specified measure, to restrict amendments to it, and to waive points of order. Requires the consent of every Senator and may be denied by a single objection. These agreements, also called "time agreements," are the Senate parallel to "special rules" from the House Rules Committee.

Waiver—A temporary setting aside of one or more rules by prohibiting points of order that might be raised to enforce those rules. The House uses special rules from the Rules Committee for this purpose. In addition, the House procedure for suspending the rules and passing a measure implicitly imposes a blanket waiver because it suspends all rules, including statutory rules that might conflict with the suspension procedure or the measure's passage.

Yielding Time —Once a Member has been recognized by the Speaker (or Chair) to speak, he controls the floor; in general, no other Member may speak without being granted permission to do so by the Member recognized. Another Member who wishes to speak will ask the recognized Member to yield by saying, **"Will the gentleman (or gentlewoman) from (STATE) yield to me?"**

Index

E

F

Great Compromise of 1787, 9
Great Society, 251

H

Hamilton, Alexander, 11, 12, 249
Hansen Committee, 93
Harkin, Harkin, 27
Harvard Business Review, 115, 117
Health and Human Services, Department of, 100
health care reform bill, 188, 194
helicopter parents, 121
*Helping a 221-Year-Old Institution Harness Cutting-Edge Communication
    Technologies*, 45, 167
Herding Cats, 32, 80
Hernández, Joseph Marion, 11
Hispanic Americans, 190
Hispanic, first elected, 11
hold, 81
honorarium, 229
hopper, 91, 111, 204, 308
House Administration, Committee on, 129
House Bill (H.R.), 309
House Chaplain, 273
House Concurrent Resolution (H. Con. Res.), 309
House Joint Resolution (H. J. Res.), 309
House majority leader, 33
House minority leader, 223
House: The History of the House of Representatives, The, 13
House Resolution (H. Res.), 309
House staff, 15
how to get a vote on an amendment, 290
Huffington Post, The, 150
Hyde Amendment, 100
Hyde, Henry, 34

I

Illinois, 27, 34, 36, 92
incivility, 12, 249, 250, 264
Indiana's Eighth Congressional District, 253

Q

R

voting by electronic device, 274
Voting Rights Act, 36, 77, 106, 257

W

Waiver, 315
Walker, Robert, 252
Walking in the Well, 286
Wallace, George, 251
Wall Street Journal, The, 230
war on women, 186, 187
war powers, 106
Washington, George, 10, 12, 75
Washington (state of), 63
Ways and Means, Committee on, 11, 39, 92, 193, 212
Weber Shandwick, 250
welfare reform, 104, 197
Whig, 11
Whip, 62, 63
White House Office of Legislative Affairs, 104
Wiggles, The, 224
Wilson, James, 34
Wilson, Woodrow, 83
Winston, David, 262
Wolfensberger, Donald, 100
women's issues, 186
Wood, Fernando, 217
Woodrow Wilson International Center for Scholars, 100
words be taken down, 285
World War I, 83
Wright, Jim, 253
Wyoming, 30

Y

Yankelovich, Daniel, 179
Yielding Time, 315
YouTube, 153, 157
You've Sent Mail: How Constituents Judge Their Representatives by the Snail Mail They Send, 167

Mark N. Strand has been the president of the Congressional Institute since 2007 and is an adjunct professor of legislative affairs in the Graduate School of Political Management at George Washington University. Strand spent nearly 24 years on Capitol Hill, most recently as chief of staff to Senator James M. Talent of Missouri (2003-07). From 2001-2002, Strand was vice president of government affairs for the American Water Works Company—the largest publicly held water utility in the United States. Prior to that, Strand served as staff director of the House Committee on Small Business when Talent was chairman. He has served as chief of staff to Talent, Bill Lowery of California and Stan Parris of Virginia. He has also been a legislative director and a press secretary. Strand obtained a B.S. in political science and history from Excelsior College of the University of New York, an M.B.A. in Marketing from the University of Phoenix in 2003, and a master's in legislative affairs from George Washington University. He completed the Stennis Congressional Fellowship in 2000. He frequently speaks to groups about congressional procedure, Hill staff, and more generally about how Congress works (or doesn't, as the case may be). He resides in Virginia with his wife Susan, and has three daughters.

Michael S. Johnson served 14 years in the executive and legislative branches of government, first on the White House communications staff of President Gerald R. Ford. He served as press secretary and later as chief of staff for former House Republican Leader Bob Michel of Illinois. Johnson entered the private sector in 1990, as a lobbyist with Texas and Ohio law firms. He served for five years as a senior vice president of APCO Worldwide, an international public affairs firm, before joining the OB-C Group in 2001. Johnson has served on the staff of every Republican National Convention from 1980-2008, has taught policy and public affairs, and continues to serve as a political and communications advisor. He is co-founder of the Congressional Institute, has served as its chairman and continues to serve on the board of directors. He writes periodic columns for the newgopforum.com. A native of Illinois who was reared and educated in South Dakota, Johnson began his career in journalism as a reporter and eventually executive editor of a small Illinois daily newspaper. He is married to Thalia Assuras and has five children.

Jerome F. (Jerry) Climer arrived on Capitol Hill in 1967 and served for two years as the legislative staff (offices had fewer personnel back then) to a freshman Member of the U.S. House, who managed to stay in office for 28 years. After a few years in the executive branch, including serving as assistant to the Secretary of the U.S. Department of Agriculture, he returned to the House as chief legislative assistant to former Congressman Tom Coleman (R-MO) and then for six years as chief of staff to former Congressman Ed Bethune (R-AR). His final five official years on Capitol Hill were served as leadership assistant to the late Congressman Guy Vander Jagt (R-MI). Then Climer co-founded the Congressional Institute, which he served as president for 20 years. After retiring in 2007 and relocating to North Carolina, he continues to serve as president of the Public Governance Institute, a 501 (c)(3) organization and heads Policy Implementation Consultants, LLC, a private consulting endeavor. In 2009, the Governor appointed him to the Edenton Historical Commission, which he chairs. He is deputy chairman of the Chowan County Tourism Development Authority, a governmental entity. He is secretary of Edenton Chowan Partnership, Inc., a public/private not-for-profit focused on economic development. To keep his political skills honed, he managed a successful campaign for a candidate for Edenton's Town Council, defeating an 18-year incumbent. In 2010 he chaired the successful reelection campaign for Senator Richard Burr in Chowan County. In 2012, he acted as the strategic planner for a county commission candidate and got his head kicked in. He says he relearned a few things.